"Although I am not to be numbered among
ness of many of Gregory MacDonald's argun
adept interweaving of biblical exegesis with r
erations. As engaging as they are provocativ
invite serious consideration and encourage f

CU00922012

Professor of New Testament]

"Gregory MacDonald has wrestled long and hard with the question that confronts all
those for whom Scripture is the supreme authority. Are they obliged to hold that God
consigns to eternal punishment those who fail to believe the gospel or can they legitimately trust that the grace of God will eventually embrace all humanity? From MacDonald's
spiritual and intellectual struggle has come this passionate and lucid advocacy of an evangelical universalism. It not only engages with key passages in the context of the overall
biblical narrative but also treats clearly the profound theological and philosophical issues
to which that narrative gives rise. At the same time MacDonald interacts thoroughly and
fairly with the major objections to universalism. Whether readers are convinced by all of
his arguments or not, they will find this book an excellent, accessible and indispensable
aid in their own attempts to grapple with what its author describes as 'a hell of a problem.'
One's only regret is that the ethos in some evangelical circles is such that the author felt
compelled to use a pseudonym."

—Andrew T. Lincoln
Portland Professor of New Testament, University of Gloucestershire

"Gregory MacDonald's defense of universalism is well argued logically, theologically, and
especially biblically. He is generous to other viewpoints but suggests that a universalist
approach to the difficult texts is more reasonable in the light of the overall structure of
the salvation story of the Bible. Evangelicals, among whom MacDonald would count
himself, will find him a civil and insightfully critical dialogue partner."

—Thomas F. Johnson
Professor of Biblical Theology, George Fox University

"With this wonderful book, Gregory MacDonald joins the growing body of Evangelical
Christians who now accept a doctrine of universal reconciliation. But I know of no one
who has set forth an equally clear, thorough and compelling case for a universalist reading
of the Bible as a whole. No Christian who reads this book with an open mind will remain
unaffected by its power and clarity of vision, and those who reject universalism as merely
heretical, or even as perversely heretical, will likely find that McDonald has addressed
their reservations and objections with ease and great sensitivity."

—Thomas Talbott
Professor of Philosophy, Willamette University, Salem, Oregon

"Here is an attempt to think through the implications of the doctrine of universalism that really tries to tackle the considerable difficulties posed by the biblical material, as well as traditional theological and philosophical arguments. Clear, well-written and engaging – MacDonald's charitable reading of his opponents is a model of fairmindedness. Those in the evangelical constituency will need to do some hard thinking in order to show why one cannot be both an evangelical and a universalist."

—Oliver Crisp
Lecturer in Theology, University of Bristol

The Evangelical Universalist

The Evangelical Universalist

Gregory MacDonald

First published in Great Britain in 2008

Society for Promoting Christian Knowledge
36 Causton Street
London SW1P 4ST
www.spckpublishing.co.uk

Originally published in the United States of America in 2006 by
Cascade Books, a division of Wipf and Stock Publishers,
199 W. 8th Ave., Eugene, OR 97401, USA

British Library Cataloguing-in-Publication Data
A catalogue record for this book is available from the British Library

ISBN 978–0–281–05988–1

10 9 8 7 6 5 4 3 2

Printed in Great Britain by Ashford Colour Press

Produced on paper from sustainable forests

For Thomas Talbott

. . . suddenly God seemed to answer me. An inward voice said, in tones of infinite love and tenderness, "He shall see of the travail of His soul and be satisfied." "Satisfied!" I cried in my heart. "Christ is to be satisfied! He will be able to look at the world's misery and then at the travail through which He has passed because of it, and will be satisfied with the result! If I were Christ, nothing could satisfy me but that every human being should in the end be saved, and therefore I am sure that nothing less will satisfy Him!" With this, a veil seemed to be withdrawn from before the plans of the universe and I saw that it was true, as the Bible says, that "as in Adam all die even so in Christ should all be made alive." As was the first, even so was the second. The "all" in one case could not in fairness mean less than the "all" in the other. I saw therefore that the remedy must necessarily be equal to the disease, the salvation must be as universal as the fall.

—Hannah Whitall Smith[1]

---

[1] *The Unselfishness of God and How I Discovered It: My Spiritual Autobiography* (New York: Revell, 1903) chap. 22 (1st ed. only); http://www.godstruthfortoday.org/Library/smith/hwsmith9.html.

Contents

Abbreviations

AB	Anchor Bible
AnBib	Analecta Biblica
BOL	Book of Life
ChrTod	*Christianity Today*
CJP	*Canadian Journal of Philosophy*
ConBNT	Coniectanea biblica: New Testament Series
ConComm	Continental Commentaries
F&Ph	*Faith & Philosophy*
HDR	Harvard Dissertations in Religion
ICC	International Critical Commentary
IJPR	*International Journal for Philosophy of Religion*
JBL	*Journal of Biblical Literature*
JSNTSup	Journal for the Study of the New Testament Supplement Series
JSOT	*Journal for the Study of the Old Testament*
JSOTSup	Journal for the Study of the Old Testament Supplement Series
JTS	*Journal of Theological Studies*
LPS	Library of Pauline Studies
LXX	Septuagint
NCB	New Century Bible
NIB	*New Interpreter's Bible*
NIGTC	New International Greek Testament Commentary
NovT	*Novum Testamentum*
NSBT	New Studies in Biblical Theology
NTS	*New Testament Studies*
NTT	New Testament Theology
PBTM	Paternoster Biblical and Theological Monographs
RelSt	*Religious Studies*
RH	Rejection Hypothesis
SBET	*Scottish Bulletin of Evangelical Theology*

SBLSP	*Society of Biblical Literature Seminar Papers*
SBT	Studies in Biblical Theology
SBTS	Sources for Biblical and Theological Study
TDNT	*Theological Dictionary of the New Testament.* 10 vols. Edited by Gerhard Kittel and Gerhard Friedrichson. Translated and edited by Geoffrey W. Bromiley. Grand Rapids: Eerdmans, 1964–76
THS	Tyndale House Studies
TynBul	*Tyndale Bulletin*
VT	*Vetus Testamentum*
WBC	Word Biblical Commentary
WUNT	Wissenschaftliche Untersuchungen zum Neuen Testament

Introduction

If the others are going to hell, then I am going along with them. But I do not believe that; on the contrary, I believe that we will all be saved, I, too, and this awakens my deepest wonder.

—Søren Kierkegaard[1]

An Autobiographical Note

HAVE YOU ever felt that soul-sickening feeling when you know you cannot worship God with sincerity any longer? Have you ever experienced the painful knowledge that the noble words of praise coming from your lips are hollow? I can recall one Sunday morning when I had to stop singing for I was no longer sure whether I believed that God deserved worship. For a believer, that is a moment of despair. Ever since I had been a Christian, I had never wavered in my conviction that God loved people, but on that Sunday I didn't know if I could believe that anymore. I was having a doxological crisis—wanting to believe that God was worthy of worship but unable to do so. The crisis was brought on by my reflections on hell. Let me explain.

I began my Christian life by affirming with a vengeance the mainstream tradition of the Church that hell was eternal conscious torment. After a few years, a friend managed to wean me onto a version of hell-as-annihilation by lending me a John Wenham book[2] and what, at the time, were theologically

---

[1] S. Kierkegaard, *Søren Kierkegaard's Journals and Papers*, trans. and ed. H. V. Hong and E. H. Hong (Bloomington: Indiana University Press, 1978) 6:557. Kierkegaard is responding to the accusation that he thinks of himself as better than others by suggesting that they are going to hell but that he is not. On the contrary, Kierkegaard says that he has little trouble believing that all *other* people will be blessed rather than eternally lost—it is *his own* blessing he has trouble believing (*Theodramatik* IV).

[2] John Wenham, *The Goodness of God* (London: InterVarsity, 1974); it was later reprinted as *The Enigma of Evil*.

1

contraband books by Basil Atkinson and Edward Fudge.[3] Not long after that John Stott 'came out' as a tentative annihilationist,[4] giving considerable credibility to our position—a position that is now thankfully considered as a legitimate 'evangelical option' by many.[5]

My crisis began some years later whilst I was reading a superb book by the philosopher William Lane Craig entitled *Only Wise God*.[6] Craig was defending a philosophical position known as "middle knowledge" (or Molinism) that seemed to allow the Christian to affirm *both* that humans have free will *and* that God can still exercise strong providential control over our actions. This is a tremendously appealing view, because it enables the Christian to hold together the biblical themes of predestination and free will, which seem to be in tension. However, as I read the book a question crossed my mind: "If God can allow us freedom and still ensure that he gets his will done, why is it that he allows anyone to go to hell?" If William Craig is right, I reasoned, God could save everyone without violating our free will! It was a great relief to find that Craig had a chapter on that very topic in the book; and I read it with eagerness but, to my horror, found it utterly unpersuasive (I will explain my reasoning in Appendix 1).

The problem Craig's book raised for me was that the main argument I had used to defend hell, at least when not going through a Calvinist phase, was that God had given humans free will, and if people choose to reject the gospel, then God would not compel them to accept it. Craig's book began to remove that argument from my armory, leaving me defenseless. It began to look like God could save everyone whether God controlled all our actions (as the Calvinist claims) or even if he does not (as the free will theist claims). I read all I could get my hands on to defend my belief in hell but to no avail—the arguments just seemed unpersuasive. William Craig had written several articles on the subject, so I read them all. In a couple of them he was criticising a Christian universalist philosopher known as Thomas Talbott. I was disturbed when I found the arguments Craig was criticizing more persuasive than his response to them. To some readers it will seem odd that I would find arguments for universalism disturbing. However, it is important

---

[3] Basil F. C. Atkinson, *Life and Immortality* (Taunton: Phoenix/Goodman n.d.); Edward W. Fudge, *The Fire that Consumes: The Biblical Case for Conditional Immortality*, rev. ed. (Carlisle: Paternoster, 1994). The Fudge edition I was loaned was the original U.S. edition.

[4] John Stott and D. L. Edwards, *Essentials: A Liberal–Evangelical Dialogue* (London: Hodder & Stoughton, 1988).

[5] The shift is seen in the fact that the British Evangelical Alliance Report, *The Nature of Hell* (Carlisle: Paternoster, 2000) acknowledges that annihilation is a legitimate evangelical position.

[6] William Lane Craig, *The Only Wise God: The Compatibility of Divine Foreknowledge and Human Freedom* (1987. Reprinted, Eugene, Ore.: Wipf & Stock, 2000).

to understand that for most orthodox Christians universalism is so far off the 'soundness' radar that it does not even register! Universalism is *so obviously* false that it can be rejected with hardly a moment's thought. After all, Scripture is clear that some (many?) will be in hell whilst universalists claim that all will be saved. Q.E.D. So finding arguments for universalism convincing seemed to be a major and unwelcome challenge to my orthodox faith. I was, and remain, committed to the truth of Scripture; so I thought that I 'knew' universalism was not true. The problem was that over a period of months I had become convinced that God *could* save everyone *if he wanted to,* and yet I also believed that the Bible taught that he would not. But, I reasoned, if he loved them, surely he would save them; and thus my doxological crisis grew. Perhaps the Calvinists were right—God could save everyone if he wanted to, but he does not want to. He loves the elect with saving love but not so the reprobate. God may love me, but does he love my mother? I was no longer sure. Could I love a God who could rescue everyone but chose not to? I could and did go through the motions, but my heart was not in it. And that was what happened—I sang and prayed; but it felt hollow and so I stopped. I no longer loved God, because he seemed diminished. I cannot express how deeply distressing this was for me—perhaps the most anguishing period of reflection on my faith I have ever experienced.

Then a seed of hope was planted in my heart. I found an article on the web by Keith DeRose, an evangelical philosopher at Yale, about universalism and the Bible.[7] DeRose argued that universalism is a biblical belief. I must confess to finding his arguments far from persuasive, but it opened up for me the impossible possibility, a hope beyond hope that he just *may* be onto something.

Some months later a student of mine was doing a piece of work on philosophical theology and hell. I put her onto the writings of the key contemporary Christian thinkers in the area. One of these was Thomas Talbott. I got in contact with him via e-mail, and he kindly sent a pre-publication article on universalism he had written and a copy of his book *The Inescapable Love of God.* Two things happened at that time. The first was that my student ended up shifting her view and defending a universalist position. As I tried to defend the traditional view with her, I became more convinced in my own mind that it simply did not work. I also read Talbott's book, and the seed of hope grew into a young plant. I was far from persuaded that universalism was a biblical position, but I did find many of Talbott's arguments either possible, plausible, or convincing. For the first time universalism really became a live option, though not one I could yet embrace.

---

[7] "Universalism and the Bible," found at http://pantheon.yale.edu/%7Ekd47/univ.htm.

Over the next year and a half I read widely on the subject and on relevant Scriptural passages to see if a plausible biblical theology with a universalist twist could indeed be constructed. My 'conversion' to universalism was not sudden but very gradual and, at times, anxious. Such a departure from the mainstream view of the church is not something to be rushed into. I do not expect readers of this book to rush to embrace universalism—in some ways I would be concerned if they did. I do however wish to sow a seed of hope.

The Nature of My Proposal

I am a hopeful dogmatic universalist. That may sound rather odd, so let me explain. I will clarify what I mean by universalist in the next section. For now, suffice it to say that a universalist believes that God will rescue all people. Some Christians describe themselves as "hopeful universalists." By this they mean that Scripture gives good grounds for real hope that all will be saved, but there is no certainty. Perhaps human freedom or God's sovereign right to determine the future rule out any certainty here. That is *not* my position, and the reason I reject it will become clear in the following chapters. Other Christians are dogmatic universalists. They argue that it is certain that God will save all. I agree but with a qualification. The theology outlined in this book is one that espouses a dogmatic universalism, but I must confess to not being 100% certain that it is correct. Thus I am a hopeful dogmatic universalist, a non-dogmatic dogmatic universalist, if you will. All theological systems need to be offered with a degree of humility, and one that departs significantly from the mainstream Christian tradition calls for even more. I hope to show that, in fact, universalism is not a major change to the tradition and that it actually enables us to hold key elements of the tradition together better than traditional doctrines of hell. Nevertheless, arrogance is out of place.

I need to make clear that when I speak of my view as a qualified dogmatic universalism I am not using dogma in the strong sense of a teaching central to the faith that all Christians ought to believe. I would never dare be so presumptuous. Origen, one of the great universalists in the early church, was clear that dogmatism was out of place in discussions on issues that fell outside the Church's Rule of Faith. He had eschatology in mind when he said this, and we would do well to follow in his footsteps.[8] Not all Christian beliefs are equally important (though you might never guess that from the way some Christians seem willing to fight tooth and nail defending every little 'truth'). Such core beliefs as are found in the Rule of Faith and the creeds are essential to the spiritual life of all authentic Christian faith, but universalism is not.

---

[8] Origen, *De principiis* 1.6.1.

I offer this theology as one that seems to me to fit very comfortably with central elements of a biblically grounded Christian faith. Indeed, I believe it does a better job of that than more traditional theologies. I hope that I will convince most readers that my views are neither heretical nor dangerous but constitute a legitimate Christian option and even a legitimate evangelical option (though here I may perhaps express a hope some years ahead of its time). I would also like to convince others that I am, in fact, more or less correct.

The Intellectual Geography of Universalisms

What do I mean when I speak of universalism? The word can be used in a range of ways, and we need to be very clear about how we are using it *and* how we are *not* using it. I have found the typology in the book *Universal Salvation? The Current Debate* to be very helpful,[9] and the following typology is that of Robin Parry and Christopher Partridge from the introduction to that book.

One can use the term universalism to indicate the view, shared by all Christians, that the gospel message is not simply for one specific group (the Jews, say) but for *all* people-groups. This kind of universalism is clearly taught in the New Testament and is anticipated, though not always perspicuously, in the Old. One can also employ the term to refer to the claim that God desires all individual people to be saved and that Christ was sent to die for each and every person. Of course, it need not follow from this that God will achieve his purpose of saving all, and so this view is compatible with the final damnation of some. This kind of universalism is, I suspect, the majority view in the Christian church but is certainly not shared by all Christians. Those who subscribe to a strong Calvinism with its doctrines of election and limited atonement would certainly deny it. Neither of these kinds of universalism are what I will be discussing in this book.

One could also think of stronger versions of universalism, according to which all individuals will eventually be saved. Here we are getting closer to our topic; but we still have some way to go yet, as there are a variety of versions of such universalisms. For instance, there could be non-Christian versions of such a view. Of course, such versions would have different understandings of what salvation was all about and how one achieved it. There are also pluralist universalists, such as John Hick. Hick believes that all people will be saved by God through whatever religious system they belong to. Such a universalism seems to be clearly unbiblical in that it marginalizes Christ's role in salvation, and it shall receive no more attention here.

---

[9] Robin A. Parry and Christopher H. Partridge, eds., *Universal Salvation? The Current Debate* (Carlisle: Paternoster; Grand Rapids: Eerdmans, 2003).

The group of views I wish to consider could be described as *Christian* Universalisms. What they have in common is that the origin of the universalist impulse and the way it is worked out theologically are integrally Christian. This needs to be stressed, because some critics speak as if the real motivations for Christian universalism lie not within Christian theology but within a "wishy-washy" pluralism or relativism. This is not only insulting but is patently false.

Christian universalists come in all shapes and sizes; and they certainly disagree with each other on many issues, as the introduction to *Universal Salvation? The Current Debate* makes clear. I want us to get concrete in our discussion, so I wish to introduce you to an imaginary representative of Christian universalism. We shall call her Anastasia. She will represent a version of Christian Universalism I consider to have plausible grounds for claiming to be a position in tune with Scripture. Let me sketch her views.

Anastasia is an evangelical Christian. She believes in the inspiration and authority of the Bible. She believes in all those crucial Christian doctrines such as Trinity, creation, sin, atonement, the return of Christ, salvation through Christ alone, by grace alone, through faith alone. In fact, on most things you'd be hard pressed to tell her apart from any other evangelical. Contrary to what we may suspect, she even believes in the eschatological wrath of God—in hell. She differs most obviously in two unusual beliefs. First, she believes that one's eternal destiny is not *fixed* at death and, consequently, that those in hell can repent and throw themselves upon the mercy of God in Christ and thus be saved. Second, she also believes that *in the end* everyone will do this. Now, not all Christian universalists would agree with Anastasia's views here, but it is her kind of universalism that I primarily have in mind when I speak of universalism.

It is important to be clear about these varieties, as one often reads criticisms that turn out only to be criticisms of *certain versions* of universalism. Consider this objection from J. I. Packer: "Modern universalism's basic idea is that no one deserves to be damned."[10] Well, that objection may well apply to some, but it is not remotely applicable to Anastasia. Similarly, many object that universalism is a way of sidestepping the offence of Christian particularity—that salvation is found in Christ alone. This is a fair objection against pluralist universalisms, but it does not touch Anastasia.

[10] J. I. Packer, "Good Pagans and God's Kingdom," in idem, *Celebrating the Saving Work of God* (Carlisle: Paternoster, 1998) 165 [161–68].

The Argument of this Book

The argument opens with an examination of the philosophical problems with traditional Christian teachings on hell. It was here that my own doubts about the tradition began, so it seems appropriate to take the reader along a route similar to my own. I argue that whether one believes that God predestines everything that happens or whether one believes that human freedom lies outside God's determining power, it is, or so I contend, well nigh impossible to understand why God would not save everybody. Reason seems to be in serious conflict with traditional theology; and this, I suggest, leads us to enquire whether we may actually have misunderstood the implications of biblical theology.

In Chapter 2 the focus moves from philosophy to the Bible and provides some introductory comments about constructing a theology that has some serious claims to being true to Scripture as a whole. I seek to answer the question: What tests must a universalist theology pass to count as biblical? The rest of the book is an attempt at arguing that universalism can pass such tests. The chapter then moves on to consider the theology of Colossians. This book, I suggest, provides the contours of a grand theological narrative with a universalist ending. It is this basic theology that I suggest can form the framework within which the rest of the Bible can be appropriated.

Chapters 3 and 4 fill in some of the detail for this grand theological story. My aim is to provide a fairly detailed biblical metanarrative that fits very nicely with the teachings of Christian universalism. Chapters Two to Four then are a unit providing a hermeneutic; a biblical-theological context for making sense of all individual passages.

Chapter 5 then takes a case study to show how fruitful such a theological grid can be. The book of Revelation is the home of the two most horrific hell passages in the entire Bible, and thus it presents a serious challenge to universalism. I argue that one can do justice to the exegesis of the book of Revelation with a universalist hermeneutic. Indeed, I argue that Revelation itself seems to presuppose a theology very similar to that outlined in Chapters Two to Four and to teach universalism! I suggest that the author invites readers to interpret the two hell passages in ways compatible with universalism.

Having suggested a way of making sense of biblical hell passages in Chapter Five, I take up the topic of hell texts in more detail in Chapter 6. There I argue that it is legitimate to understand the biblical teaching about hell as compatible with an awful *but temporary* fate from which all can, and ultimately will, be saved.

Chapter 7 finally sets out some of the theological benefits of Christian universalism and responds to some remaining objections. I argue that the problem of evil, though by no means made easy, is made significantly *easier*

than on traditional views. I also argue that the pastoral benefits are significant. Christian universalism yields a theology of hope, of divine love, and
presents a vision of the victory of God that has significant advantages over
the tradition, with its eternal hell. It also yields an inspiring ecclesiology and
missiological motivation. Indeed, it accentuates the love and grace of God
without diminishing his severity and wrath. It lifts the saving work of Christ
to new heights without losing sight of judgment. And, returning to the open-
ing of this introduction, it inspires a new understanding of worship and provides the inspiration for heartfelt devotion to our great God—Father, Son
and Holy Spirit.

CHAPTER ONE

A Hell of a Problem

THE TRADITIONAL position [is] . . . that God will be all in all despite the damnation . . . of many of his creatures . . . [T]he universalist asserts: "The God I believe in, the God I see in Christ, could not be all in all in these conditions: such victory could not be the victory of the God of love."

—Bishop J. A. T. Robinson[1]

When Biblical Interpretation and Reason Clash

IT HAS long been recognized that Christian theology is guided by several key sources of wisdom: Scripture, tradition, reason, and experience. Of these, the Protestant churches agree that Scripture is the most authoritative. These four sources, however, inter-relate in such complex ways that one cannot claim to "just read the Bible" without paying attention to tradition, reason, and experience. In an ideal world, the four sources would beautifully dovetail and lead to clear conclusions. However, it is a common experience for the Church to be faced with situations in which Scripture *seems* to conflict with one or more of the other sources. What do we do in such situations if we are committed to a divinely inspired Scripture? We first ask whether reason, tradition, or experience may not be misleading or mistaken. We then also consider whether we may have misunderstood Scripture, for even a commitment to an inspired Bible is not a commitment to inerrant *interpretations*. Reason can play a role in exposing misinterpretations of the Bible. It is this role that I want to draw attention to in this chapter.

In the history of the Church it is not hard to find cases in which prevailing interpretations of the Bible were changed in the light of reason. One has

---

[1] J. A. T. Robinson, *In the End God: A Study of the Christian Doctrine of the Last Things* (London: James Clarke, 1950) 102.

only to think of how the Copernican revolution led to a new understanding of texts such as Psalm 93[2] or how modern cosmology has led to new ways of reading Genesis 1.[3] On the non-scientific front, one thinks of how Aquinas's metaphorical interpretations of biblical statements about God's changing his mind were acceptable because his philosophy told him that they could not be literally true (for God is timeless). Most evangelicals, myself included, are quite happy with such a use of reason to guide interpretation.

In this chapter I wish to apply this method to the doctrine of hell. The mainstream Christian tradition speaks clearly on this issue, as does traditional interpretation of several key biblical texts. All who fail to accept the gospel of Jesus Christ, so the tradition goes, will be condemned to eternal, conscious torment in hell. The moment of death is the moment after which there are no more chances to receive God's mercy. Within the tradition there has always been a minority report in favor of annihilation or universalism, but the main thrust of the tradition is clear. I think that the reflective Christian ought to start by taking the tradition as the default position—it should be assumed to be correct unless good grounds can be found to reject it. To jettison such a long-lasting and clear tradition is something that ought to be done cautiously and reluctantly. The Christian biblical scholar, philosopher, or theologian should *begin* then by attempting to defend this tradition. Many have rightly done so. However, Protestants do not, in theory, recognize tradition, nor interpretations of the Bible, as infallible; so we must be open to the *possibility* that we have made a mistake here.

I shall argue that philosophical attempts to defend the tradition to date have failed to present a convincing case. I shall further argue that philosophical arguments for universalism have considerable force. This produces a conflict between reason and traditional interpretations of the Bible. The reflective Christian should re-examine the Bible and theology to see if they are not, in fact, compatible with some form of universalism. If such an attempted re-reading fails, then they must return to philosophy and try again to make reason fit the Bible. I, however, shall argue in the following chapters that a universalist interpretation of the Bible can work; and, if it does, reason will have played a crucial role in exposing our misinterpretations and pointing us to a truer understanding of Scripture.

---

[2] See Colin A. Russell, *Cross Currents: Interactions between Science and Faith* (Leicester: InterVarsity, 1985) chap. 3; Nicholas Wolterstorff, *Divine Discourse: Philosophical Reflections on the Claim That God Speaks* (Cambridge: Cambridge University Press, 1995) 209ff.

[3] I have non-literal readings in mind. Though such interpretations can be traced back at least as far as Augustine there can be no doubt that scientific discoveries have rightly promoted their plausibility.

General Problems With the Traditional Doctrine of Hell

There are several problems that all attempts to justify the traditional doctrine must run up against, so I shall deal with these first, before looking at problems connected with specific defenses.

The Problem of the Justice of Infinite Retribution

Any roughly traditional doctrine of hell is parasitic upon a philosophy of punishment usually known as the retributive theory of punishment. This theory holds that the punishment of a criminal is justified, *not* on the basis of its rehabilitative effect, *nor* on the basis of its crime-deterring impact, but on the grounds that *the criminal deserves it*. Clearly, punishing sinners in the traditional hell is not going to rehabilitate them, nor deter them from future sins. God punishes the sinners in hell *because they deserve it, because justice is served in this way*.

Central to the retributive theory of punishment is the notion that the punishment must fit the crime. A punishment too lenient or too harsh does not serve the cause of justice. But it is here that the problem lies. According to the traditional doctrine, hell is everlasting, conscious torment. What *possible* crime is a finite human capable of committing that would be justly punished in *this* way? Many find the idea absurd, because it is hard to see how even the most hideous crimes humans commit could be balanced by the traditional eternal punishing. The upshot of this is that the traditional doctrine seems to require a theory of punishment that ends up undermining it.

I am aware of two approaches that try to circumvent this problem; and, it seems to me, both are problematic. The first solution is that of St. Anselm, who argued that as God is infinitely great and as any sin is an offence against him, then any sin incurs infinite demerit. The only fitting penalty for an offense against an infinite being is an infinite punishment—everlasting punishment.[4] There are two common objections to this argument. The first is that it is based on a view of crime we no longer subscribe to. Marilyn Adams points out that the social background to this argument is that of a feudal society in which the gravity of a crime is determined by both the offense and the social status of the victim. Adams objects that Anselm's argument carries little weight today, as we no longer consider the legal seriousness of a crime to be influenced by the social status of the victim.[5] In a recent essay Oliver Crisp has vigorously defended the Anselmian tradition against this kind of objection.[6] He agrees with Adams that the social status of the victim does not

---

[4] Anselm, *Cur Deus Homo*, chap. 22.

[5] Marilyn Adams, "Hell and the Justice of God," *RelSt* 11 (1975) 433–47.

[6] Oliver Crisp, "Divine Retribution: A Defense," *Sophia* 42.2 (2003) 36–53.

make any difference to the seriousness of the crime. However, we should not simply jettison Anselm's argument for that reason. We also typically consider that crimes committed against humans are more serious than crimes committed against cats or mice. So we do usually recognize an ontological difference between humans and lesser species that makes crimes against human more liable to punishment. Given this common intuition, there is nothing obviously out of date with the claim that God is ontologically greater than humans and that crimes against God are more serious than crimes against humans. Indeed, God is infinitely great, and thus crimes against him may possibly incur infinite demerit and deserve infinite punishment.

It seems to me that Crisp may have successfully rescued Anselm from the first objection, though problems remain with his response. For instance, it is not obvious that a sin against God's infinite honor incurs an infinite demerit. Suppose that John has 10 units of honor. Imagine further that Philip ignores John in public whilst Simon spits in John's face. Both have offended against his honor, but the amount of demerit incurred is surely not 10 units in both cases. The nature of their crimes plays a key role in deciding their desert. So also it is with God. It does not necessarily follow from the claim that God has infinite honor that *any* crime against him is infinitely bad. This is because the gravity of an offense is determined not merely by the status of the offended party but also by the nature of the offense.[7]

The second objection to Anselm is that his theory makes all sins equally bad, and most people consider this consequence to be counter-intuitive. Thomas Talbott writes:

> . . . if *every* sin is infinitely serious and thus deserves the same penalty as every other sin, namely everlasting torment, then . . . the idea so central to the retributivist theory, that we can grade offences, collapses—as does the idea of an excessive punishment and that of fitting lesser punishments to lesser crimes. Many Christians do, it is true, speculate that gradations of punishment exist in hell; some, they suggest, may experience greater pain than others. . . . But even this seems inconsistent with the idea that *every* sin against the infinite God is infinitely grave and therefore equal to every other sin . . . .[8]

---

[7] In the end this critique rests on an intuition and Crisp's intuitions are different from my own. Crisp feels that the creator-creature relationship is unique in such a way that whilst my objection applies to relationships between creatures it does not apply to the relationship between creatures and God. I think that it does but in the end we are simply *asserting* contrary intuitions. In defense of my own let me simply point out that in Scripture not all sins are considered equally bad nor do they all incur equal punishment.

[8] Thomas Talbott, *The Inescapable Love of God* (Boca Raton, La.: Universal, 1999) 154–55. Talbott gives additional reasons for rejecting Anslem's theory (see too Adams, "Hell and the Justice of God"). J. Kvanig also argues that the "punishment model" for hell defended by

Crisp has responded to this objection also. It does not follow from the claim that all sinners are punished infinitely that they are punished equally. He asks us to imagine two sinners, Trevor and Gary. "Both are consigned to hell forever. Both suffer an infinite punishment in hell. But Trevor is only punished for one hour a day whereas Gary is punished for twelve hours a day. Clearly, in this state of affairs they are both punished infinitely but not equally."[9]

Let us, for argument's sake, grant that Crisp is correct to say that God could punish all sinners infinitely without all punishments being equal. The degrees of punishment he retains in his view of hell require sins to be gradable in terms of their seriousness. The very bad sins would merit severe punishments for infinity and the mild sins would merit mild punishment for infinity. The problem is that it is hard to give an account of how sins can be distinguished in degrees of seriousness if we begin, as Crisp does, from the claim that all sins incur *infinite* demerit. You cannot get worse than that. The very claim seems to flatten out any attempt to distinguish between degrees of sin. So it seems to me that Crisp has to make a stronger case that allows him to consider all sins as equally bad and yet also to allow him to distinguish lesser from greater sins. If he cannot do so, the standard objection remains and renders Anselm's view implausible.

A more recent attempt to deal with the problem of the injustice of ev-

---

Anselm and others is unworkable. To defend a roughly traditional view of hell he adopts a "choice model" in which hell is simply what people choose as their destiny and God has to respect that choice, "Heaven and Hell," in *Companion to the Philosophy of Religion*, ed. Philip L. Quinn and Charles Taliaferro (Cambridge, Mass.: Blackwell, 1997) 562–68.

[9] There is an objection to this line of argument. If pains are commensurable, that is to say, if pains can be measured by the same standard, then over an infinite period of time Gary has suffered an infinite amount of pain and so has Trevor. But this means that, odd as it may sound, Trevor and Gary have suffered the same amount of pain as each other (i.e., an infinite amount) and Crisp's argument fails. The objection to Crisp fails, however, because Trevor and Gary only experience pain in a potentially infinite way rather than an actually infinite way thus at no point in their experience will they have ever experienced an infinite duration of pain—there will always be more to come. But here another problem raises its head, because justice is only served when Trevor and Gary have served their infinite sentence yet at no point in the future will that have happened. There will always be more punishment required for justice to be satisfied so we end up with a theory of divine punishment in which justice is *never* satisfied *fully* (and that is the case even though we may rather suffer Trevor's punishment than Gary's if we were forced to choose). One way out of this problem is to embrace a highly controversial view of time according to which time can be divided up into smaller and smaller units infinitely. If this idea of "dense time" is embraced then there is an infinite amount of time between any two moments in time and God could punish someone infinitely in one hour, one minute, one second, or less. See Nathan Oaklander and Quentin Smith, *Time, Change, and Freedom* (London: Routledge, 1995). I do not wish to sidetrack into such matters except to register an inclination to reject such notions of time.

erlasting torment is to suggest that God only punishes sins with a temporary
punishment but the damned are so furious at God that they rage against his
treatment of them, thus sinning some more. This warrants yet more punishment; and a vicious circle is set up of sin, punishment, sin, punishment,
which spirals on for eternity.[10]

However, this view seems incompatible with a biblical theology according to which in the coming age God *destroys* sin from his creation. On the
vicious circle argument, God creates a situation in hell in which sin is not
merely *punished* for eternity but actually *perpetuated for eternity*. But why
would God wish to create a situation in which many of his creatures rebel
against him forever? Hell does not *have* to be that way. For instance, God
could make those in hell fully aware of the weight of their crimes and the
righteousness of his judgment. Such sinners would suffer but would recognize that they fully deserve the punishment they are receiving and would not
rage against God. Or, God could annihilate those in hell, eradicating both sin
and sinner. Alternatively, as I will argue later, God could restore those in hell
and redeem them from sin. In all these ways justice is still done, but sin is not
perpetuated.[11] And any of these three alternatives seem preferable to the view
according to which sin is never *removed* from creation but merely contained
in a kind of stasis chamber where it is perfectly balanced by punishment.

Given the profound problems of everlasting conscious torment, two alternatives have become increasingly popular:

> (a) Hell is everlasting; but, from the perspective of the damned, it
> is not that bad a place to be.[12]

---

[10] D. A. Carson seems to envisage such a scenario in *The Gagging of God: Christianity Confronts Pluralism* (Grand Rapids: Zondervan; Leicester: Apollos, 1996) 533–34.

[11] On which, see now, Talbott, "Freedom, Damnation and the Power to Sin With Impunity," *RelSt* 37 (2001) 417–34.

[12] Consider Jerry L. Walls: "Those in hell may be almost happy, and this may explain why they insist on staying there. They do not, of course, experience even a shred of genuine happiness. But perhaps they experience a certain perverse sense of satisfaction, a distorted sort of pleasure" (*Hell: The Logic of Damnation* [Notre Dame: Notre Dame University Press, 1992] 128). Walls has nuanced, qualified and defended his view in "A Philiosophical Critique of Talbott's Universalism," in Parry and Partridge eds., *Universal Salvation?*, 105–24. Consider C. S. Lewis: "Hell is hell, not from its own point of view, but from the heavenly point of view" (*The Problem of Pain* [New York: MacMillan, 1944] 114). Possibly not dissimilar is Stump's Thomist approach according to which for God to annihilate the wicked would be a great evil and thus not an option open to him. Given that some freely choose to fall short of their human nature he can only save them by over-riding their freedom which, says Stump, he would also be wrong to do. Thus God loves them in the best way open to him by treating them according to their freely chosen, sinful natures. God is showing his love to the damned by preserving them in hell (Stump, "Dante's Hell, Aquinas' Moral Theory and the Love of God," *CJP* 16 (1986) 181–96). See too Richard Swinburne, *Providence and the Problem of Evil* (Oxford:

(b) Hell as annihilation, perhaps preceded by temporary torment.

Both *may*[13] succeed in bypassing *this* problem, though (a) seems to be unbiblical. One may properly understand biblical descriptions of hell metaphorically, but they certainly portray the inhabitants as consciously and seriously suffering.

The Problem of the Joy of the Redeemed

A second general problem with any view in which some are damned concerns the eschatological bliss of the redeemed. Not all pleasures are as worthwhile as each other. The pleasures of a woman who mistakenly thinks she has saved a friend's life are not as worthwhile as the pleasures of a woman who actually has done so. The pleasures of the sadist are worth less than Mother Theresa's. The redeemed surely experience the *most valuable* kind of happiness. Thomas Talbott has developed an argument first used by Schleiermacher that, I propose, can be set out as follows:[14]

> 1. Let us say that supremely worthwhile happiness is a kind such that (a) it could survive the complete disclosure of truth about the universe, and (b) one possesses it only when one is filled with love for others.

> 2. Supremely worthwhile happiness cannot rest on deception or false factual beliefs (given 1.a),[15] nor can it exist if there are people we know of but do not love (given 1.b)

> 3. Love can jeopardize our happiness if those we love suffer, especially if they suffer everlastingly with *no hope* of salvation.

> 4. Therefore, to have supremely worthwhile happiness, I must be able to know about the genuine fate of those I love and remain happy.

Clarendon, 1998).

[13] It is a moot point whether annihilation does indeed circumvent the injustice criticism; see T. Gray, "The Nature of Hell: Reflections on the Debate Between Conditionalism and the Traditional View of Hell," in *Eschatology in Bible and Theology: Evangelical Essays at the Dawn of a New Millennium*, ed. Kent E. Brower and Mark W. Elliot (Downers Grove, Ill.: InterVarsity, 1997) 231–41.

[14] There is no evidence that Talbott was aware of Schleiermacher's argument when he devised his version.

[15] Talbott is following Swinburne in this claim, Swinburne, "A Theodicy of Heaven and Hell," in *The Existence and Nature of God*, ed. Alfred J. Fredosso (Notre Dame: Notre Dame University Press, 1983) 40.

5. I can only know the fate of those I love and remain happy if
their fate is ultimately a blessed one.

6. Therefore, the redeemed can only have supremely worthwhile
happiness if ultimately no one they love is damned eternally.

William Lane Craig has responded to this argument by denying 1.a. He maintains that supremely worthwhile happiness is the kind that *would be* diminished *if* the full truth about the universe were made known *but not necessarily
the kind that can survive such a revelation.* The saved, says Craig, could be
both supremely happy (in the sense of having no sadness) and have supremely
worthwhile happiness (in the sense of being subject to diminished happiness
if they were aware of the fate of the lost) so long as they were unaware of the
fate of the damned.[16] I concur with this critique. Craig suggests two possible
ways in which such ignorance of the fate of the damned could arise:

• God could wipe their memory of those they love, or

• the beatific vision may be so all-consuming that they may
simply never turn their thoughts to them.

But Talbott's argument is not so easily defeated, as both Craig's suggestions are deeply problematic.[17] We must realize that a "Craigian memory-
wipe" would lead to the obliteration and deformation of *huge* chunks of my
past (perhaps most of it). This would make it hard for God to avoid deceiv-
ing me for the following reason: Suppose that I experienced the saving love
of God as a result of various interactions with people who end up damned.
For instance, suppose I was converted through an evangelist who was only
a pseudo-believer, one who proclaimed the true gospel whilst not truly believing it himself. How could God allow me to retain true beliefs about my
conversion, or my secular life prior to it, whilst at the same time blotting out
all memory of all those who are damned? The answer, it seems to me, is that
he can only do so by allowing me to locate the true belief fragments within a
broader web of false beliefs. Thus, I may have the true memory of hearing the
gospel proclaimed to me but falsely "remember" that it was someone else who
told it to me (a genuine believer) or that the person who preached to me was
actually a believer. This makes deception unavoidable unless God wipes out

---

[16] William Lane Craig, "Talbott's Universalism Once More," *RelSt* 29 (1993) 297–308.

[17] Talbott says that the memory-wipe option would be tantamount to deception bringing
me joy by forever hiding from me the horrible (even if deserved) fate of those I cherish. Craig
denies that such a memory-wipe would be a deception as the saved hold no false beliefs about
the damned—they hold no beliefs about them at all. Again, I think that Craig is right, but
further trouble awaits him (see main text).

all memory of our pre-parousia life. But how could we worship the Lamb who has redeemed us by his blood (Rev 5:9) if we have no memory of our sin nor of our redemption? The only alternative is to have a memory full of so many holes that that my memory would be fragmented and lose the narrative continuity so essential to a sense of self-identity. It would be hard not to try to fill in the blank spaces and infer the existence of the unsaved and this, on Craig's account, would destroy my heavenly bliss.

Talbott points to another problem with the memory-wipe option. Nobody who really loves someone else would want to remain blissfully ignorant of a loved one's fate, even if the fate is horrible. And they would not choose to have their memory blanked out in this way. It would perhaps seem to be cruel rather than merciful (as Craig thinks) for God to act like this.[18] On top of that, the Bible hints that the saved are indeed aware of the fate of the damned (Isa 66:24). Thus, I judge a memory-wipe a deeply problematic proposal that is better rejected.

The beatific vision of God's love does not make us *less* aware of the pains of others but *more*. It makes no sense to me to imagine that we shall be so full of God that we will forget others, let alone hate them or even love them less (1 John 4:20). God could stop me loving those I love at present. He could make my heart callous so that I am not tormented by their pains. But would the God who loves his enemies (Matt 5:43-48) perform such heart-hardening surgery? To suggest that he would is, at the very least, deeply problematic. Thus, both the memory-wipe option and the beatific vision option offer little hope of escape from Talbott's argument.

It has been claimed by some theologians that the redeemed will look upon the sufferings of the damned and rejoice in God's just punishment of the wicked.[19] Pastor John K. La Shell writes:

> How will the gloriously transformed saints respond when they see people they loved on earth cast into hell? They will not look on them as their beloved "Mother" or "Aunt Matilda." They will see human beings stripped of their attractive shell, enemies of God cursing their beloved Savior. Hence their former affection will be turned to utter rejection. We will then rejoice at the destruction of all who have opposed our heavenly husband, the Lord Jesus Christ.[20]

---

[18] Talbott, *Inescapable Love*, 194.

[19] For instance, Jonathan Edwards, "The End of the Wicked Contemplated by the Righteous"; Robert Murray McCheyne, "The Eternal Torment of the Wicked, Matter of Eternal Song to the Redeemed" (see D. Strange, "A Calvinist Response to Talbott's Universalism," in Parry and Partridge, eds., *Universal Salvation?*, n.63).

[20] *ChrTod* (July 8, 2002) 8. Such sentiments can be found in many classical theologians also.

This is a view judged by many Christians to be repulsive and unworthy of serious consideration. If God himself does not rejoice in the death of the wicked (Ezek 33:11) or in the pain he sometimes has to inflict (Lam 3:31-33), how could his people? Even if the glorified saints rejoiced that justice was served (and the book of Revelation indicates that they will), they could not find pleasure in the sufferings that such justice required if they love the damned in the way that God does.

Thus, given the problems with the claim that the redeemed will forget the lost, I think that Talbott's eschatological bliss argument remains a difficulty for all traditional views.

In conclusion, all views of hell as eternal conscious torment suffer from two generic problems. First, the punishment seems out of proportion to any crimes humans can commit. Classical attempts to avoid this conclusion seem to lead to the problem of making all sins as bad as each other—a morally problematic position. Second, it is hard to see how God could give the redeemed perfect happiness if some of their loved ones are in hell forever. Views of hell as annihilation may possibly be able to bypass the first criticism, but the second remains a difficulty (even if not so acute a difficulty as it is for eternal conscious torment views). It is time to move beyond generic problems to consider attempts to defend hell that originate in divergent theological traditions.

Calvinism and Hell

The various defenses of hell differ as a result of their views of freedom. There are two main families of views when it comes to the philosophy of free will: compatibilist and libertarian.[21] To simplify: the libertarian maintains that for a person to act freely the following two conditions must be met:

> 1. the action is one the person *wants* to perform;

> 2. the person could choose to perform *or not perform* the action
> (i.e., the agent is not causally determined to perform the action).

The compatibilist will accept 1 and deny 2. To the compatibilist human freedom and moral responsibility are compatible with causal determinism. For the sake of argument, I shall assume that both views of freedom are plausible candidates for the truth.

---

[21] For the record, I am aware that there is another option—hard determinism (a view which embraces a libertarian understanding of freedom but denies that anyone has such freedom because all human actions are, according to the view, determined)—but this is not a live option for a Christian.

Now, assuming compatibilist views of freedom (as most Calvinists will), consider the following argument:

> 1. God, being omnipotent, *could* cause all people to freely accept Christ.

> 2. God, being omniscient, *would know how* to cause all people to freely accept Christ.

> 3. God, being omnibenevolent, would *want* to cause all people to freely accept Christ.

Now 1–3 entail:

> 4. God *will* cause all people to freely accept Christ.

From which it follows that:

> 5. All people *will* freely accept Christ.

Thus, a strong view of divine providence, combined with the claim that God loves and desires to save all people, leads to a convincing argument for universalism.[22] However, most who have held such a strong view of providence are most certainly *not* universalists (Augustine, Aquinas, Luther, Calvin, etc.). They maintain that 5 is false. But if 1–3 entail 4 and 4 entails 5, how can they do this? By denying 3. God, according to the Calvinist, *does not love all people and want to save them*. If he did then he would. Rather, he loves the elect—his chosen people. It is *them* he loves, was for *them* he died, and it is *they* he will save.

At the level of logic, then, the problem of hell seems to be solved. Setting aside the generic problem discussed above, God is not *unjust* in sending people to hell.[23] The real problem for the Calvinist solution is not with God's *justice*[24] but with his *love*. The claim that God does not love and wish to save all is a *very* hard pill for the Christian to swallow. It seems to entail a denial of the claim that God's *nature* is to love his creatures (as 1 John 4:8, 16b seems to teach),[25] that Christ died for all people (as 1 John 2:2 seems to teach), and

---

[22] For a powerful statement of the case for Calvinist universalism see Oliver Crisp, "Augustinian Universalism," *IJPR* 53 (2003) 127–45.

[23] At least, not unjust if we think of justice as purely retributive. If we wish a richer notion of justice involving rehabilitation then God may be unjust in condemning people without hope of restoration (see Talbott, *Inescapable Love*, chap. 9).

[24] At least, not if justice is understood as retribution.

[25] See Talbott, *Inescapable Love*, chap. 7. An appeal to the doctrine of common grace to alleviate this difficulty is of limited value. Whilst it allows you to say that God "loves" all his creatures in a limited capacity (enough to bestow certain blessings) it does not allow you to

that God desires to save all (as 2 Pet 3:9, 1 Tim 2:4, and Ezek 33:11 seem
to teach). According to theists, God is the greatest possible being. In light
of the biblical emphasis on the supreme value of love, it seems plausible to
think that a being that loves *all* is greater than a being who loves some but
not others. Thus, it seems plausible, from a Christian perspective, to see the
Calvinist solution to the problem of hell as requiring a diminished view of
God's greatness, and diminishing God's greatness is the *last* thing a Calvinist
wants to do. A God who loves all seems more worthy of worship than a God
who does not.

The Calvinist may say that by saving some and not others God is making clear that salvation is of *grace* and thus undeserved. God did not *have* to
save anyone. That he chooses some is wonderful. That he does not choose
all is not unjust. In reply, let me note, first, that it is unclear why the "grace
not works" aspect of salvation requires any to be damned. Surely we could
all be recipients of such grace without it becoming less gracious.[26] We could
also all *realize* that we are saved by grace apart from works without anyone
being eternally damned. Second, the scenario seems frighteningly close to
the following analogy: imagine a man whose sons suffer from a disease that
makes them constantly disobey him (original sin). One day, as a result of
this, the sons fall through the ice on a pond their father had warned them
not to walk on. They begin to drown. They have brought their fate upon
themselves. Being afflicted with the disease, they are too stupid to even respond to their father's calls to grasp the safety ring he has thrown in (the
gospel). The man has the solution: a ray gun he has will cure his sons of
their disobedience and enable them to grasp the ring (irresistible grace). He
could, thus, save both; but, to make the point that he does not *have* to,
he only saves one. This story is shocking! We would think that if the father *could* save both and loved both then he *would* save both. If he did not
we would not say, "Oh well done, you, for saving one of your sons." We
would be shocked by a father who did not love his sons enough to help
them when he could. Is God like that? Even if they deserve what they get,
how could a *loving* father let them die when it is in his power to help?[27]

---

say that God loves all his creatures enough to wish to bring about their ultimate good. But the
"love" shown in common grace is not the robust love that 1 John speaks of when it says that
"God is love." It is more akin to a limited divine generosity.

[26] Perhaps it would be even more gracious.

[27] Some would claim that God, unlike the father, has no moral obligations to us. Even
universalists like Marilyn Adams accept this. However, following William Dumbrell (*Covenant
and Creation* [Exeter: Paternoster, 1984]), I believe that in the act of creation God covenants
himself to his creation and takes upon himself obligations towards us. So even if one thinks
(mistakenly, in my view) that God has no moral obligations to us one can still think he has
chosen to bind himself to creation and to humans in particular.

Is the Calvinist paying too high a price to maintain a traditional doctrine of hell?[28]

The Calvinist may argue that God chooses to display his glory in creation and that he displays both the glory of his love and the glory of his justice. His love is displayed in his treatment of the elect and his justice in the treatment of the damned. Both demonstrate the glory of God, and hell is thus a necessity to display the fullness of that glory. However, it is somewhat ironic that construing Calvinism in such a way that God *has* to show the glory of his justice by punishing many in hell seems to limit God's sovereign freedom to save all *should he so desire*. On top of that, this traditional line of argument is unsuccessful as a defense of hell. According to Calvinists all people deserve hell. However, God has acted in the cross of Christ in such a way as to enable the elect to be saved. Calvinists usually hold to a penal substitutionary view of the atonement, according to which God places the punishment for our sins upon Christ instead of upon us. In this way God can save the elect because their sins have already been paid for. In the cross justice is served (sin is punished) and love is shown (a way of salvation is opened). But on this view God could save everyone whilst still showing the glory of his love and his justice at Calvary. All he need do is make Christ's death sufficient and efficient for all. Hell then becomes unnecessary for the display of the fullness of God's glory, and the argument collapses in on itself. Justice is no impediment to God's saving everyone.[29] For that reason the Calvinist ought to abandon this strategy for defending hell.

I have been supposing that God loves everyone and wants to show mercy on all. Indeed, I have hinted that I believe that if God did not love and try to save everyone, he would be less than perfect. Calvinists will not agree to this. God *has* to be just, they maintain, but he does not *have* to be merciful. He *has* to punish unforgiven sin, but he does not *have* to forgive sin. This is a common view among theologians, but it ought to be seen as problematic for a *Christian* view of God. To subordinate divine love to divine justice so

---

[28] There is a specific problem for the Calvinist connected to the psychological possibility of worship. Talbott again: "I cannot both love my daughter as myself and love (or worship wholeheartedly) a God whom I believe to have done less than he could to save her from a life of misery and torment. For necessarily, if I truly love my daughter, then I will disapprove of any God whom I believe to have done less than his best for her, less than I would have done if I should have the power; and necessarily, if I disapprove of God, then I do not truly love him" ("Providence, Freedom and Human Destiny," *RelSt* 26 [1990] 239).

[29] Alternatively, if hell is required to be inhabited why need it have more than one inhabitant and why could that not be Satan? A more sophisticated version of the argument in the main text has since been produced by Oliver Crisp ("Augustinian Universalism"). To Crisp it is a serious problem for Calvinism and one which he would very much like to find a solution to. So far he has not found a solution.

that God *has* to be just but does not *have* to love is odd for a Christian who confesses that God *is* love. The Calvinist will maintain that this argument is confused because the logic of mercy and justice are different. If a person is just, she or he will be consistently just and cannot simply waive justice on occasions for the sake of convenience. If God is just, he *has* to act justly *all* the time; for that is what it *is* to be just. Mercy is not like that. Mercy is, by definition, something one can choose to give or not to give. Paul Helm writes: "If God cannot but exercise mercy as he cannot but exercise justice, then its character *as mercy vanishes*. If God has to exercise mercy as he has to exercise justice then such 'mercy' would not be mercy."[30] I suggest that Helm is correct in seeing a certain asymmetry between justice and mercy but mistaken in claiming that if God *has* to show mercy then it cannot be true mercy he shows. It could be that it is in God's nature that he desires to show mercy to all. After all, Christians claim that God is love and that he loves his enemies. For God to be love, it would seem to be the case that he has to love all his creatures. This is because if it is God's very essence to love, then God cannot but love, in the same way that if God's essence is to hate evil, then he cannot but hate evil. And if God loves all he has created, then he will want to show saving mercy to all his creatures. Thus he has to show mercy to all *in the sense* that his love for all "psychologically" motivates him to do so. God does not have to show mercy in the sense that some law or force *external to him* compels him to—that would indeed eradicate the merciful character of such acts as Helm rightly notes. But it is perfectly intelligible to claim that he does have to show mercy in the sense that, as the liturgy says, "it is *his nature* always to have mercy."[31] None of this implies that God has to show us mercy *in the sense that we deserve mercy*, for clearly that would destroy the meaning of mercy. We do not deserve mercy, and God does not owe it to us. Nevertheless, it is his nature to show mercy to the objects of his love, and in that sense he does have to show us mercy.

In conclusion, the Calvinist's view of divine sovereignty, combined with the view that God loves and desires to save everyone, leads inevitably to universalism. However, Calvinism, combined with the traditional view of hell as it almost always has been, inevitably leads to deeply troubling waters: a God who *could* save everyone but chooses instead to send some to suffer eternal torment in hell to demonstrate the glory of his justice (a glory he could have demonstrated without sending anyone to hell). Many Christians have found this view too difficult to handle and rejected Calvinism. Many committed

---

[30] P. Helm, "The Logic of Limited Atonement," *SBET* 3.2 (1985) 50.

[31] Given Helm's compatibilism, it is very easy to suppose that God must display mercy by reason of an inner necessity (his divine nature) and yet still act freely in doing so. My thanks to Thomas Talbott for pointing this out.

Calvinists struggle regularly with these issues. To my mind, Christian reason seems to lead either to Calvinist universalism, or away from Calvinism.

Freewill Theism and Hell

The basic freewill theistic way to defend the traditional doctrine of hell is to deny that God can always get his will done. God's will, says the freewill theist, is that all people *freely* (in a libertarian sense) choose to accept the salvation God offers in Christ. God *does* love and *desire* to save all. However, he will not *force* his salvation on people. He wants them to choose it *freely*. Thus, God must respect the free choices of those who reject salvation and who, by default, choose hell.

There is an objection that applies to all freewill theists' attempts to justify a traditional doctrine of hell that is worth making at this stage. It could be argued that an all-loving God will try all that he can to elicit freely a positive response to the gospel; but, if all else fails, he would be justified in not leaving people free in a libertarian sense with respect to their salvation.[32] This is preferable to allowing them to suffer in everlasting conscious torment. This criticism boils down to a value judgment. When you see that a person you love has *irrationally* chosen to do *irreparable* harm to himself or herself (in the case of the traditional doctrine of hell such harm amounts to suffering unbearable torment forever and ever), is freedom *so sacrosanct* that you are not justified in interfering with it? Certainly, we often limit the choices of our younger children in such cases; but should we for our *adult* children? Before answering negatively, consider the following scenario: your adult son or daughter, through persistent irrational and self-destructive choices, is about to enter a realm where they will suffer unbearably day and night forever and ever. You have tried every way you know to persuade them out of it. Your last resort is to use an implant you have had placed in their brain to over-ride, temporarily, their self-destructive desires, allowing them to "choose" to avoid this terrible fate. Once they have entered the realm of salvation, the device will cease working; but they will have tasted the goodness of salvation and will freely choose it for themselves. Would you be willing to do that? I know that I would, and I suspect that any loving parent would. It is hard to see that libertarian freedom is *so* precious that it cannot be temporarily overridden in such dire circumstances. Eric Reitan writes,

---

[32] Marilyn Adams thinks that we often idolize free agency by thinking it to be so valuable that God would accept any unredeemable horror rather than override it on occasion ("The Problem of Hell: A Problem of Evil for Christians," in *A Reasoned Faith*, ed. E. Stump [Ithaca: Cornell University Press, 1993] 301–27). She is ambiguous about how God will save all but invokes the mystery of God—he will do it "somehow" (323).

Libertarian freedom as described[33] does not seem worth having. In fact, as described, I sincerely hope that I lack it. The capacity to eternally act against all my motives would introduce into my life a potential for profound irrationality that I would rather do without. And if I exercise my libertarian freedom as described above, dooming myself to outer darkness without reason, I sincerely hope that God would act to stop me—just as I hope a friend would stop me if I decided to leap from a rooftop for no reason. I would not regard the actions of that friend as a violation of any valuable freedom, but would see it as a welcome antidote to arbitrary stupidity.[34]

This objection alone is perhaps sufficient to undermine *all* of the following freewill theistic theodicies of hell. However, you may feel that our libertarian freedom is *that* important, so I will not labor the point.

We shall consider two varieties of freewill theism: Open Theism and Molinism.[35]

Open Theism and Hell

Traditionally, theologians have thought that God knows the future with 100% accuracy (whether he be timeless or everlasting) and guides his creation, knowing the consequences of all his choices. However, it has become increasingly common to find theologians who talk of "risky providence."[36] Human freedom, being unpredictable from antecedent conditions, throws a spanner in the works for God's knowledge of the future and thus also for his providence. In creation God takes a risk—the world he creates may be one in which no one ever sins. It may be one in which people do sin, but all are saved. It may be one in which some are saved and some are lost. It may even be one in which *all* are lost. God does not know, prior to creating, what percentage of his creatures will be damned. He *hopes* that none will be and will work to that end. He knows that all may be. It is a gamble.

---

[33] It was described as "the ability to choose x even when you see absolutely no good reason for doing x, very good reasons for not doing x and no compelling desire to do x."

[34] Reitan, 137, in Parry and Partridge.

[35] A third position is that of the Arminian. Arminians believe that God chooses to give humans libertarian free choices and refuses to interfere with them (both Open Theists and Molinists concur here). However, they do not think God has the providential control Molinists claim but they do think that he knows the future completely (contra Open Theism). The problem of hell for the Arminian is that, on their view, God created the world knowing in advance that many (most?) people he created would be damned to hell. Granted, the choice was theirs but it is arguably problematic to believe that God went ahead with creation knowing that for many (most?) it would end in disaster.

[36] For example, Clark Pinnock, Keith Ward, William Hasker, John Sanders, and Greg Boyd.

The main problem this view faces is that, when one considers just *how awful* the traditional doctrine of hell is, God was taking a terrible risk in creating. When the outcome *could* be one that is ultimately tragic for some (many? most? all?) of those God creates, there are serious questions about whether God could be considered good or wise in creating. If, as many Christians think, the majority of the human race will be damned, then one could argue that God gambled with the eternal destinies of his creatures and, for the most part, lost! This is hardly a fitting way to think of the God and Father of our Lord Jesus Christ!

The Open Theist may reply that there is very little risk that all will be lost because God is so skilful in his interactions with creation that he is almost certain that he can woo many to accept him. The analogy of the skilful chess player is often used to illustrate this. The skilful chess player can be certain that he will beat the novice even if he does not control the novice's choices and even if he does not know every move the novice will make. The Chess Master can adapt his moves to fit those of the novice and win anyway. This analogy may work with Molinism (on which see below), but it seems out of place here. To *really* win God would have to achieve his purpose of saving *all*.

Some have claimed that God has won the victory so long as he has achieved his purpose of giving all people *the opportunity* to accept salvation freely and saving those who do accept it. Thus, God's victory is compatible with the damnation of some. This will not do, because such an understanding of victory makes it possible to claim that God has won the victory and achieved his purposes in salvation even in the event that all people reject salvation and are condemned to hell. Such a notion of victory seems empty. Unless God saves all people, we must say that he has not achieved the *total victory* he seeks. If it is true that *many* (or even most) are damned, then it seems he is no Chess Master, but more like a reckless novice. And if God's knowledge of the future is diminished by human free will, then God cannot be *sure* that *anyone* will *freely* respond to the call to salvation.[37] Thus, I judge Open Theism to be riddled with problems when it comes to justifying hell.

---

[37] Talbott indicates another problem: Arminians believe what Talbott calls the Rejection Hypothesis (RH): "Some persons will, despite God's best efforts to save them, freely and irrevocably reject God and thus separate themselves from God forever." But if RH is true and God, though knowing all that is logically possible, does not know what future choices his creatures will make we have a problem: On this view "neither God nor anyone else could ever have a reason to believe that some sinners are beyond the possibility of restoration; nor could anyone have reason to believe that RH is true; nor would RH in fact be true; nor would it be so much as possible that RH is true"; Talbott, "Providence, Freedom and Human Destiny," *RelSt* 26 (1990) 233. See the article for the argumentation.

Molinism and Hell

A small but growing number of philosophers are embracing a view known as Molinism. According to this view, there are three logical (not temporal) moments in God's knowledge. First of all, there is God's natural knowledge—that is, his knowledge of every logically possible state of affairs (or every possible world). Second, there is God's middle knowledge—that is, his knowledge of what any possible creature would freely choose in any possible circumstance in which it made a free choice. For instance, in God's natural knowledge he knows that there is a logically possible world in which I am faced with the decision of whether to follow Christ and I choose to do so. There is another logically possible world identical to the previous one right up to the moment of my decision in which I choose not to follow Christ. In his middle knowledge God knows what I would *actually freely choose if I was ever in such a situation.* God knows that, if faced with this decision in the set of circumstances in question, I would freely choose to follow Christ. I would not *have* to choose Christ. I could choose otherwise (i.e. there is a possible world in which I do choose otherwise); but, as a matter of contingent fact, I would not do otherwise. If God wants me to follow Christ, he knows that he must instantiate the circumstances in which I freely choose to do so. In this way God preserves our (libertarian) freedom and does so without risk. So God chooses to actualize the possible world in which he gets his will done. The final moment in his knowledge is his free knowledge—that is, his knowledge of the actual world he has chosen to create.

This view holds great promise, if it can be made to work,[38] in that it claims to be able to reconcile libertarian freedom (which many find attractive) and no-risk providence. However, it also gives rise to an obvious objection to the doctrine of hell:[39]

> 1. God, being omniscient, knows, via his middle knowledge, how to bring all people to accept salvation freely in Christ.[40]

---

[38] Whether Molinism can be made to work is hotly contested. Contemporary philosophers who defend it include Alvin Plantinga, Alfred Freddoso, Thomas Flint, and William Lane Craig. Opponents include David Hunt, William Hasker, and Robert Adams. The debate rages on.

[39] This formulation is borrowed from William Lane Craig.

[40] Francisco Suarez, a sixteenth century Jesuit priest who defended Molinism seems to have believed that God, via his middle knowledge, knows exactly what graces each possible free creature would need to win their free consent to the gospel (*gratia congrua*). Suarez himself, however, combined this with a more Augustinian doctrine of election such that God only chooses to offer such efficacious graces to his elect. On Molina and Suarez see William Lane Craig, *The Problem of Divine Foreknowledge and Future Contingents From Aristotle to Suarez,* Brill's Studies in Intellectual History 7 (Leiden: Brill, 1988) chap. 8.

2. God, being omnipotent, is able to actualize a possible world in which all persons freely accept salvation in Christ.

3. God, being omnibenevolent, wants to bring all people to salvation through Christ.

Points 1–3 entail that if God creates creatures with free will, then all people will be brought to salvation through Christ. Thus, 1–3 are inconsistent with:

4. Some persons do not receive Christ and are eternally damned.

If, however, one were to reject proposition 2 because one thought that God could not actualize a possible world in which all persons freely choose to accept salvation in Christ, then we could add proposition 5:

5. God prefers a world in which there are no persons at all to a world in which there are persons some of whom fail to receive Christ (and are damned).

Proposition 5 is also inconsistent with proposition 4. And if 5 does not seem compelling, we could substitute 6.

6. God prefers a world, W, in which any people who do not accept salvation in Christ freely (in a libertarian sense) will nevertheless accept it freely (in a compatibilist sense) to a world, W*, in which those who do not accept salvation in Christ freely (in a libertarian sense) are condemned to hell for eternity.[41]

Now the world W in proposition 6 could be actualized, because it allows for God to *determine* the free choices of those who do not freely choose in a non-determined, libertarian sense. Proposition 6 is also incompatible with proposition 4, and proposition 6 seems, to me at least, to be likely to be true.

Thus we seem to have, for those Christians who accept middle knowledge, a conclusive disproof of the traditional doctrine that some people will be damned for eternity. If 2 is true, then God could have created a world in which everyone chooses, of their own free will, to receive Christ. Being omniscient, he would know which world this was. Being omnipotent, he could actualize it. Being omnibenevolent, he would want to do so. If 5 is true, then, even *if* it is not possible for God to create a world in which all people *freely*

---

[41] Presuming that there is a world in which libertarianism and compatibilism are both possible (and I think that they are). But if the reader thinks that such a world is not possible, then we could replace (6) with (7) "God prefers a world, W, in which any people who do not accept salvation freely (in a libertarian sense) will have their freedom temporarily interfered with so that they do accept salvation to a world, W*, in which those who do not accept salvation freely (in a libertarian sense) are condemned to hell for eternity."

receive Christ (i.e., if 2 is false), God would rather create *no world at all* than a world in which some of his beloved creatures are eternally damned. Thus, if 5 is true, no one would go to hell everlastingly. Similarly, if 6 is true (or 7, see n. 41) then hell will also be emptied. In other words, if the God of traditional theism exists, no one would be damned for eternity. For a critique of William Lane Craig's attempt to refute this argument see Appendix 1.

So it seems that both Calvinism and Molinism fit very well with universalism but hit rough waters when combined with a traditional doctrine of hell. Suppose, though, that we reject both Calvinism and Molinism. Could God preserve our freedom and still secure the salvation of all?

Thomas Talbott has objected to the whole notion that a person can make a *fully informed* free decision to reject the gospel.[42] If he is right, then there is no possible world in which a person who makes a fully informed decision to accept the gospel would choose otherwise. This argument warrants an explanation.

First a note on free will: Talbott writes, "If someone does something in the absence of any motive for doing it *and* in the presence of an exceedingly strong motive for not doing it, then he or she displays the kind of irrationality that is incompatible with free choice. A necessary condition of free choice, in other words, is a minimal degree of rationality on the part of the one who acts freely."[43] Suppose that a child who can experience pain like everyone else puts his hand into a fire with no motive for doing so and a very strong motive for not doing so. We would be utterly perplexed. Such an act would be totally irrational and, with a lack of any motives, one for which the child should not be blamed. There may be irrational forces controlling his action but we would probably not consider it free.

Clearly people can, and regularly do, freely reject the gospel as a result of being ignorant, misinformed, or deceived. But what would it mean for someone who is *adequately* or *fully* informed about the gospel to reject it freely? Can we even make sense of such a suggestion?

> If God is our loving creator, then he wills for us exactly what, at the most fundamental level, we want for ourselves; he wills that we should experience supreme happiness, that our deepest yearnings should be satisfied, and that all of our needs should be met. So if that is true, if God wills the very thing we *really* want for ourselves, whether we know it or not ... what might qualify as a motive for someone making a fully informed decision to reject God? Once one has learned, perhaps through bitter experience, that evil is always destructive, always

---

[42] Talbott, "The Doctrine of Everlasting Punishment," *F&Ph* 7 (1990); "Providence, Freedom and Human Destiny," *RelSt* 26 (1990).

[43] Talbott, *Inescapable Love*, 184–85.

contrary to one's own interest as well as to the interest of others, an intelligible motive for such rebellion no longer seems even possible. The strongest conceivable motive would seem to exist, moreover, for uniting with God. So if a fully informed person should reject God nonetheless, then that person, like the boy in our story above, would seem to display the kind of irrationality that is itself incompatible with free choice.[44]

If a person's choices are as self-destructive and irrational as those of the boy, we would generally see no problem in restricting his or her freedoms and making some decisions for the person's own good. A person who made a fully informed decision to reject the gospel would be acting in such a self-destructive and irrational way that it is hard to consider the choice free in any true sense. In such a case, would it not be justified to override the decision?[45]

Craig complains that Talbott underestimates the power of sinful people to resist God in quite irrational ways.[46] This objection is easily overcome, because Talbott could simply maintain that nobody is in a position to understand the gospel adequately, due to the epistemically blinding power of sin. However, God's Spirit can overcome the effects of sin and enable a person, any person, to understand. Thus, apart from God's gracious work by his Spirit, nobody is ever adequately informed. But God, being omnibenevolent, will eventually bring all into this position and then a rejection is unimaginable. Craig more or less concedes this point when he objects that, "It may well be the case that for some people the degree of revelation that would have to be imparted to them in order to secure their salvation would have to be so stunning that their freedom to disobey would be effectively removed . . ."[47]

Craig seems to be concerned that, on Talbott's view, our libertarian freedom is removed, and he is not alone in this concern. Talbott seems to deny that anyone *fully* informed about the gospel could reject it; but, if that is so, could their choice be said to be free? It is certainly free in a compatibilist

---

[44] Ibid., 185.

[45] I ought to clarify that by "fully informed" I do not simply mean that a person has had enough information communicated to them. I also mean that this information is *epistemically compelling* for them. To illustrate the difference, the disciples were informed by the women who went to the empty tomb that Christ was risen, but this information was communicated to them in a far more compelling way in their own encounter with the risen Lord. Talbott's notion of being "fully informed" implies that the information is *imparted in a compelling way that elicits belief.*

[46] Craig, "Talbott's Universalism," *RelSt* 27 (1991) 297–308; see too "Talbott's Universalism Once More," *RelSt* 29 (1993) 497–518. Kvanig, Sanders, and Walls make a similar objection.

[47] Craig, "Talbott's Universalism," 300. Jerry Walls also concedes this point (*Logic of Damnation*, 129, 133).

sense, for the person does what she or he wants to do; but it is not free in a libertarian sense.[48] Talbott does believe that many of our choices are free in a libertarian sense, but the *fully informed* choice to accept the gospel is not one of those.[49] But why is that a problem? It seems that St. Paul was probably in such a position of revelation that his ability to reject Christ was severely diminished. So what? Did God do him an injustice? In the Bible God seems far less concerned with preserving human libertarian freedom through ever-lasting 'epistemic distance' than many modern philosophers do. Epistemic distance may play an important role in God's economy, but only as a tem-porary measure. By so revealing himself, God is not forcing an agent to act against free will but simply clarifying the situation in such a way that the will changes. Why should this worry us? Such compulsion is totally unlike forcing someone against his or her will.[50]

It is somewhat ironic that if one grants Talbott's arguments about free-dom, then a sinner in hell experiencing the real consequences of rejecting God will become better informed of the true significance of his or her life-choices, making continuing to resist God increasingly difficult and, at some point, psychologically impossible. The only way for God to keep the damned continually choosing to resist him forever is by shielding them from the real consequences of their actions, thus denying them the possibility of making a *fully informed* decision. But by doing this, God is arguably interfering with their freedom! Hence, if God respects the freedom of those in hell and per-mits them to experience the full reality of their freely chosen condition, they will learn the true meaning of separation and will in the end choose to em-

---

[48] Eric Reitan thinks that Talbott's view of freedom is neither libertarian nor compatibilist but a third view which he calls "rational freedom" (Reitan, "A Guarantee of Universal Salvation?"). Talbott calls himself an "unrepentant libertarian" in that he sees indeterminism (and thus to some extent randomness) as essential to our *emergence* as free moral agents. However, he also wishes to identify an insight in compatibilism according to which moral freedom requires that we learn from our mistakes in a rational way that shapes our moral character and makes certain decisions psychologically impossible. Thus randomness plays an *increasingly diminishing* role in our free choices ("Libertarian Freedom and the Problem of Hell," paper delivered at the 52nd Annual Wheaton College Philosophy Conference, October 21, 2005). The nuances of Talbott's evolving philosophy of freedom are too subtle to explain here.

[49] It ought to be added that perhaps most people who choose to accept God's salvation in Christ do not do so when "*fully* informed" and so they still could choose otherwise and remain free in a libertarian sense.

[50] "The very idea of a freedom-removing revelation rests on a mistake, as does the idea that we are free only for as long as God keeps us in the bondage to ignorance. I fail to see how a knowledge of the truth, even when it renders certain actions psychologically impossible, in any way restricts one's freedom to perform such actions—as if those in possession of the beatific vision are no longer free agents" (Talbott, "Craig on the Possibility of Eternal Damnation," *RelSt* 28 [1992] 502).

brace him. Whether that final choice to embrace God is understood as a free choice will depend upon how one conceives of freedom. But one cannot freely choose a life apart from God unless God permits one to experience the very life that one has freely chosen to live.[51]

Nevertheless, many still want to claim that it is crucial that rejecting the gospel is *always* a possibility when the choice is made to accept it. To suggest, as Talbott does, that the loss of libertarian freedom in a *fully informed* choice for Christ is not a problem, is too much for some. They want to retain the libertarian freedom in every choice for the gospel, and this entails that rejection is always a possibility, even if only a very slim one.

Eric Reitan argues that, even if we wanted to uphold the random element in libertarian choice at all costs (and it is not remotely clear why we should),[52] it is still possible for God, for all intents and purposes, to guarantee that all would be saved, so long as God always leaves the doors open for the lost to turn and be saved. Briefly, his argument runs as follows.[53] Imagine a box of pennies all facing heads-up. Imagine that the heads-up side is covered with superglue so that if the penny ever lands tails-up it will stick in that position. Imagine further that the box is shaken every few seconds indefinitely. Suppose, further, that for any penny facing heads-up when the box is rattled there is a 50% chance it will land tails-up and 50% chance it will land heads-up.[54] In this situation we would expect that if this shaking went on forever *all the pennies would eventually end up facing tails-up.* As time goes on the probability of any penny remaining heads-up approaches zero. This situation is analogous to the situation of people in hell (pennies facing heads-up) who at any moment could choose in a random, non-determined way to accept salvation (face tails-up). Even if we wish to preserve the random element in free choice (represented by the behavior of the pennies upon the shaking of the box), one would expect hell to empty over time. Suffice it to say that, in my view, even *if* his strategy fails to prove that freely resisting God for eternity is impossible (if freedom is understood to require a random, non-determined

---

[51] See Talbott, "Libertarian Freedom and the Problem of Hell."

[52] This is because the element the libertarian is so keen to hang on to boils down to a completely random and arbitrary element in human choice and it is not clear why we would even want that let alone seek to preserve it at all costs (Reitan, "A Guarantee of Universal Salvation?").

[53] For full presentations with the mathematics explained more adequately see Reitan, "Universalism and Autonomy: Towards a Comparative Defense of Universalism," *F&Ph* 18 (2001) 222–40; "Human Freedom and the Impossibility of Eternal Damnation," in Parry and Partridge, eds., *Universal Salvation?*; and "A Guarantee of Universal Salvation?".

[54] Even if the odds are changed to, say, a 1% chance that the pennies will land tails-up and thus the dice are loaded against Reitan, his argument still works, given enough time (you can do the mathematics yourself).

ingredient), it does establish that, even with radical libertarian freedom, it is *incredibly* unlikely that any will remain lost.

It may be objected that Reitan's argument relies upon the assumption that sinners have no limit on the time God allows them to repent, and this is an assumption that the mainstream Christian tradition denies. This is indeed so, but in defense of Reitan we should note that the traditional view that there are no chances to repent after death is also very hard to defend. What possible reason would God have for drawing a line at death and saying, "Beyond this point I will show no mercy to those who repent and turn to Christ"? Clearly, his mercy and love do not justify such a stance; and, given traditional Christian views of justice and atonement, neither does his justice.[55] There is no obvious reason why God would draw the point of no return at death (or anywhere at all). There is, however, a good reason for thinking that he would not—namely, he is loving, gracious, and merciful and will accept all who turn to him in repentance. This is not to suggest that God somehow owes it to the lost to leave the door open forever, but it is to suggest that his love would seem to motivate him in this direction. Contemporary philosophers who defend the point of no return view often argue that the door to hell is locked from the inside and that God would, in principle, accept any of the damned who repented; but, in fact, none (few?) of them will ever do so. But this is also deeply problematic. What is it about death that would fix humans against God in a way that they were not previously fixed? Why should it be that from that moment on change is impossible? Why would the *Christian* God abandon people in this condition and effectively give up trying to rescue them? If one says that change is possible, then one opens the door for the possibility of post-mortem salvation and is already moving beyond the mainstream Christian tradition.[56] Indeed, given Talbott's argument above about the impossibility of making a fully informed rejection of the gospel, it seems to me that, given an omnibenevolent God, hell would not last *forever* for anyone.

A Final Word About Appeals to Mystery

It may be that the traditionalist will appeal to mystery at this point. He may grant that he cannot see any way in which traditional punishment in hell can be defended but still maintain that it is just and good. "God, after all, is beyond our ken, and we should not presume to be able to understand

---

[55] If God can be just when justifying the ante-mortem ungodly (Rom 3:26) then it is not clear why he would be unjust to justify the post-mortem ungodly.

[56] Jerry Walls sees salvation from hell as possible though diminishingly likely as our characters harden against God.

everything about him. The fact of the matter," he may say, "is that Scripture teaches everlasting hell, and so we must accept it. The things that have been revealed belong to us and to our children but the hidden things belong to the LORD and we must rest content with that." I do have some sympathy with this position, but it is surely a last resort. The secret things may well belong to the Lord, but that which has been revealed can be known to be true; and it is on the basis of those revealed things that I have argued for universalism and against everlasting hell. The premises in my arguments all rely on traditional Christian claims about God, and it is those very claims that seem to conflict with traditional views of hell and yet fit so well with universalism. I would suggest that these arguments ought, at the very least, to make us wonder if we have not misunderstood certain biblical teachings on hell. Only if we are absolutely certain that we have not done so should we appeal to mystery. I hope to show in the rest of this book that we have indeed misunderstood the implications of the Bible's teaching on this subject.

Some universalists also appeal to mystery in a way that I find most unsatisfying. Hopeful universalists want to say that Christians can legitimately hope that God will save all, but they cannot be certain. But why may we not be certain? Two kinds of argument tend to be given. Some universalists appeal to human freedom as the complicating factor, but we have already seen that freewill reasons for rejecting universalism are seriously wanting. Others appeal to God's sovereign freedom. "Who are we to say that God *must* save all? In the end the decision is God's alone and he has not revealed it to us." In no way would I wish to deny God's mystery or his sovereign freedom, but I must confess to finding this argument perplexing. As I argued in the Calvinism section above, not saving all people seems utterly out of character with the kind of God revealed to us in Jesus Christ. Indeed, I shall argue that it looks as if the Bible does teach universal salvation or, at least, that universal salvation can be legitimately inferred from what the Bible teaches. So suggesting that God in his sovereign freedom may not choose to save all is as perplexing to me as saying that God in his sovereign freedom reserves the right to break his covenant or to do evil. That said, as I mentioned in the introduction, I am a hopeful-certain-universalist. Thus although my theological system is one in which it is certain that God will save all, I confess to being only too aware of my limits. Thus I am not totally certain that my theological system is correct, and I certainly do not wish to suggest that it is the *only* legitimate Christian view.

In conclusion, theologians and philosophers have offered many ingenious attempts to justify the traditional doctrine of hell, but all such attempts are riddled with problems. Universalism, on the other hand, is a compelling view that has a clear edge over its competitors as far as philosophical arguments go. This ought to concern Christian theologians, for we seem to have a clear clash of biblically guided reason with Scripture and tradition. The first move of a Christian theologian must be to try to defend the Church's teaching on hell; but, given the severe problems in the many attempts to defend hell, the theologian is justified in returning to Scripture to ask whether it actually supports a doctrine of eternal damnation, as has traditionally been thought. Could a Christian theology that is grounded in the Bible be universalist?[57]

---

[57] My thanks to Professor Thomas Talbott and Dr. Oliver Crisp for their invaluable feedback on earlier versions of this chapter.

CHAPTER TWO

Universalism and Biblical Theology

Christ is the first-born among many brethren—Christ is the
first-born of the new humanity—Christ is the first-born of
the whole creation: Jesus is Israel's messiah—Jesus is the son of
man of the nations—Jesus is the head of the reconciled cosmos.

—Jürgen Moltmann[1]

I HAVE VERY gradually and reluctantly come to the view that there is a serious conflict between traditional interpretations of the Bible and reason. I
ought to restate that by reason I do not refer to human autonomous reason
but reason informed by the self-revelation of God testified to in the Bible. We
must be open to the possibility that we have misread the Bible. It is time that
Christian biblical scholars looked again at this question.

Reason, I suggest, would lead us to *seek* a universalist interpretation of
specific biblical texts. Typically such an interpretation is ruled out *a priori*
and thus not even considered. We need to ask of texts whether they can be
read in a way compatible with universalism. We need to look again at these
so-called universalist texts (Rom 5:18; 1 Cor 15:22; Col 1:20; Phil 2:11; Eph
1:10) and ask whether they may *actually* mean what they seem to mean when
taken at face value. We need to think again about biblical teachings on God's
judgment, especially post-mortem judgment. Are these texts compatible with
universalism (i.e., the possibility of redemption from hell)?

The arguments in the last chapter, I suggest, also lead us to *prefer* a
universalist interpretation if a plausible one is available. If a traditional interpretation of a passage and a universalist one reach hermeneutical stalemate,
then reason would lead us to prefer the universalist interpretation. This may
sound dubious to some, but it is perfectly proper to seek the best fit among

---

[1] Jürgen Moltmann, *The Way of Jesus Christ: Christology in Messianic Dimensions*, trans.
Margaret Kohl (San Francisco: HarperSanFrancisco, 1990; London: SCM, 1993) 275.

reason, Scripture, tradition, and experience. In fact, it is simply a reversal of current evangelical bias.

Evangelical theology lays great store by the claim that this or that teaching is well grounded in the Bible. But what exactly do we mean by that? I suggest that universalism has a claim to being biblical if:

(a) It has *positive support* from scripture. This could be the case if:

I.   *It is explicitly taught.* There are several texts that *seem* to do this (e.g., Rom 5:18; 1 Cor 15:22; Col 1:20; Phil 2:11). Now, evangelicals need to seek a theological unity in biblical teachings, and so I see nothing wrong in the attempts made by those convinced that the Bible teaches a traditional view of hell to interpret these texts in a non-universalist way. The problems with hell discussed in Chapter 1 will, or so I would argue, give a positive inclination towards the universalist interpretations of them.

II. *It can be reasonably inferred from what is explicitly taught.* That is what I shall try to do in this book; for it seems to me that biblical teachings on God's love, his desire for universal salvation, and his providence point towards universalism. It ought to be noted that this inference of universalism can be perfectly proper *even if the biblical authors themselves never made it.* It has long been recognized by evangelicals that a teaching can claim to be biblical if it can be legitimately inferred from other teachings that are directly taught in the texts.

III. *It is consistent with the biblical meta-narrative.* Most of the debates for and against universalism in the past have been proof-text debates. The universalist will quote his or her favourite texts to prove that universal reconciliation is taught in the Bible. The traditionalists will counter with their own proof texts that show that some people are condemned to hell. Obviously such texts are important and will have to be considered. Nevertheless, the debate needs to move into a new arena. The Bible is the single story of God's creating and then redeeming his world, and any claim that universalism (or traditionalism) is biblical must show how it fits in with the broader picture of Scripture and makes sense of the broader themes. The theology that best fits the rest of the jigsaw has good claims to be the right theology for the job. I shall argue that universalism fits well within the biblical meta-narrative and that it coheres very well with the Bible's central teachings. It is only within the broader context of biblical theology that we can address the specific texts pro and contra adequately.

(b) It *does not conflict* with what is explicitly taught in the Bible. This would include such biblical doctrines as salvation by grace, through faith in the atoning work of Christ, as well as individual texts on hell. It is here that many feel universalism can be sunk without trace; for although universalism is compatible with the gospel message, it cannot be reconciled with the hell texts (e.g., Matt 25:45; 2 Thess 1:6-9; Rev 14:11; 20:10-15). Now, if universalism is to have a claim to being biblical, it must indeed be able to present a plausible interpretation of such texts. The question is then, "Does any of the Bible's teaching on hell substantially contradict universalism?" The answer is affirmative if and only if the Bible teaches that hell lasts forever. I shall argue in chapters 5 and 6 that it does not.

It is worth adding at this point that if some texts remain that perplex the universalist, this need not pose a serious obstacle to the acceptance of universalism. Virtually all the key Christian beliefs have some texts that seem to run against them. We may well maintain that, properly interpreted, they do not actually contradict what we take to be the clear teachings of other texts. Nevertheless, we are content to hold firm our faith in the central Christian claims *in spite of some awkward texts.* It may help to give a couple of examples of what I have in mind here. Calvinists are prepared to live with some very awkward texts, such as Hebrews 6:4-6, Arminians, likewise, live with their own problematic texts, such as Romans 8:29-30. All Christians find Jesus' attitude to the Syro-Phonecian woman in Mark 7:24-30 to be difficult, yet it does not lead them to give up their belief that Jesus intended his message to reach out beyond Israel at the right time. Similarly, the claim in Proverbs 8:22 that God created his own wisdom has not led any orthodox Christians to think that there was a time before God was wise nor that God created his Son (who is God's wisdom incarnate). Many Protestants have found Jesus' teachings in the parables that *seem* to teach salvation by works to be confusing, yet it has not led them to abandon the Pauline teaching of justification by faith. My point is that all Christians are prepared to tolerate some problematic texts without surrendering their beliefs. Of course, they ought to try to understand those texts aright, but they do not suspend all belief until *all* the detailed problems are resolved. I suggest that the universalist should behave no differently in this respect. Only if the problem texts are significantly serious or numerous should they start to worry. Of course, there is no scientific measure here. The point at which a universalist should start to worry will differ from one universalist to another. Theology is an art, and a false precision is misleading. At this point it will be helpful to outline some hermeneutical

observations by Christian philosopher Thomas Talbott.[2] Talbott asks us to
consider three propositions:

> 1. It is God's redemptive purpose for the world (and therefore his
> will) to reconcile all sinners to himself.

> 2. It is within God's power to achieve his redemptive purpose for
> the world.

> 3. Some sinners will never be reconciled to God, and God will
> therefore either consign them to a place of eternal punishment,
> from which there will be no hope of escape, or put them out of
> existence all together.

Now, this set of propositions is inconsistent in that it is impossible to believe
all three of them at the same time. If, for instance, 1 and 2 are true, then 3
must be false; for if God *wants* to save everyone and *can* save everyone, then
everyone will be saved, and 3 will be false. If, on the other hand, 3 is true,
then 1 or 2 (or both) must be false. That is to say, if God does not save everyone, it is either because he does not want to (thus 1 is false) or because he
cannot (thus 2 is false).[3]

Now, observes Talbott, the interesting thing is that we can find theological arguments and biblical texts that *seem* to support all three propositions.
Thus, we find several texts that seem to affirm that God does indeed want to
save all (e.g., 2 Pet 3:9; 1 Tim 2:4; Ezek 33:11), that God can accomplish his
purposes for creation without having human free will throwing a spanner in
the works (e.g., Eph 1:11; Job 42:2; Isa 46:10b, 11b), and that some will be
damned forever (e.g., Matt 25:46; 2 Thess 1:9; Eph 5:5). But here, then, is a
problem for all evangelicals; for, when taken at face value, the Bible *seems* to
teach three things which *cannot* all be true. So either we affirm that the Bible
is contradictory, or we must attempt to reinterpret one of those three sets of
texts so that the contradiction is removed. Traditional evangelicals have taken
the latter move; but then the question has arisen; "Which set of texts do we
try to reinterpret?" evangelicals have tended to consider proposition 3 as beyond dispute and so have gone on to reject either 1 or 2. Thus we find the
classical division within evangelicalism between Calvinists and Arminians.
Calvinists affirm 2 and 3 but reject 1. They argue that, as God is sovereign
and controls everything that happens, if he really wanted to save everyone,

---

[2] Thomas Talbott, *The Irresistable Love of God* (Boca Raton, La.: Universal, 1999) chap. 4.

[3] The freewill theist will object that perhaps God wants to save all and can save all but does
not do so because he wants to save all with, and not against, their wills. God will not force his
salvation on people (though he could). I have already discussed freewill theodicies in chap. 1
and so shall not revisit the matter here.

Nor sure about this — seems to me that God does limit
himself by the way he has chosen to relate to mankind — we
an not automatons and there are limits to what he can do
to shift around events to make them work for us.

then he would. Given that he does not, it follows that he does not want to. God chooses to save a limited group of people (the elect) and not everyone. The Calvinist then has to reinterpret texts that seem to teach that proposition 1 is true. Arminians, on the other hand, affirm 1 and 3 but reject 2. They believe that God wants to save everyone; but, because of human free will, he is unable to get his will done, and so some end up damned. Consequently, Arminians have to reinterpret texts that support proposition 2. Talbott asks us to consider a third option: universalism. Universalists affirm 1 and 2 but reject 3. In their thinking, God wants to save all and has the power to do this (without destroying our freedom). Universalists thus have to reinterpret the hell texts. But they are in a situation *no different* from Calvinists or Arminians in this respect. "*Every* reflective Christian who takes a stand with respect to our three propositions *must* reject a proposition for which there is at least some *prima facie* biblical support."[4] Some evangelicals have objected that some universalist interpretations of texts seem rather strained. In many cases I agree, and I shall attempt to avoid such forced interpretations in this book. Nevertheless, traditional evangelicals (both Calvinists and Arminians) are guilty of exactly the same "crime" and so ought to be more cautious when pointing the finger. It is important to try to give level headed and plausible interpretations of biblical texts. Agnosticism is better than torturing texts to suit our theological needs.

Some comments about a systematic theology that seeks, at the same time, to be biblical are in order at this point. The biblically minded systematic theologian is looking for theological grids, or stories, or doctrines that are *taught clearly in some biblical texts and are broad enough to serve as organising categories for considering the teachings of other biblical texts (without doing violence to them).* Let me give just one example. The Christology of Mark's Gospel is, in traditional Christian terms, quite low. Jesus in Mark is a human being. He is also the Messiah, the King of Israel, and he is the Lord; but there is nothing in Mark that would lead us to believe that Mark wanted to communicate the idea that Jesus is the second person of the divine trinity made flesh, as later Christian theology claimed.[5] John's Gospel is the Gospel that comes closest to traditional Christian dogmatics. In John, Jesus is the Logos who was with God and yet *was* God (1:1), the source of all creation (1:2), the divine "I am" (8:58) who can be called "Lord and God" (20:28). He is also a real human being. John's Logos was "made flesh" (1:12). Now the system-

---

[4] Ibid., 47.

[5] Mark does claim that Jesus is the "Son of God" (1:1) and identifies Jesus with Yahweh returning to Zion foretold by Isaiah but this still falls short of thinking of Jesus as John's pre-existent "Word made flesh" or Paul's pre-existent creator being made in the likeness of humanity.

atic theologian will not want to claim that all New Testament authors had a Johannine Christology. As we have just noted, there is no reason to think that Mark wanted to communicate such a Christology. What the traditional systematician will note is that John's Christology is broad enough to contain Mark's. John's Jesus, like Mark's, is a real human Messiah. Affirming John's Christology is not to deny Mark's but to place it within a broader framework.[6] This is exactly what the church did at the great councils. Both texts are inspired, both can be accepted on their own terms, *and* both can be accepted together if John is given theological priority in terms of the broad dogmatic framework. One key hermeneutical move I wish to make in this book is to find a broad theological grid that allows me to make sense of a wide range of themes and texts. Chapters 3–5 will set out that grid. What I would like to note at this point is that this move allows me to say without embarrassment that some biblical authors may not have been universalists. Indeed, it seems to me more than likely that they were not. However, the universalist grid I will suggest is both biblical and broad enough to accommodate what such authors taught about final judgment. So when I claim that universalism is biblical, I do *not* mean that all biblical authors were universalists but that the universalist tendencies of some authors provide the big picture within which we can happily accommodate the teachings on hell of all the biblical writers. Such, at any rate, is my claim. Whether I succeed I leave to the reader to judge.

It is appropriate to make clear that any attempt to read the Bible as a whole is an activity of the *readers* of the text and not something that the text itself does for us. The diverse texts invite such a way of reappropriating them, but the hard work is left to the readers. Christian readers are situated in communities with traditions of interpretation that guide such seeing the Bible as a unity. The reading traditions prioritize certain themes, texts, and intertextual relations. The locating of a text within the Christian canon, for instance, changes the frame within which Christians try to make sense of the book and sets up some privileged intertexts that the original authors may not have had in mind. So, one issue that will loom large later in this book is how we can make sense of biblical texts about hell in ways that are consistent with other theological themes that are strong in the canon. The question is, "How can *we Christian readers* be true to these texts as part of the teaching of the whole canon?" That is not simply a question that is able to stop with

---

[6] I am not saying that we must read John into Mark nor that we should not allow Mark to set his own agenda or that we should not be sensitive to his emphases. I am saying that a Christian reader must not read Mark in such a way as he contradicts John. I am also saying that it is not inappropriate for a Christian theological reader to read Mark in the light of John, and, thus, in ways that Mark would not have expected.

historical-critical exegesis but one which must push further to uncover the logic of biblical teaching, even when a biblical author may not have explored the ideas in such ways.

Scripture must retain its place as the primary locus of authority in any hermeneutical spiral of understanding; so if such a review of the Bible does not plausibly yield to a universalist interpretation, then we need to return to philosophy and try to see how we can make sense of the everlasting damnation of the lost. If, on the other hand, a reasonable biblical case can be made for universalism, then the philosophical arguments discussed in Chapter 1 would significantly amplify the claims of universalism to be authentically Christian and biblical. This book is an attempt to argue that universalism has strong claims to being well grounded in biblical revelation.

Christ, Cosmos, and Church: The Theology of Colossians

I am going to begin my examination of biblical theology with a discussion of the teaching of Paul in Colossians on Christ, the cosmos, and the church. I begin with Colossians because it seems to me to provide the contours of a very helpful theological grid for making sense of a vast range of biblical teachings and it shows how the main structures of my proposal for a universalist twist to biblical theology fit together. In other words, it provides a very broad theological web within which the teachings of other texts can be fitted without doing violence to them. We shall fill in the grid some more in Chapters 4 and 5.

Let us enter Colossians through the magnificent gates of the Christ-hymn in Colossians 1:15 ff. N.T. Wright has suggested that the structure of the hymn can be brought out as follows in the diagram on the next page.[7] This passage is a poem that, both in terms of its structure and its content, bears testimony to the Jewish monotheistic worldview that gave it birth. In this worldview, Wrights points out, there is one God who creates the world. This God is in a covenant relationship with Israel, ". . . and he will, in fulfilling that covenant, reclaim and redeem his whole creation from that which at present corrupts and threatens it."[8] I would like briefly to examine the poem under the themes of creation, fall, and redemption.

---

[7] N.T. Wright, "Poetry and Theology in Colossians 1:15-20," in idem, *The Climax of the Covenant: Christ and the Law in Pauline Theology* (Edinburgh: T. & T. Clark; Minneapolis: Fortress, 1991) 99–119.

[8] Ibid., 108.

15a	**Who is** the image		
15b		Of God, the invisible	
15c		**Firstborn** of every creature	
16a			**Because in him** were created all things
16b			*In the heaven and in the earth*
16c			The seen things and the unseen
16d			Whether thrones or lordships
16e			Whether rulers or authorities
16f			All things **through him and to him** were created
17a	*And he* is before all things		
17b		And all things hold together in him	
18a	*And he* is the head		
18b		Of the body, the church.	
18c	**Who is** the beginning		
18d		**Firstborn** from the dead ones	
18e		So that he might become in all things himself pre-eminent	
19a			**Because in him** was pleased
19b			All the fullness to dwell
20a			And **through him** to reconcile **all things to him**
20b		Making peace by the blood of his cross [through him]	
20c			*Whether things on the earth or things in heaven*

Creation

The poem is emphatic in its claim that *everything* that exists (God excluded) was created "in Christ." Christ created "*all* things." The "all" of "all things" is then expanded upon to show that it encompasses all things "in heaven and on earth, visible and invisible." That is to underscore the breadth of Christ's creating work. Not content with that, the poem expands the "invisible" order in terms of "thrones, dominions, rulers, and powers." The poem then restates the point yet again: "all things have been created through him" (v. 16). Christ not only brought creation into existence but he also sustains it in being: "in him all things hold together" (v. 17).

Christ brings the universe into existence and sustains it in existence. More than that, he is the goal of creation. "All things," we are told, "have been created . . . for him." This world, says the poet, belongs to Christ. And that includes the principalities and powers that are so hostile to him. They too were made *by* God's beloved Son (v. 14) and *for* God's beloved Son. As Wright points out, this poem is a Jewish monotheistic confession.[9]

It is because Christ created everything that he can be said to be "before all things" (v. 17) and the "firstborn of all creation" (v. 15). Not firstborn in the sense of "created first" (God's wisdom was not created) but in the metaphoric sense of "pre-eminent." In Old Testament times, the firstborn son was the pre-eminent son in the family. Christ is pre-eminent in creation because he created it all, sustains it all, and is the goal of it all.

Fall

Christian theology places an emphasis on the doctrine of the fall of humanity into sin. There is no mention of a fall in this poem, but it is clearly presupposed, both within the poem and in the rest of Colossians. Notice first of all the principalities and powers. There is no hint in the poem that they are hostile or fallen; they are simply a part of God's good creation. However, it is clear elsewhere in the letter that the writer conceives of them as enemies of Christ. Thus, in 1:13 he writes that believers have been transferred by God "out of the kingdom of darkness," and in 2:15 he speaks of the defeat of these powers by Christ at his cross. Clearly, we must imagine some fall of these powers after their original creation. They were created "for Christ," but they are presently in a state of rebellion and hostility. This basic hostility of the

---

[9] Ibid., 107. Even the focus on Christ here, as opposed to God, is not unJewish. It has been noticed by many a NT scholar that the teaching about Christ in this passage is modeled on Jewish teaching about God's wisdom. See for instance, James D. G. Dunn, *The Epistle to the Colossians and to Philemon* (Carlisle: Paternoster; Grand Rapids: Eerdmans, 1996).

powers is underscored in Ephesians 6:10ff., where believers are said to be in a battle against them.[10]

Colossians does not simply presuppose an angelic fall. Humans too are seen as culpable and in a sinful state. Thus in 1:21 Paul says of his readers, "You were once alienated and hostile in mind because of your evil deeds." Hostility to God is the characteristic of the fallen human (cf. Rom. 8:7-8). And, of course, the whole doctrine of redemption, which is so central to Colossians, only makes sense against the background of a creation that needs redeeming. The poem goes on from Christ's pre-eminence in creation to his pre-eminence in redemption. Between the two parts, the readers are expected to understand that God's good creation has become corrupted and alienated. It is this problem that God solves in Christ's cross.

Redemption

The poem moves on to celebrate Christ's pre-eminence in the new creation. It is not to be thought that he was not pre-eminent already or that he becomes pre-eminent twice but rather that in the resurrection and reconciliation he becomes *in fact* what he already was *by right* in creation: first in all things.

It is his death and resurrection that effect the reconciliation. He made peace "through the blood of his cross," and "he is the firstborn from among the dead." The cross as the means of salvation also comes out clearly in 2:15, where Christ strips the hostile authorities of their power, making the way for salvation open. We shall return to this text later when we consider objections to the view being set out here.

The next thing to notice about the salvation is that it extends as wide as creation.[11] This is highlighted by both the verbal and the thematic parallels between v. 16 and v. 20. Indeed, the very structure of the poem draws the hearer to read the two verses together.

> For in him were created all things, in the heavens and on the earth . . .
> all things were created through him and for him. (v. 16)

---

[10] There has been much debate amongst New Testament scholars on the issue of whether these principalities and powers are angelic beings of some sort or human power structures (or both the human structures and the spiritual powers behind them). It seems to me that the weight of evidence is against those who see the powers as no more than human power-structures; but little hangs on that debate as far as this book goes, and so I will pursue the question no further.

[11] See Eduard Schweizer, *The Letter to the Colossians,* trans. Andrew Chester (Minneapolis: Augsburg, 1982) 260–77 for a helpful discussion of universalism and Colossians 1.

> . . . and through him to reconcile all things to him, making peace through the blood of his cross (through him), whether things on the earth or things in the heavens. (v. 20)

James Dunn comments:

> What is being claimed is quite simply and profoundly that the divine purpose in the act of reconciliation and peacemaking was to restore the harmony of the original creation, to bring into renewed oneness and wholeness "all things," "whether things on earth or things in the heavens."[12]

What is of interest from a universalist perspective is that the poem is quite unambiguous about the extent of the reconciliation Christ has effected through his cross. The "all things" that are reconciled in v. 20 are, without any doubt, the same "all things" that are created in v. 16. In other words, every single created thing. It is not "all without distinction" (i.e., some of every kind of thing) but "all without exception" (i.e., every single thing in creation).

The word Paul uses to describe the act of reconciliation is *apokatallasso*. This verb occurs only here, in 1:22, and in Ephesians 2:16. In 1:22 we read, "But now he has *reconciled* you [i.e., the believers] by Christ's physical body through death to present you holy in his sight, without blemish and free from accusation." Clearly, the reconciliation spoken of here is the restoration of a harmonious relationship between the believers and God. The Ephesians reference speaks of the overcoming of hostilities between Jews and Gentiles "in Christ":

> For he himself is our peace, who has made the two [i.e., the Jews and Gentiles] one and has destroyed the barrier, the dividing wall of hostility, by abolishing in his flesh the law with its commandments and regulations. His purpose was to create in himself one new man out of the two, thus making peace, and in this one body to *reconcile* both of them to God through the cross, by which he put to death their hostility (Eph 2:14-16).

This reconciliation is also effected through the cross and is probably best thought of as part of the social outworking of the cosmic reconciliation spoken of in Colossians 1. Like *katallasso* (Rom 5:10; 1 Cor 7:11; 2 Cor 5:18-20), the verb *apokatallasso* presupposes some kind of rupture in relationship that is then repaired. The damaged relationship, says Paul, between God and a fallen creation is restored in Christ.

Seeing the clear universalist implications of this verse, some have argued that "reconciliation" simply denotes a restoration of divine order to the uni-

---

12 Dunn, *Colossians*, 104.

verse. This can mean salvation for some (believers), but for others it speaks of their punishment (demons and the unbelievers). In other words, some are "reconciled to God" by being punished in hell. This interpretation simply will not do. That reconciliation should be seen in salvific terms is underscored by the fact that the poem expands on the notion of reconciling all things in terms of making *peace* through the blood of his cross. The reconciliation of all things brings peace with God—a notion that, for Paul, clearly expresses salvation. The same connection between reconciliation (*apokatallassein*) and peace is found in Ephesians 2:14-16 (quoted above), and there it is quite clear that the reconciliation is a positive state of affairs for those reconciled. The association of peace with God and reconciliation and salvation can also be found in Romans 5:1, 10. One could hardly imagine Paul supposing that one of Christ's enemies suffering eschatological punishment was in a state of peace with God! Further, Paul goes on in vv. 21-22 to apply this notion of reconciliation to his readers. He says, "And you, once alienated and enemies in mind in works that are evil, he has now reconciled in the body of his flesh through his death, to present you holy and unblemished and blameless before him . . ." Here again reconciliation retains its salvific meaning. The word itself and the context make it abundantly clear that Paul speaks of salvation when he speaks of reconciliation and that, as long as a being remains hostile to God, it cannot be said to have been reconciled to him. The context also makes it abundantly clear that Paul sees Christ as effecting the salvation of all creation.

A second traditionalist attempt to get around this problem is to maintain that, although the passage does envisage the salvation of all creation as God's *desire,* it does not follow that God will ever bring his desire into a reality. David Powys writes that

> without coercion universal reconciliation would not be achievable. The only possible interpretation of this verse is that the "all things" is a reference to intent rather than actual achievement. This is a fully satisfactory interpretation which has the advantage of not requiring the violation of human free will.[13]

This also will not do. Paul does not think that this redemption is something that God *hopes* will come to pass in the future. He maintains that it is something *already* accomplished in Christ. In Christ the whole of creation is *already* reconciled! Now obviously, this salvation has not worked its way through the whole of creation yet. All who are outside of Christ remain hostile, as the readers once were; but Paul's focus on God's providential outworking

---

[13] David J. Powys, *"Hell": A Hard Look at a Hard Question—The Fate of the Unrighteous in New Testament Thought* (Carlisle: Paternoster, 1997) 337.

of his eternal purposes in history would lead him to maintain that God will indeed accomplish his purposes in Christ. Paul knows nothing of a theology in which God does not ultimately achieve his purposes. The full redemption Christ has bought will one day manifest itself in all its fullness. Powys' claim that his interpretation is "the only possible interpretation of this verse" is a stunning claim. Perhaps he means that a universalist interpretation *cannot* be right, and so this one *must* be. And why cannot a universalist interpretation be right? Presumably because it would require God to "violate human free will." We have seen in Chapter 1 that this is not so. Instead of being the only possible interpretation, this proposal is a poor contender when placed along-side the universalist interpretation.

It has been argued that Paul simply cannot mean what he seems to say in this passage. Several reasons are often given for this. Howard Marshall points out that the reconciliation Paul speaks of is clearly conditional on faith (1:21-23). Those who are in Christ by faith share in it; but if they cease to believe, they cease to experience reconciliation in him.[14] In a similar vein N. T. Wright argues that Paul could not intend for this to be understood as an endorse-ment of universal salvation, for elsewhere he is very clear that salvation is only for those in Christ.[15] This is indeed correct, but it hardly counts against a universalist interpretation. The universalist will happily concur that reconcili-ation is only for those who are in Christ through faith. There is no salvation outside of Christ, and one is included in Christ through faith. However, the universalist will also maintain that, in the end, everyone will be in Christ through faith. Marshall will object that 1:21-23 seems to presuppose the very real possibility that Christians can be excluded from Christ and thus from the salvation in him. He reasons that this would not be the case if universalism were correct. In reply, first let me say that Paul is very clear in Colossians that salvation is only found in Christ. The world outside of Christ does not share in it, and clearly any Christian who steps outside of Christ (i.e., ceases to be a Christian) will move from life into death (cf. Rom 8:13; 11:22; 1 Cor 9:27; 10:11-12; Gal 5:4). This is a very foolish move. However, it does not fol-low that this condition is necessarily final. The Christ-Hymn would indicate otherwise. Second, given the clear uniting perspective of Colossians, Hillert argues that: "there is no basis for interpreting the *ei*–clause ['if'–clause] as a condition or a warning. Rather, the author reminds his readers of the basis for their faith and hope, which they are held to share with all creation."[16]

[14] I. Howard Marshall, "Does the New Testament Teach Universal Salvation?," in *Called to One Hope: Perspectives on the Life to Come*, ed. J. Colwell (Carlisle: Paternoster, 2000) 17–30.

[15] N. T. Wright, *Epistles of Paul to the Colossians and to Philemon*, Tyndale New Testament Commentaries (Leicester: InterVarsity; Grand Rapids: Eerdmans, 1986).

[16] Sven Hillert, *Limited and Universal Salvation: A Text Oriented and Hermeneutical Study of*

Others draw attention to 2:15, where we read that Christ has defeated the powers at the cross. It is argued that the cross brings defeat for them and not salvation. Thus, we cannot understand reconciliation as implying universal restoration. Again, it seems to me that this observation is both right and wrong. Yes, Christ defeated the opposing powers at the cross. He broke their hold over creation and thus opened the doors of salvation. But it does not follow from this that they are not saved. They had to be defeated in their hostility before they could be reconciled. Their defeat at the cross opens the way for their reconciliation. After all, it is hardly plausible to interpret the reconciliation of the principalities and powers in 1:20 in terms of their eschatological punishment. 1:20 clearly refers to their deliverance. That this is effected through their defeat at Calvary is no problem for the universalist.

So there is no overriding reason internal to Colossians to reject the most natural interpretation of the reconciliation of the cosmos in Colossians 1. Given the somewhat strained nature of the major non-universalist interpretations, we have added reason to opt for the universalist reading of Colossians 1.

Church and Cosmos

Many modern commentators consider that the original text Paul is utilizing in 1:18 read "and he is the head of the body" and that Paul has added the words "the church" to explain what he has in mind by "the body." The suggestion is that originally "the body" referred to the cosmos. It was common in Greek thought to think of the cosmos like a giant body with a rational soul. Plato speaks of the cosmos as God's body,[17] and the Orphic fragment 168 describes Zeus as the head of his cosmic body. Philo too speaks of the divine reason (*logos*) as the head of his body—the cosmos.[18] The Christian hymn thought by some to lie behind the Pauline adaptation posited *Christ* as the head of the cosmic body, and this was simply another way of making the same point found earlier on—he is pre-eminent in creation because he is the origin of creation. The theological question is, "What is the theological impact of the addition of these two words?" It seems that the Church is equated with the cosmic body of which Christ is the head (cf. Eph 1:22-23).

Two Perspectives in Paul, ConBNT 31 (Stockholm: Almqvist & Wiksell, 1999) 228. Lincoln writes, "The conditional construction translated as 'providing that . . .' need not express doubt that they will do so. But it does make clear that cosmic reconciliation is not some automatic process; it works itself out in history in relation to the response of faith, and that response entails not abandoning the content of faith" ("Colossians," *NIB* [Nashville: Abingdon, 2000] 11:606 [551–670]). Indeed so.

[17] *Timaeus* 31b, 32a, 32c

[18] *De Somnis* 1.128

> In that case we have to speak here . . . of the church under Christ's headship being depicted as the microcosm which mirrors (or should mirror) the divinely ordered cosmos, the assembly of Israel's wilderness wanderings anticipatory of and preparatory for the new state of society in the eschatological promised land, the church as the greenhouse in and by means of which the green shoots of God's purposes in and for creation are brought on.[19]

Christ's headship over creation parallels his headship over the church; the one provides a model for the other.

Paul's thought runs in this hymn from Christ's pre-eminence in creation to his pre-eminence in new creation. The Church, as the beginning of the new creation, is thus obviously set in parallel to the original cosmic creation. The parallel in the hymn can be seen as set out below.

Creation	New Creation
Christ is the firstborn of all creation (v. 15c)	Christ is the firstborn from the dead (v. 18d)
Through him all things were created . . . (v. 16a)	**Through him** to reconcile **all things** to him (v. 20a)
. . . in the heaven and in the earth (v. 16b)	. . . whether things on earth or things in heaven (v. 20c)
So that he might become in all things himself pre-eminent (v. 18e)	

Clearly, vv. 15-17 speak of Christ's priority in creation, and then vv. 18-20 speak of his priority in new creation in such a way to draw the two into parallel. The Church is the equivalent in the new creation of the cosmos in the original creation. This could be thought to narrow Christ's role as mediator; creation is now replaced in God's plans by a mere sub-section of it (the Church). But this interpretation would run counter to the fact that the scope of the new creation in v. 20 is as wide as the original creation in v. 16. The "all things" that were created are the same "all things" that will be reconciled. It is better to see the Church as the beginning of the new creation—the first fruits. Rather than narrowing the mediating role of Christ from creation to Church, we must instead see Paul as making claims of cosmic significance for the Church.[20] Thus, it is no accident that Paul transforms cosmic-body lan-

---

[19] Dunn, *Colossians*, 96.

[20] Ibid., 96. See also Dunn, "The 'Body' in Colossians," in *To Tell the Mystery: Essays on New Testament Eschatology in Honor of Robert H. Gundry*, ed. Thomas E. Schmidt and Moises Silva, JSNTSup 100 (Sheffield: Sheffield Academic, 1994) 163–81.

guage into church-body language. To see the significance of this more clearly
we need to look briefly at the realized eschatology of Colossians.

Realized Eschatology

A feature of considerable importance in the theology of Colossians is the tension between realized and future eschatology. The final victory of God over
the hostile powers has already occurred at the cross. Paul writes that

> When you were dead in your sins and in the uncircumcision of your
> sinful nature, God made you alive with Christ. He forgave us all our
> sins, having cancelled the written code, with its regulations, that was
> against us and that stood opposed to us; he took it away, nailing it to
> the cross. And having disarmed the powers and authorities, he made
> a public spectacle of them, triumphing over them by the cross. (2:13-
> 15)

That the cross is decisive is seen in the use of the aorist tense in 1:13 and 1:22
indicating the finished nature of the action.[21]

> For he *has rescued* us from the dominion of darkness and *brought* us
> into the kingdom of the Son he loves. (1:13)

> But now he *has reconciled* you by Christ's physical body through death
> to present you holy in his sight, without blemish and free from ac-
> cusation. (1:22)

The future salvation Israel had hoped for has *already been accomplished* in
Christ and is experienced by the church as *a present reality* in Christ. The
eschatological promised land Israel would enter has been entered now by the
church (1:12).[22] And yet the eschatology of Colossians is not *so* realized that
it loses sight of a still future completion of salvation. Creation is still not,
on the whole, experiencing the salvation achieved in Christ. Thus, Paul can
write in 1:24, "Now I rejoice in what was suffered for you, and I fill up in my
flesh *what is still lacking in regard to Christ's afflictions*, for the sake of his body,
which is the church." This text reflects the apocalyptic belief that the new age
will begin once a predetermined amount of suffering by the saints has been
endured. Christ's death triggers this suffering but the suffering awaits a future

---

[21] The aorist tense implies that the cross-work of Christ was decisive, but it does not imply
that the work of reconciliation is finished; for clearly Colossians sees an on-going work in
which the reconciliation won through the cross is appropriated by creatures.

[22] The language of the promised land was understood by many Jews at the time as an
eschatological promise of resurrection life beyond the grave (Dan 12:13; Wis 5:5; *Shemoneh
'Esreh* 13; Dead Sea Scrolls: 1QS 11:7-8; 1QH 11:10-12). This "promised land" of Israel's was
being inherited by the Christians, says Paul.

completion. Thus Christ in the believers is spoken of as "the *hope* of glory" (1:27). This glory is the glory of God shared by Adam and then lost (Rom 3:23), but which is restored through Christ (Rom 8:17-21). In a very clear future looking statement Paul says, "When Christ, who is your life, appears, then you also will appear with him in glory" (Col 3:4). So the glory is a future reality experienced now, in hope, as Christ-in-us.

The reconciliation of creation is thus already achieved in Christ and yet is only experienced as a reality by those in Christ by faith. This comes out in 1:22 when, having spoken of the reconciliation of the whole creation achieved through the cross, Paul says of the Christians, "but now he has reconciled you by Christ's physical body through death to present you holy in his sight, without blemish and free from accusation." Observe first that Paul directly connects the experience of the Christians in Colossae to the vision for the whole of creation in 1:15-20. They are experiencing the reconciliation he has just spoken of. They are the first to taste the reconciliation that has been won for all. The Church, then, is a present sign of the reconciliation that the whole creation will one day experience. It is clear that in Colossians reconciliation is only found in Christ (1:13-14) and that, for now, not all are in Christ; but the vision presented in the hymn is a vision in which one day all will be.

Gospel proclamation and living ("walking worthily of the Lord, wholly pleasing to him, bearing fruit in every good work" 1:10) are ways for the Church to bring about the goal of universal reconciliation.[23] The Church must live by the values of, and proclaim the coming of, the kingdom age in the present evil age as a sign to a hostile world. Here is a vision of the people of God according to which the future reconciliation of creation is already (beginning to be) worked out and in which the members of the community need to live out, in their social relationships, a model of the future (Col 3:8-15). Andrew Lincoln expresses this idea eloquently:

> Perhaps the real challenge of this hymnic material lies in its depiction
> of the church as the forerunner of a reconciliation that will be cosmic
> and universal in scope . . . The worldwide community of believers is
> meant to be a microcosm in which the divine purpose in reclaiming
> the entire creation is anticipated and through which, as a reconciled
> and reconciling community, that purpose is furthered. If this is the
> case, then the most urgent task of Christians is to play their part in

---

[23] "That the Church has a role in [the reconciliation of the whole creation] is implied in the correlation of 1:18a with 1:20. And when we include the earlier talk of the gospel 'in all the world . . . bearing fruit and growing' (1:6), and the subsequent talk of the age-old mystery being made known among all the nations (1:27), the implication becomes clear: it is by its gospel living (1:10) and its gospel preaching (1:27) that the cosmic goal of reconciled perfection will be achieved (1:28)"; Dunn, *Colossians*, 104.

> making the church a place of healing for broken relationships, where
> divisions caused by class, race, wealth, education, age, gender, nation-
> ality, or religious traditions are overcome, and an agent of peace and
> justice in situations of conflict . . . .[24]

The message proclaimed by the community of Christ speaks of the destiny of
humanity. Paul writes of "the word of truth of the gospel," for the gospel message unveils the truth about human destiny stored up in heaven (1:5)[25] in the
sure hope it holds forth.[26] This gospel message is the means by which people
enter into the reconciliation and hope (1:22-23), and it is being proclaimed
and is bearing fruit "all over the world" (1:6). This worldwide proclamation
is certainly an exaggeration as a description of the reality in Paul's day. But it
is not, I suggest, mere hyperbole. Paul's eschatological vision is one in which
the gospel is proclaimed to the entire creation, and he sees his own mission
as part of that eschatological scenario. Thus he can speak of it in terms that
are stunningly triumphalist. This is even clearer later in Colossians 1 when he
writes, "This is the gospel that you heard and that *has been proclaimed to every
creature under heaven*, and of which I, Paul, have become a servant" (1:23). In
other words, Paul's gospel mission is the means of bringing about the reconciliation of creation spoken of in the hymn. Of course, this is not a description of the actual state of affairs, and yet Paul's realized eschatology allows
him to speak of it *as if* it were so already in his own mission. Thus Lincoln
can speak of "the present Gentile mission as anticipating the completion of
the worldwide proclamation."[27]

Now, for Paul, a crucial part of the eschatological restoration brought
by Christ is the reconciliation of Jew and Gentile in Christ. We shall explore
this theme in more detail in Appendix 2, but suffice it to note at this point
that the social unity of Jew and Gentile in the Church is an eschatological
anticipation of the new age and a prophetic sign to the world.

What we find in Colossians, then, is a theology that locates the origin of
creation, the revelation of God, and the salvation of world in Christ. It recog-
nizes the massive rupture introduced into the world through sin, and it sees
the solution to this problem in the death of Christ. It requires a response of
obedient faith to share in Christ and in the inheritance of eternal life. It offers
no hope of a nice God letting everyone into heaven no matter how they live
or what they believe. However, in spite of that, it holds before us a confident

---

[24] Lincoln, "Colossians," 611.

[25] Which is not to be confused with a hope to go to heaven. The hope is merely kept in
heaven until Christ returns (so N. T. Wright, *New Heavens, New Earth: The Biblical Picture of
Christian Hope* (Cambridge: Grove, 1999).

[26] Dunn, *Colossians*, 60–61.

[27] Lincoln, "Colossians," 607.

hope in the salvation of the whole creation. It is God's covenant purpose that his world will one day be reconciled in Christ. For now, only the Church shares in that privilege, but this is not a position God has granted his people so they can gloat over the world. On the contrary, the Church must live by gospel standards and proclaim its gospel message so that the world will come to share in the saving work of Christ. This is the outline of the evangelical universalist theology I wish to commend to the reader. Appendix 2 seeks to show the presence of the same kind of theology in the book of Ephesians.

This chapter has set out to argue that Colossians works with a vision of reconciliation for the whole creation. We have seen that this vision is perfectly compatible with a strong doctrine of sin (see Appendix 2 for a fuller development of this in relation to Ephesians), with a Christ-centred account of salvation, with the necessity of faith, with the current division between the elect and those lost in sin, and with a high ecclesiology. This vision, I suggest, can provide the contours for an evangelical, gospel-centred universalism. Chapters 4 and 5 will fill out this meta-narrative by tracing God's purposes in election from Abraham, through Israel, to Christ and beyond.

CHAPTER THREE

Israel & the Nations in the Old Testament

Turn to me and be saved, all you ends of the earth; for I am God, and there is no other. By myself I have sworn, my mouth has uttered in all integrity a word that will not be revoked: Before me every knee will bow; by me every tongue will swear. They will say of me, "In the LORD alone are righteousness and strength." All who have raged against him will come to him and be put to shame. But in the LORD all the descendants of Israel will be found righteous and will exult.

—Yahweh (Isa 45:22-25)

CHAPTERS 3 and 4 need to be read together to appreciate how they provide the framework for a biblical, universalist theology. Many of the individual observations are fairly commonplace in recent biblical studies. What I think has been missed, however, are the universalist implications when these observations are put together.

In this chapter I intend to trace God's plan for the redemption of creation from Abraham through to the end of the Old Testament. This is essential scene-setting for the next chapter, in which the implications in terms of universal salvation will become clearer.

Israel and Adam

Our story begins with Adam and Eve in the Garden of Eden. In the beginning, Genesis tells us, God created humanity and blessed them (Gen 1:28). In this story humanity was created in the divine image to rule over creation (Gen 1:26-28). They experienced an openness in their relations with each other and knew a deep intimacy with God as they walked together in the cool of the day (Gen 3:8). Abundant provision and blessing was theirs (Gen 2:16), and they threw it all away. By crossing the line they had been commanded not to cross, they found that blessing gave way to curse, and humanity was expelled from the divine presence in Eden to keep them from gaining access to the tree of life (Gen 3:22-24). Genesis 4–11 traces a downward spiral of sin and violence. First Cain kills Abel (4:1-16), then Lamech threatens retribution that far outweighs any scales of justice (4:23-24) until the violence is so great God sends the flood (6:11) and starts with a "new Adam"—a man named Noah. However, this "Adam" still has sin rooted in his heart (8:21), and it is not long before the spiral starts again, culminating in the tower of Babel (11:1-9).

Until this point, God has been concerned with the world of nations—with humanity as a whole. However, a decisive change in the biblical plot line occurs in Genesis 12:1-3. Now God calls out an individual, Abram, setting in motion a story that continues to this day. The divine promise to Abram is so crucial to Scripture that it is worth repeating:

> The LORD had said to Abram, "Leave your country, your people and your father's household and go to the land I will show you. I will make you into a great nation and I will bless you; I will make your name great, and you will be a blessing. I will bless those who bless you, and whoever curses you I will curse; and *all peoples on earth will be blessed through you.*"

God was promising three things to Abram: descendants ("I will make you into a great nation"), land ("go to the land I will show you"), and relationship with God ("I will bless you"). David Clines has shown how these three elements are emphasized over and over again throughout Genesis and the rest of the Pentateuch, making it hard to miss their centrality.[1] God, from this point, focuses his attention and his affections on Abraham and his descendants, the nation of Israel.

To understand more clearly the significance of Abraham and his descendants, we need to appreciate the connections within the Old Testament between Abraham/Israel and Adam. Wright has drawn attention to the way that Genesis sets Abram up as a new Adam and Israel as a new humanity in him. He uses three lines of evidence. First of all, there is the idea of blessing. This is present in the creation of humanity (Gen 1:28) and is very prominent in the promises to the patriarchs (Gen 12:2; 17:2, 6, 8; 22:16ff.; 26:3ff., 24; 28:3; 35:11ff.; 42:27; 48:3ff.).[2] Second, there is a strong emphasis on reproductive

---

[1] David J. A. Clines, *The Theme of the Pentateuch,* 2nd ed., JSOTSup 10 (Sheffield: Sheffield Academic, 1997).

[2] Wright is not alone in seeing these connections. See, for example, Wenham, *Genesis 1–15,* WBC 1 (Waco, Tex.: Word, 1987) 282.

fruitfulness in the creation story (Gen 1:28) and in the promises to the patriarchs, although there has been a shift from a command to a promise. Third, the command to humanity to have dominion over creation (Gen 1:28) is transformed into a promise that Abraham's descendants would possess the gates of their enemies (Gen 22:17). The connection is made stronger when one pulls in other Old Testament books such as Daniel. In Daniel 7 we see Israel described as "one like a son of man"[3] ruling over the beasts of the earth (the nations who oppressed them). The connections with humanity ruling over creation in Genesis 1 are clear, and Israel is given the role of Adam. The Adam-Israel link was made more explicit in Second Temple Judaism and is, arguably, presupposed by Paul in his letters.[4]

Not only is Abraham a new Adam and Israel a new humanity, but the promised land of Canaan is a new Eden. Gordon Wenham and Gregory Beale have drawn attention to a number of parallels between the garden of Eden and the Israelite sanctuary linked with Moses and Solomon.[5] For instance, God walks "to and fro" both in Eden (Gen 3:8) and in the sanctuary (Lev 26:12; Deut 23:15); cherubim guard the tree of life both in Eden (Gen 3:24) and the holy of holies in the sanctuary (Exod 25:18-22; 1 Kgs 6:23-28); both Eden and the Sanctuary are entered from the east (Gen 3:24); the menorah in the tabernacle is probably a stylized tree of life, like the tree in Eden; Solomon decorated his temple with botanical and arboreal imagery, giving it a garden-like appearance (1 Kings 6–7); as Adam, the first priest, was to "till and keep" the garden (Gen 2:5), so the Levites are to "till and keep" the sanctuary (Num 3:7-8; 8:26; 18:5-6); just as a river flowed from Eden, so Israel's visionaries saw a river flowing from the Jerusalem temple (Ps 46:5; Ezekiel 47); gold and precious stones were connected with Eden and the sanctuary (Exod 25:7; 28:9-14; 1 Chr 29:2). Beale argues that just as the temple had three parts (the outer court, the holy place, the most holy place) so also did Eden (outside

---

[3] The "one like a son of man" (Dan 7:13-14) is described as "the saints of the Most High" (7:18). In other words, he is a personification of Israel. For a defense of this interpretation see N. T. Wright, *The New Testament and the People of God* (London: SPCK; Minneapolis: Fortress, 1992) 291–97. Alternatively, he may well be a High Priest figure entering the Holy of Holies surrounded by clouds of incense. Even if this is so, he does so as a representative of Israel. For a defense of this view see C. Fletcher Louis, "The High Priest as Divine Mediator in the Hebrew Bible: Dan 7:13 as a Test Case," *SBLSP* (1997) 161–93.

[4] On which see N. T. Wright, "Adam, Israel and the Messiah," in *The Climax of the Covenant: Christ and the Law in Pauline Theology* (Edinburgh: T. & T. Clark; Minneapolis: Fortress, 1992).

[5] Gordon J. Wenham, "Sanctuary Symbolism in the Garden of Eden Story," in *"I Studied Inscriptions From Before the Flood": Ancient Near Eastern Literary and Linguistic Approaches to Genesis 1–11,* ed. Richard S. Hess and David Toshio Tsumara, SBTS 4 (Winona Lake, Ind.: Eisenbrauns, 1994); G. K. Beale, *The Temple and the Church's Mission: A Biblical Theology of the Dwelling Place of God,* NSBT 17 (Downers Grove, Ill.: InterVarsity, 2004) 66–80.

of the garden = the outer court; the garden next to Eden = the holy place, Eden itself [i.e., the area where the water flowed from] = the most holy place). However, it is not merely the temple that parallels Eden, but the whole land of Canaan, which, in the symbolism of holy space, shares in the holiness of the temple at its heart. This is seen in part in the Edenic brush strokes with which the descriptions of Canaan are lavishly painted (Num 13:20-27; Deut 8:7-9; 11:9, 11-15; 26:15). It comes out more clearly in the way judgment on Israel's land is depicted in terms of the destruction of Eden (Joel 2:3) and post-exilic restoration is portrayed as a return to Eden (Isa 11:6; 51:3; Ezek 36:35). Ezekiel is of interest here for he is clearly familiar with the Eden traditions in some form (28:1-19, 31). He speaks of the restoration of Israel in terms clearly reminiscent of the creation of Adam. The lifeless bodies in the valley are animated by the breath of life from God (Ezekiel 37; Gen 2:7). This army of Adams then returns to a restored land like Eden (36:35) in which the Sanctuary is restored and from which the life-giving river flows into the desert garden (40–48). Various other texts concerning Israel's post-exilic restoration make use of the water and garden imagery (Isa 58:11; Jer 31:12) as well as new creation imagery (Jer 3:16; 23:3; Ezek 36:11; Zech 10:8), which makes the Canaan–Eden link stronger.

Once we open up the possibility of such typology in Genesis 2–3, the story there takes on new dimensions. Just as Israel is created outside the land and brought in by Yahweh, so Adam is created outside Eden and placed in it by Yahweh (Gen 2:8). As Israel is to fill the land subdue their enemies, so Adam is told to fill the earth and subdue the animals (Gen 1:28). As obedient Israel will enjoy abundant blessing, so too will obedient Adam. As God gave his commands to Israel via Moses, so he gives Adam a command not to eat from the tree of the knowledge of good and evil (Gen 2:16-17). As Israel disobeys and incurs divine oracles of judgment and curse from the prophets, so Adam disobeys and brings a divine oracle of judgment and curse from the Lord (Gen 3:14-19). As Israel is expelled from the Promised Land for not keeping torah, so Adam is expelled from Eden for not keeping the command of Yahweh. It is hard not to see that the reader of Genesis 2–3 is intended to see Adam as a type of Israel.

This conclusion is strengthened by the probable covenant connections in the Eden story. Dumbrell has argued plausibly that the covenant with creation connected with Noah (Gen 6:18; 9:8ff.) is not a new covenant but the perpetuation of a covenant *already established* in creation.[6] God renews this covenant with Noah, his new Adam.[7] This would indicate that the first

---

[6] William Dumbrell, *Covenant and Creation*, (Exeter: Paternoster) 11–46.

[7] On the Noah–Adam connections see Wenham, *Genesis 1–15*.

Adam was in a covenant relationship with God (compare Hos. 6:7) and puts the icing on the cake of the Adam–Israel link.

What I have argued so far is that the Eden story was shaped to prefigure Israel's own story. However, in the canonical context this is reversed, so that Israel's story becomes a retelling of Adam and Eve's story. Humanity, in Adam, lost the blessing; but Israel, in Abraham, is the vehicle through which God restores it (diagram 1). Adam and Eve's expulsion finds its echo in Israel's exile, and, as we shall see, Israel's return foreshadows and precipitates humanity's restoration.

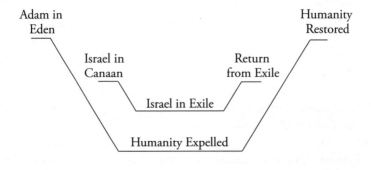

Diagram 1

Israel and the Nations

Being God's chosen people is both a privilege and a responsibility. Israel alone is chosen from all the nations of the earth (Deut 14:2; 4:37; 7:6-7; 10:15) to be Yahweh's firstborn son (Exod 4:22), his "treasured possession"[8] (Exod 19:5), the apple of his eye (Deut 32:9-10). "He has declared that he will set you in praise, fame, and honor high above all the nations he has made and that you will be a people holy to the LORD your God, as he promised" (Deut 26:19). Israel was chosen, not because of its power or status, but out of the sheer love of God.

> For you are a people holy to the LORD your God. The LORD your God has chosen you out of all the peoples on the face of the earth to be his people, his treasured possession. The LORD did not set his affection on you and choose you because you were more numerous than other peoples, for you were the fewest of all peoples. But

---

[8] The term *segullâ* (Deut 7:6; 14:2; 26:18) is used to describe the jewels in a king's treasury (1 Chr 29:3; Eccl 2:8).

it was because the LORD loved you and kept the oath he swore to
your forefathers that he brought you out with a mighty hand and redeemed you from the land of slavery, from the power of Pharaoh king
of Egypt. (Deut 7:6-8)

This election brought with it great obligations to keep the covenant laws
(Exodus 19–24), which were not seen as a burden but an honor and a joy
(Psalm 119).

Most of the Old Testament is focused on Israel and its covenant relationship with Yahweh. It would be easy to think that God had given up on
the nations and had replaced his concern for them with a concern for Israel.
This, however, would be a serious mistake. It is clear, even at the origins of
the nation of Israel, that Abram and Israel are elect *for the sake of the nations*.
Abram is singled out in order that the divine blessing, which humanity had
lost in Eden, can be recovered. This is clear, in part, from the divine promise
itself ("you will be a blessing. I will bless those who bless you, and whoever
curses you I will curse; and *all peoples on earth will be blessed through you*")
and also by the way the placing of the story following Genesis 1–11 identifies
God's call to Abram as God's way of dealing with the problem of the nations.
The promise that all nations would be blessed in Abraham's descendants is
repeated four more times in Genesis (18:18; 22:18; 26:4; 28:14).[9] The idea
of Israel being elect for the sake of the nations is also hinted at in that other
key moment in the formation of the nation—the institution of the covenant
at Sinai.

Then Moses went up to God, and the LORD called to him from
the mountain and said, "This is what you are to say to the house of
Jacob and what you are to tell the people of Israel: 'You yourselves
have seen what I did to Egypt, and how I carried you on eagles' wings
and brought you to myself. Now if you obey me fully and keep my
covenant, then out of all nations you will be my treasured possession.
Although the whole earth is mine, you will be for me *a kingdom of
priests* and a holy nation.' These are the words you are to speak to the
Israelites." (Exod 19:3-6)

The Israelites are to function as a kingdom of priests; that is, like priests,
they will mediate between God and the peoples of the earth. This mediation
seems not to have been one in which Israel had to go out to the nations and
convert them to Yahwism. Rather, Israel had to focus its attention on keeping
its own house in order, by following the commands of the torah, which, in
turn, would function as a witness to Yahweh that the nations would marvel

---

[9] It is also echoed in Ps 72:17; Isa 19:24-25; Jer 4:2; Zech 8:13.

at. Israel would keep the torah's commands, and Yahweh would bless them and answer their prayers. The nations would watch and wonder.

> Observe them carefully, for this will show your wisdom and under-
> standing to the nations, who will hear about all these decrees and say,
> "Surely this great nation is a wise and understanding people." What
> other nation is so great as to have their gods near them the way the
> LORD our God is near us whenever we pray to him? And what other
> nation is so great as to have such righteous decrees and laws as this
> body of laws I am setting before you today? (Deut 4:6-8).

> The LORD will establish you as his holy people, as he promised you
> on oath, if you keep the commands of the LORD your God and walk
> in his ways. Then all the peoples on earth will see that you are called
> by the name of the LORD, and they will fear you. (Deut 28:9-10)

Clearly, obedience to Yahweh was central to Israel's mandate.

In a similar way, Yahweh's mighty acts on behalf of Israel, performed in the sight of the nations, would testify to Yahweh's greatness and mercy. For instance, Yahweh powerfully delivers Israel from Egypt, so making his name known amongst the nations (Exod 9:16; 2 Sam 7:23; Neh 9:10; Ps 106:8; Isa 63:10, 12; Jer 32:20; Dan 9:15). Similarly, his drying up the Jordan for Israel to cross over is "so that all the peoples of the earth may know that the hand of the LORD is mighty" (Josh 4:24), and the post-exilic restoration of Israel demonstrates to the nations that Yahweh alone is God (Ezek 36:22-23)—"all the earth will see the salvation of our God" (Isa 52:10; cf. 40:3-5).

It is not clear that this "blessing of the nations" involved their coming into any kind of relationship with Yahweh themselves as is seen from the fact that they also come to know that Yahweh is God when he lays waste to them in judgment (Ezek 25:7, 11, 17; 30:19, 25-26). It seems that they were merely educated in the wonders of Yahweh's laws and the power of Yahweh's arm to save and judge. However, some Old Testament texts do develop the idea in such a way that the nations themselves enter into a relationship with Yahweh.

> This is what Isaiah son of Amoz saw concerning Judah and Jerusalem:
> In the last days the mountain of the LORD's temple will be estab-
> lished as chief among the mountains; it will be raised above the hills,
> and all nations will stream to it. Many peoples will come and say,
> "Come, let us go up to the mountain of the LORD, to the house of
> the God of Jacob. He will teach us his ways, so that we may walk in
> his paths." The law will go out from Zion, the word of the LORD
> from Jerusalem. He will judge between the nations and will settle dis-
> putes for many peoples. They will beat their swords into ploughshares

and their spears into pruning hooks. Nation will not take up sword against nation, nor will they train for war any more. Come, O house of Jacob, let us walk in the light of the LORD. (Isa 2:1-5)

"If you will return, O Israel, return to me," declares the LORD. "If you put your detestable idols out of my sight and no longer go astray, and if in a truthful, just, and righteous way you swear, 'As surely as the LORD lives,' *then the nations will be blessed by him and in him they will glory.*" (Jer 4:1-2)

In the Isaianic vision, the nations, having seen God's laws modeled in Israel, are themselves drawn to the temple to learn his ways and walk in his paths. This inspirational thought leads the prophet to call urgently to the sinful Israel of his day, "Come, O house of Jacob, let us walk in the light of the LORD," for the vision will only come to pass if Israel is itself obedient to the torah. That notion is even stronger in the Jeremiah text, with its "if . . . then . . ." structure. It also includes a clear and significant allusion to the divine promise in Genesis 12 that the nations would be blessed through Abraham's descendants.

The notion of the nations flowing in pilgrimage to Mount Zion to worship at the Temple is one picked up in numerous Old Testament passages, being especially prominent in Isaiah (Isa 2:1-4; 11:10-12; 18:7; 60:1-16; 61:5-6; 66:12, 18, 23). Similarly, several Psalms call the nations to worship Yahweh and can envisage a time when that will happen:[10] "Praise the LORD, all you nations; extol him, all you peoples. For great is his love towards us, and the faithfulness of the LORD endures forever. Praise the LORD" (Psalm 117). "*All the nations you have made will come and worship before you,* O Lord; they will bring glory to your name. For you are great and do marvelous deeds; you alone are God" (Ps 86:9-10). Psalm 67 is worth quoting in its entirety:

> For the director of music. With stringed instruments.
> A psalm. A song.
>
> May God be gracious to us and bless us
>   and make his face shine upon us,
> that your ways may be known on earth,
>   your salvation among all nations.
> May the peoples praise you, O God;
>   may all the peoples praise you.
> May the nations be glad and sing for joy,
>   for you rule the peoples justly

---

[10] See also Pss 22:27-29; 47:7-9; 68:29; 72:9-11; 102:21-22; 122:3-4; 138:4-5.

and guide the nations of the earth.
May the peoples praise you, O God;
    may all the peoples praise you.
Then the land will yield its harvest,
    and God, our God, will bless us.
God will bless us,
    and all the ends of the earth will fear him.

Yet again, God's blessing Israel is the means by which the nations are drawn into worship with Israel.

Another significant text about Israel's mission to the nations is found in Isaiah 42:1-7.

> "Here is my servant, whom I uphold, my chosen one in whom I delight; I will put my Spirit on him and he will bring justice to the nations. He will not shout or cry out, or raise his voice in the streets. A bruised reed he will not break, and a smoldering wick he will not snuff out. In faithfulness he will bring forth justice; he will not falter or be discouraged till he establishes justice on earth. In his law the islands will put their hope." This is what God the LORD says—he who created the heavens and stretched them out, who spread out the earth and all that comes out of it, who gives breath to its people, and life to those who walk on it: "I, the LORD, have called you in righteousness; I will take hold of your hand. I will keep you and will make you to be a covenant for the people and a light for the Gentiles, to open eyes that are blind, to free captives from prison and to release from the dungeon those who sit in darkness."

This is the first of the so-called Servant Songs (Isa 42:1-7; 49:1-9; 50:4-11; 52:13—53:12). There has been much debate about the identity of the Servant in these texts, but I think that the case for an identification with Israel, albeit presented in a Davidic role, in the first Song is very strong.[11] So what is the

---

[11] The more plausible suggestions include Cyrus (so John D. W. Watts, *Isaiah 34–66*, WBC 25 [Waco: Word, 1987]), Deutero-Isaiah (so R. N. Whybray, *Isaiah 40–66*, NCB [Grand Rapids: Eerdmans, 1975]), a Davidic Messianic figure (so J. H. Eaton, *Festal Drama in Deutero-Isaiah* [London: SPCK, 1979]; A. Motyer, *The Prophesy of Isaiah* [Leicester: InterVarsity, 1993]); a new Moses figure (so G. P. Hugenberger, "The Servant of the LORD in the Servant Songs of Isaiah," in *The Lord's Annointed: Interpretation of Old Testament Messianic Texts*, ed. P. E. Satterthwaite et al. [Grand Rapids: Baker; Carlisle: Paternoster, 1995] 105–40); and Israel. The servant is clearly a royal figure (see H. G. M. Williamson, *Variations on a Theme: King, Messiah and Servant in the Book of Isaiah* [Carlisle: Paternoster, 1998] 132–35) but contextually Israel is explicitly identified with the servant (Isa 41:8-9; 42:19; 43:10; 44:1-2, 21, 26; 48:20) and given that Isaiah 55:3-5 confers the Davidic role upon the nation, the royal imagery becomes understandable (so Williamson, *Variations*, chap. 4). The Servant is Israel personified as a royal figure. This explains all the parallels between descriptions of the servant and the King as well

mission of Servant-Israel (Isa 41:8) to the nations? He is to bring forth "justice to the nations" and "establish justice on the earth." This justice, despite scholars' disagreement as to its meaning, is clearly seen as a positive thing to benefit the nations.

Second, we read that "in his law (*torah*) the islands will put their hope." Here there are clear echoes of Isaiah 2:1-4, in which the *torah* goes out from Zion to the nations. This *torah* need not be interpreted as the Mosaic law; the term is much broader than that and merely designates "teaching." It should be noticed that this is not something oppressive for the islands. They put their hope in this teaching just as in Isaiah 2. This seems clearly to indicate some positive mission to the nations.

Third, he will be "a covenant for the people." There is some debate about whether the people referred to are Israel or the nations. I shall argue later that the Gentile nations are referred to, and we shall simply assume that conclusion for now. It seems that Israel functions as mediators of some sort of covenant between Yahweh and the nations.

Fourth, "he will be a light for the Gentiles, to open eyes that are blind, to free captives from prison and to release from the dungeon those who sit in darkness." Here Servant-Israel is to free Gentiles from captivity and darkness—yet another image with a positive outcome for the nations.[12]

Israel's Exile–Restoration and the Light to the Gentiles

Israel fell short of God's calling for her. She did not keep the law of Moses (Isa 42:24) and thus incurred divine covenant curses (Isa 42:22-25) of escalating

---

as those between the servant and Israel (features too numerous to list here).

[12] Many scholars have seen vv. 6-7 as being about someone with a mission to Israel rather than Israel's mission to the nations. They see the "bruised reed" and "dimly burning wick" in v. 3 as the exiles and they notice that v. 6 speaks of "a covenant to the people" and not "to the peoples" (Deutero-Isaiah's normal designation for the nations). In 49:8 the phrase "covenant to people" is clearly applied to Israel. On this view those to be released from prison are the exiles. Finally in Isaiah 40–48 Israel is portrayed as blind so they seem the obvious candidates for the Servant's eye-opening ministry. I think that this view is mistaken. First, that the prisoners in v. 7 are the nations is clear, because the description of the release of the blind prisoners is an explication of what it means to be a light to the nations (v. 6). Israel may be blind, but so too are the nations (44:9-20). Israel only becomes blind to the extent that she becomes like them. Second, although it is unexpected to find "people" ('*ām*) in the singular as a term for the nations, the previous verse (v. 5) provides a parallel where '*ām* refers to all humanity. Third, it seems likely that the two phrases "covenant to people" and "light to the nations" parallel each other and thus refer to the same group. Fourth, the "dim wick" and "bruised reed" are vague descriptions and do not clearly refer to the exiles. Finally, the prima facie evidence for the Servant being Israel in 42:1-7 is strong. However, I do think that these scholars have picked up some important clues that will help us understand the text better. I explain this in footnote 15.

seriousness until the curse reached its climax in the exile in Babylon (Deut 28:15-68 portrays exile as the climax of the covenant curses). Israel, who was to be a light to the blind nations, became blind herself (Isa 42:16, 18-25). Israel, who was to release the captives, became captive herself. Israel, who was to help the broken reed, was herself broken. Even after so much corrective punishment, Israel is still stubborn-hearted (Isa 46:8-13) and wearies Yahweh (Isa 43:24). This divine critique of his people reaches a climax in Isaiah 48, in which Israel's stubbornness (v. 4) and continued devotion to idols (v. 3) lead Yahweh to despair at their short sightedness (v. 18). Israel, instead of fulfilling her Servant mission to the nations, became in need of such Servant ministry herself. In its present state, God's people cannot be the source of blessing to the nations as Yahweh had intended.

But here, in the midst of such a hopeless situation, Isaiah sees hope. Israel is still God's servant, his chosen one, the offspring of Abraham (Isa 41:8). Yahweh is still their God, who has chosen them and will not cast them off (Isa 41:10). Though they are blind, he will lead them (42:16) and keep them through trial (43:1-2), for he loves them (43:3-4). The exiles will be gathered (43:5-7) and their enemies destroyed (41:11-12). Blind Israel is still his witness (43:8-13), although not whilst she remains in her blind state.[13] Thus blind Israel *will* be Yahweh's servant, but *not in her present blind state*. There will be a new exodus (43:14-21) with provision for the journey (43:19-21; 41:18-20) that will change everything. God promises to pour out his Spirit on their descendants so that they will honor him (44:1-5), bringing about the change required for Israel to fulfill her divine mission. God will be glorified in Israel, but only in a *restored* Israel.[14] When Israel is restored, the nations will come in chains to them, confessing that Yahweh alone is God and that the idols are nothing (45:14-17; 55:5). The Gentiles will acknowledge Yahweh and be saved (45:20-25), and Israel's Servant mission will be completed (2:1-5).[15]

---

[13] In Isa 43:10 Israel "knows" and "understands" in contrast to blind Israel who do "not understand" (41:25).

[14] One may also note how restored Israel can be contrasted with idolaters (44:12-20) who remain blind and their witnesses (the idols) "who neither see nor know" (44:9).

[15] This outline of the calling, failure, and hope for Israel presented in Isaiah 40-48 helps us to understand an odd expression in the first Servant Song. God says to the Servant, "I will keep you and will make you to be *a covenant for the people* and a light for the Gentiles." Yahweh speaks of the Servant being a covenant for the nations and yet we would have expected him to say "a covenant for the peoples" rather than "a covenant for the people." Elsewhere in Isaiah the nations are referred to as "peoples" (except 40:5 and 42:5) whilst in 49:8 the expression "covenant for the people" is applied to Israel. I suggest that the singular "people" was used deliberately in 42:6 so that although it is clearly a reference to Israel's servant mission to the Gentiles *it also invites a second level reading in which Israel itself is the recipient of the Servant's ministry*. She needs restoring before she can fulfill her role.

The important conclusion from this discussion is that in the Old Testament story God's mission to the nations through Israel can only be completed after God has restored Israel. The return from exile is depicted as the restoration of Israel and thus the trigger for the pilgrimage of the nations. This is depicted in diagram 1. Israel's exile parallels the expulsion of humanity from Eden and Israel's return prefigures and precipitates the restoration of the nations.

But how is Israel to be restored? We shall see the New Testament answer to this question in the next chapter. However, the book of Isaiah does drop clear hints that are worth sketching briefly. I shall argue that God sends an individual[16] who takes upon himself the Servant mission of the nation and acts as the Servant to Servant-Israel. The crucial shift occurs after the clear structural break between Isaiah 40–48 and 49–55.[17] The second Servant Song in 49:1-13 functions as a hinge between 40–48 and 49–55, and we find a shift in the Servant's identity. On the one hand, he is clearly identified *with* Israel (v. 3) whilst, on the other, he is clearly *distinguished from* Israel (vv. 5-6).[18] Wilcox and Paton-Williams argue that throughout vv. 1-7 the Servant is Deutero-Isaiah himself. He embodies Israel's calling and destiny and has a mission to Israel. From this point on in the book, the nation of Israel is never again referred to as Servant. Whilst remaining agnostic about who the oracle refers to (the prophet himself, a messianic figure, or whatever), I think that Wilcox and Paton-Williams are correct in seeing here the transference of Israel's mission onto an individual. From now on, the Servant Songs portray the destiny of an individual in whom Israel's story is writ small. This is an important theme that we do not have time to develop, so we need to be content with a few observations. The individual Servant in Isaiah 49:8-13 does for Israel what Israel was to do for the nations. He is a "covenant for the people" (Israel) just as Servant-Israel was called to be "a covenant for the people" (i.e., the Gentiles) in 42:6. As Israel was to release Gentile prisoners in 42:7, so

[16] Or a remnant within Israel—it is impossible to say for certain, although there are problems with the remnant theory because in 50:10 the Servant seems to address the remnant in such a way as to distinguish them from the Servant (even if they are the "servants" of Isaiah 56–66).

[17] On the break see the references in Williamson, *Variations*, 147 n.58.

[18] Numerous explanations have been made to account for this peculiar phenomenon. Among the ones that I think do not work are the following: (a) Delete the word "Israel" from v. 3. The problem is that the mss evidence is overwhelmingly in favour of retaining the word and the metre and syntax are not improved by its removal. (b) Watts suggests that vv. 1-4 are about servant Israel whilst vv. 5-6 are about Darius, the Persian ruler. However, v. 5 continues with the same first person speaker as vv. 1-4 and uses the same imagery ("called from the womb"), indicating that there is no change of speaker. If there is a change if speaker, it has been well hidden by the redactor. To this we may add that the Servant in 49:5-6 is the same as that in 42:1-7 (n.b. light to the nations) and if the case in 42 for Israel is strong, then the same goes here (to be fair to Watts he sees the Servant in 42 to be a Persian ruler also).

now she finds her own prisoners released by this Servant to the servant (49:9). By bringing about a new exodus (49:9-12) the Servant brings about the restoration of Zion (49:13ff.); but the question remains—how will he achieve this. The answer, I suggest, is found in the most famous Servant Song of all: 52:13—53:12. There, the Servant embodies in his own story Israel's exilic suffering and restoration in the imagery of death and resurrection. This can be illustrated in diagram 2.

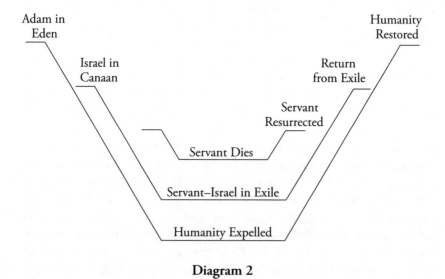

Diagram 2

The Old Testament prophets portrayed Israel's exile in terms of a metaphorical death and resurrection (esp. Ezekiel 37; Hos 6:2; Isa 26:29), so the use of such imagery for the individual Servant in the exilic context of Isaiah 40–55 is suggestive of Israel's exile and restoration. We cannot explore now how this embodiment of Israel's destiny is thought to bring about her restoration, but we should note that the death and resurrection of this Servant are followed by oracles of Zion's restoration (Isaiah 54), which, given their location, suggests that this salvation for Zion is achieved by the Servant's work in Isaiah 53. Chapter 55 then portrays the mission of Israel completed as the nations come running to Israel (55:3-5).

The Fate of the Nations: Judgment Then Salvation

We have seen that the nations will be brought to worship Yahweh through a restored Israel. Israel, according to Isaiah 40–55, would be restored by an act of divine grace in a second exodus and by means of an individual who embodies the nation's identity and destiny. Israel's story is one of judgment and mercy, destruction and salvation, exile and restoration, death and then life. The story of the nations in the Old Testament is parallel to Israel's—divine judgment followed by divine mercy mediated somehow through the Servant of Yahweh.

Destruction

The theme of the destruction of the nations is common in the Old Testament. Sometimes this is simply the destruction of a particular nation whilst at other times a universal destruction of all the nations is envisaged.

> Come near, you nations, and listen; pay attention, you peoples! Let the earth hear, and all that is in it, the world, and all that comes out of it! The LORD is angry with all nations; his wrath is upon all their armies. He will totally destroy them, he will give them over to slaughter. Their slain will be thrown out, their dead bodies will send up a stench; the mountains will be soaked with their blood. All the stars of the heavens will be dissolved and the sky rolled up like a scroll; all the starry host will fall like withered leaves from the vine, like shriveled figs from the fig-tree (Isa 34:1-4).

This oracle is directly connected with Israel's return from exile as is seen by its close connections and juxtaposition with Isaiah 35. God destroys the nations, thus delivering Israel from exile. The salvation of the nations, then, must be portrayed as being *subsequent* to this destruction. The wounding precedes the healing.

Salvation

One of the most important Old Testament texts about salvation for the Gentiles is Isaiah 45:20-25. It clearly reflects a post-judgment salvation for the nations.

> Gather together and come;
> > assemble, you fugitives [or "survivors"] from the nations.
> Ignorant are those who carry about idols of wood,
> > who pray to gods that cannot save.
> Declare what is to be, present it—
> > let them take counsel together.
> Who foretold this long ago,
> > who declared it from the distant past?
> Was it not I, the LORD?

> And there is no God apart from me,
>> a righteous God and a Savior;
>>> there is none but me.
> Turn to me and be saved,
>> all you ends of the earth;
>>> for I am God, and there is no other.
> By myself I have sworn,
>> my mouth has uttered in all integrity
>> a word that will not be revoked:
> Before me every knee will bow;
>> by me every tongue will swear.
> They will say of me,
>> "In the LORD alone are righteousness and strength."
> All who have raged against him will come to him
>> and be put to shame.
> But in the LORD all the descendants of Israel
>> will be found righteous and will exult.

Here Yahweh addresses the survivors from the nations.[19] That is, he speaks to those who have survived the divine judgments, perhaps on Babylon. These survivors are idolaters, but Yahweh challenges them to see the futility of their gods and that he alone is God. He then calls to the nations to turn to him and be saved.[20] The salvation in mind is at least analogous to Israel's own (see 45:17, which is the only other occurrence of the Niph'al of *yasha'* in Second Isaiah). Then, in this salvific context, Yahweh swears by himself an irrevocable oath that *every* knee will bow down before him and *every* tongue will confess him as God. That this is no forced subjection of defeated enemies is clear for the following reasons. First, we see that God has just called all the nations to turn to him and be saved, and it is in that context that the oath is taken. Second, the swearing of oaths in Yahweh's name is something his own people

---

[19] Snaith ("The Servant of the Lord in Deutero-Isaiah," in *Studies in Old Testament Prophecy Presented to Professor Theodore H. Robinson*, ed. H. H. Rowley [Edinburgh: T. & T. Clark, 1950]) interprets this as a reference to the exiles who had escaped from the nations. This is part of his project of seeing no salvation for those outside Israel in Deutero-Isaiah. For a critique see A. Gelston, "Universalism in Second Isaiah," *JTS* 43 (1992) 387 [377–98].

[20] Some scholars have argued that Second Isaiah is narrowly nationalistic and sees no salvation for the nations (e.g., Snaith, De Boer, Lindars, Orlinsky, Wilson, Barstad and Whybray). This is something of a reaction against an earlier simplistic account of the kind of universalism found here. The truth seems to be found in mediating positions such as those of A. Gelston, W. A. M. van Beuken ("The First Servant Song and Its Context," *VT* 22 [1972] 1–30; "The Main Theme of Trito-Isaiah: The Servants of Yahweh," *JSOT* 47 [1990] 67–87); and Williamson, *Variations*.

do, not his defeated enemies. Third, those who confess Yahweh go on to say, "In the LORD alone are righteousness and strength," which sounds like the cry of praise from God's own people.

Many scholars do not think that here Yahweh takes an oath to save *all* who have survived.[21] This is because the text goes on to say, "All who have raged against him will come to him and be put to shame. But in the LORD all the descendants of Israel will be found righteous and will exult." Those who are put to shame are said to be those who do not turn and accept the offer of salvation. This, I suggest, is to misunderstand the text. The contrast is between those who are shamed and Israel. The shamed ones are the nations, and so, on the common interpretation, it looks like the text teaches that *none* of the nations are saved! The same contrast is found in the near context of Isaiah 45:16-17, which contrasts those who make idols (they will be put to shame) and Israel (saved with everlasting salvation and never put to shame). Here again those who are ashamed are *all* the nations. If this shaming excludes them from salvation, then, presumably, none of the nations turn to Yahweh and are saved, which flatly contradicts the teaching of Isaiah elsewhere (e.g., 60:1ff.; 66:18-23; 2:1-4), and the divine oath becomes something of a joke. We may better understand the contrast when we appreciate that the nations throughout Second Isaiah are idolaters. When they turn away from idols to Yahweh as the one true God, they do so ashamed of their past. Israel, on the other hand, is vindicated and rejoices. This reading is reinforced when we consider a text such as Ezekiel 16, in which Yahweh says that after Israel's period of idolatry he will redeem them, and they will be ashamed: "Then, when I make atonement for you for all you have done, you will remember and be ashamed (*bôsh*) and never again open your mouth because of your humiliation, declares the Sovereign LORD" (Ezek 16:63). Being ashamed of past idolatry is not an inappropriate response for those Yahweh redeems from such things.[22]

Alternatively, some interpreters speak of this divine oath as something Yahweh merely *hopes* will happen—a possible future, but one conditional upon the response of the nations. Granted that this future depends on the nations' turning to Yahweh, it does not follow that this is only a *merely possible* future. Yahweh swears an oath that this is what *will* occur. In Second Isaiah the theme of the power of Yahweh's word is pervasive.[23] This word

---

[21] E.g. Gelston, "Universalism in Second Isaiah," 391; Beuken, "The Confession of God's Exclusivity by all Mankind: A Reappraisal of Is. 45:18-25," *Bijdragen* 35 (1974) 335–56.

[22] Rightly J. N. Oswalt, *The Book of Isaiah Chapters 40–66* (Grand Rapids: Eerdmans, 1998) 225.

[23] See D. Pao, *Acts and the Isaianic New Exodus,* WUNT 2/130 (Tübingen: Mohr/Siebeck, 2000) chap. 5 for the Isaiah's teaching and how the book of Acts makes use of it.

lasts forever (40:8) and will not return to God without accomplishing what he sent it for (55:10-11), so it is not possible that one should envisage that the divine oath to ensure universal worship will remain unrealized. The oath stands alongside other texts in second Isaiah in which there is universal recognition of Yahweh's sovereignty (40:3-5; 45:3, 6, 14; 49:7, 26; 52:10; 55:5).

A similar story of destruction followed by healing is found in the astonishing Isaiah 19. Here we read of Egypt and Assyria, Israel's archetypal enemies:

> In that day five cities in Egypt will speak the language of Canaan and swear allegiance to the LORD Almighty. One of them will be called the City of Destruction. In that day there will be an altar to the LORD in the heart of Egypt, and a monument to the LORD at its border. It will be a sign and witness to the LORD Almighty in the land of Egypt. When they cry out to the LORD because of their oppressors, he will send them a savior and defender, and he will rescue them. So the LORD will make himself known to the Egyptians, and in that day they will acknowledge the LORD. They will worship with sacrifices and grain offerings; they will make vows to the LORD and keep them. The LORD will strike Egypt with a plague; he will strike them and heal them. They will turn to the LORD, and he will respond to their pleas and heal them. In that day there will be a highway from Egypt to Assyria. The Assyrians will go to Egypt and the Egyptians to Assyria. The Egyptians and Assyrians will worship together. In that day Israel will be the third, along with Egypt and Assyria, a blessing on the earth. The LORD Almighty will bless them, saying, "Blessed be Egypt my people, Assyria my handiwork, and Israel my inheritance." (Isa 19:18-25)

This passage follows a description of divine punishment on Egypt. The Lord strikes them *and then* heals them. That is the pattern for the nations as it was with Israel. What is astonishing is the manner of the healing. Israel's archenemies convert to the service of Yahweh and worship him on an equal footing with Israel herself. In the light of the fierce prophetic oracles of judgment on Egypt (esp. Ezekiel 29–32) and Assyria (esp. Nahum; Ps 139:21) this is all the more stunning. Indeed, it is perhaps the most astonishing oracle in the Old Testament about the destiny of the nations.

Sometimes the salvation of the nations is depicted in less egalitarian ways. A common motif is of the nations coming in chains and bowing before Israel and even licking the dust. The roots of this image seem to lie in the Davidic traditions, in which the Davidic King rules from Zion, the seat of God's universal rule (Ps 99:1-3). Although the Davidic King's rule was not, unlike Yahweh's, universal, the theological hyperbole often spoke as if it would be.

> He will rule from sea to sea
>> and from the River to the ends of the earth.
> The desert tribes will bow before him
>> and his enemies will lick the dust.
> The kings of Tarshish and of distant shores will bring tribute to him;
>> the kings of Sheba and Seba will present him gifts.
> All kings will bow down to him
>> and all nations will serve him (Ps 72:8-11)

The kings of the nations become client kings of the Davidic king enthroned in Zion (cf. Zech 9:10; Mic 5:4; Ps 2:8). The ideal Davidic king thus becomes the mediator of Yahweh's universal rule over the nations. Now in Deutero-Isaiah this Davidic role in relation to the nations is passed to the nation of Israel as a whole as it reappropriates its Servant mission after return from exile (Isa 55:3-5). Hugh Williamson suggests that the clue to the two models of Israel's relation to the nations (partners-in-worship and ruler-subjugated peoples) lies with this insight.[24] He pictures the connections as follows. The prevalent Old Testament hierarchy of

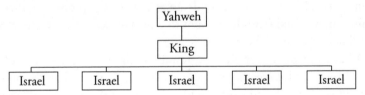

becomes

In both diagrams the mediator (king and people) is at the same time in a position of privilege in their relationship with God and responsibility to mediate blessing to those below them on the hierarchy. Those at the bottom of the hierarchy also have both privileges in sharing in the blessings and responsibili-

---

[24] This claim is defended by Williamson, *Variations*, chap. 4.

ties to be obedient to the mediator. This understanding generates two kinds of oracle regarding Israel's relations with the nations: universalistic and egalitarian ones on the one hand, and nationalistic ones on the other. However, in interpreting the nationalistic oracles in canonical context, one needs to see that the political submission of the nations to Israel, often pictured in terms of military defeat and subjection, is actually the means by which they come to share in the blessing of Israel.[25] This is clear from texts in which the submission of the nations to Israel is in the context of the Gentiles' seeing that Yahweh alone is God (Isa 49:7; 45:14; 55:5). Gelston says: "In each of these passages we read of a voluntary submission to Israel, motivated by the recognition that Israel's God is the only God, and the terms of the submission contain more than a hint of a quest for God."[26] The New Testament clearly interprets the subjection texts through the grid of the blessing texts to the point that any national superiority for Israel is eliminated.[27] Israel is still seen as privileged mediator (see Romans) but not in such a way as to imply superiority.

Conclusions

In summary, we have argued that the Old Testament, when read as a whole, sees Yahweh's plan as the salvation of all the nations through Israel, his new humanity. Israel herself actually ends up as part of the problem rather than the solution, but God sends his servant to servant-Israel in order to enable her to fulfill her mission to the nations.

What kind of universalism is found in the Old Testament? One in which ultimately all humanity without exception acknowledges the universal sovereignty of Yahweh and worships him. But is this the salvation of each and every individual who has ever lived? The answer to that question, which may surprise the reader, given where I am heading, is no. There is a reason for this; and it is not, as some suggest, that the Old Testament does not deal with that question directly. While it is true that the Old Testament is interested primarily in groups (Israel and national groups) rather than individuals,[28] this does

---

[25] See D. W. Van Winkle, "The Relationship of the Nations to Yahweh and to Israel in Isaiah xl-lv," *VT* 35 (1985) 446–58; and A. Gelston, "Universalism in Second Isaiah."

[26] Gelston, "Universalism in Second Isaiah," 386.

[27] See how Revelation 21 makes use of Isaiah 60 by stripping it of its political subjection overtones. See also Pao (*Acts and the Isaianic New Exodus*) on how Acts modifies the Isaiah traditions to which it is so indebted by passing over the nationalist texts. However, I suggest that this is not simply a matter of ignoring such texts but of re-interpreting them in light of the salvation oracles.

[28] Rightly T. Johnson, "A Wideness in God's Mercy: Universalism in the Bible," in Parry and Partridge, eds., *Universal Salvation?*, 79.

not mean that we cannot infer the fate of individuals. We have seen that the ultimate vision for humanity is one in which all humanity worships Yahweh; and, thus, it anticipates a future in which each individual does. The reason that I think the Old Testament does not envisage the salvation of all individuals who have ever existed and is thus not universalist in the strong sense of the word is that it has no conception of life after death, at least until the very end of the Old Testament period (Dan 12:2). Thus, the universal salvation only extends to those who are living—the "survivors of the nations" (Isa 45:20). That is why Isaiah 66:23-24 can envisage a valley of dead bodies existing alongside the salvation of *all* humanity. In the next chapter we shall see how the belief in life after death leads to theological moves that drive towards a stronger universalism that embraces all humanity, past, present, and future.

CHAPTER FOUR

Christ, Israel, and the Nations in the New Testament

*For in [God's] union with this one man [Christ] He has
shown His love to all and His solidarity. In this One He
has taken upon himself the sin and guilt of all, and therefore
rescued them all by higher right from the judgment which they
had rightly incurred, so that He is really the true consolation of
all. For in the death of this One it has taken place that all who
had incurred death by our sin and guilt have been released
from death as He became a Sinner and Debtor in our place,
accepting the penalty and paying the debt.*

—Karl Barth[1]

IN THIS chapter I shall argue that Jesus, in his Messianic role, fulfils the calling of Israel in his own person. In his death Israel's exilic curse reaches its climax, and in his resurrection Israel returns from exile. Jesus is also the second Adam who reverses the curse of expulsion from Eden by his execution and enables the restoration of humanity by his resurrection. As in the Isaianic plot, this restoration of Israel in the Servant precipitates the restoration of Zion and the pilgrimage of the Gentiles. However, unexpectedly, this true Israel, this new humanity in Christ composed of Jew and Gentile, is restricted to the church. These insights are not unusual in biblical scholarship and hardly amount to universalism. What is usually missed, though, is that the church is only a foretaste of the redemption of Israel and the pilgrimage of the nations. We shall see that the New Testament anticipates a future fulfillment in which "all Israel will be saved" and the nations will come to worship before the one who sits on the throne and the Lamb.

---

[1] Karl Barth, *Church Dogmatics*, trans. G. W. Bromiley and T. F. Torrance (Edinburgh: T. & T. Clark, 1956–76) 3:613.

Jesus as Israel

The insight that throughout the New Testament Jesus is portrayed in terms that recall the nation of Israel and its mission is so commonplace I shall not spend long defending it. The kinds of evidence appeal can be made to include the fact that many titles for Jesus have strong associations with Israel. For instance, Jesus' use of the title Son of Man was influenced by Daniel 7 (e.g., Mark 14:62), where it refers to Israel or Israel's representative. By playing the role of the Son of Man, Jesus is playing the role of Israel. The title Son of God is also linked in the Hebrew Scriptures to the nation of Israel, God's son (Hos 11:1), and to the king of Israel (Ps 2:7) as the representative of the nation. This could suggest that Jesus, in his role as messianic king of Israel, represents and embodies the destiny of that nation. Now the title Son of God did evolve during the New Testament period and afterwards into something closer to the later title God the Son, but its messianic connections are still clear in places.[2] This insight helps explain some otherwise peculiar Christian interpretations of the Old Testament, such as when Matthew takes the words of Hosea 11:1, "out of Egypt I called my son," which in their context refer to the exodus of the Israelites, and applies them to Jesus' flight to Egypt after the death of Herod (Matt 2:15). Once it is perceived that for Matthew Jesus is Yahweh's son *because he is embodying the story of Israel,* this apparent mis-use of an Old Testament text begins to make sense. The title Messiah/Christ could also suggest one who represents the whole nation before God;[3] and, in light of our arguments in the previous chapter, thinking of Jesus as Isaiah's Servant of Yahweh, as the early Christian certainly did (Mt 3:17/Isa 42:1; Mark 10:45/Isa 53:10; Acts 8:30-35/Isa 53:7-8), *is* to think of him as one who fulfils the story and mission of Israel. On top of this, we can see how the Gospels can tell the story of Jesus in such a way as to parallel the story of Israel. For instance, after Jesus is baptized he goes into the wilderness for fort-ty days before crossing the Jordan into Israel to begin his mission just as Israel went into wilderness for forty years before crossing the Jordan into Canaan. However, where Israel failed its testing in the wilderness, Jesus succeeds.

Not only is Jesus, as the Messiah of Israel, the one who represents the nation, but in his death and resurrection Israel's exile and return are pictured and achieved. Although the suggestion is controverted, I think that there are good reasons for believing that many Jews in the Second Temple period

---

[2] Because the title Son expressed the relationship between Jesus and the Father, it naturally evolved to express the unique intimacy between Father and Son in such a way that Christ's divinity also became associated with the title. One can see this is the use of the title Son in John's Gospel in particular.

[3] See N. T. Wright, *The Climax of the Covenant: Christ and the Law in Pauline Theology* (Edinburgh: T. & T. Clark; Minneapolis: Fortress, 1991) chap. 3.

did not consider that Israel's exile had ended when the Jews returned from Babylon under Cyrus.[4] Consequently, many Jews were looking to God to deliver them from exile even though they were living in the Promised Land. Once this is conceded, the way is open to seeing Jesus' death as paralleling Israel's exile in the same way that Israel's exile parallels Adam and Eve's expulsion. N. T. Wright has argued convincingly, to my mind, that Paul's claim in Galatians 3:13 that Christ has redeemed "us" from the curse of the law by becoming a curse for us makes a direct link between Jesus' death and the exile.[5] The supreme curse of the law was exile (Deut 28); and, as I have already indicated, many Jews in Paul's day considered Israel still to be in exile. According to Wright, such Jews would take Paul's reference to the "curse of the law" as a reference to their ongoing exile. On the cross, Jesus takes the exilic curse to its terrifying climax and destroys its power.

> Because the Messiah represents Israel, he is able to take on himself Israel's curse and exhaust it . . . The crucifixion of the Messiah is, one might say, the *quintessence* of the curse of exile, and its climactic act . . . He is Israel going down to death under the curse of the law, and going through that curse to new covenant life beyond.[6]

This makes perfect sense of the logic of Paul's argument in Galatians 3:13-14 when he writes,

> Christ redeemed us [i.e., Jewish Christians] from the curse of the law [i.e., exile] by becoming a curse for us, for it is written: "Cursed is everyone who is hung on a tree." He redeemed us [i.e., Jewish Christians] in order that the blessing given to Abraham might come to the Gentiles through Christ Jesus, so that by faith we might receive the promise of the Spirit.

Now it is true that New Testament prefers to speak in terms of the language of a "new exodus" rather than the language of return from exile when imagining the salvation brought about by Christ. However, it is critical to appreciate that the language of the exodus as used in the New Testament *is filtered through Isaiah 40–55* where it is clearly used to picture the return from exile. Consequently, "new exodus" language in the New Testament is not an alternative to "return from exile" language—it *is* "return from exile" language.

---

[4] See N. T. Wright, *The New Testament and the People of God*, (London: SPCK; Minneapolis: Fortress, 1992); C. Evans, "Jesus and the Continuing Exile of Israel," in *Jesus and the Restoration of Israel*, ed. Carey C. Newman (Downers Grove, Ill.: InterVarsity, 1992) 77–100; for a convenient summary see David Pao, *Acts and the Isaianic New Exodus*, WUNT 2/130 (Tübingen: Mohr/Siebeck, 2000) 143–46.

[5] N. T. Wright, "Curse and Covenant: Galatians 3:10-14" in idem, *Climax*, 137–56.

[6] Ibid., 151–52.

In Christ's death and resurrection Israel's exile reaches its climax and Israel is restored (the new exodus occurs). This precipitates the salvation of Israel, anticipated in the Jewish believers, which, in turn, leads to the salvation of the Gentile nations, anticipated in the believing Gentiles and the eschatological giving of the Spirit. In other words, just like in the Old Testament plotline discussed in the last chapter, Jesus restores Israel, enabling the nations to come and worship with them in a new age of *shalôm*. The blessing of Abraham that God had always intended to be mediated to the world through Israel was now set loose in Christ!

The above observation can be briefly supported by two other arguments. First, it has often been said that Jesus innovatively added the idea of a suffering Son of Man (Mark 8:31; 9:9; 10:33, 45) to Daniel's glorified and vindicated Son of Man. However, once it is seen that Daniel's Son of Man *represents* Israel, it becomes clear that in Daniel 7 Israel *both* suffers *and* is vindicated (Dan 7:21-23); so Jesus is not being especially innovative here. What is interesting, and what has often been missed, is that the Son of Man allusions to Daniel 7 make Jesus' death and resurrection-ascension an embodiment of Israel's suffering and vindication. Second, as soon as one concedes that the early Christians, and Jesus himself, understood his role to be that of the Servant of Yahweh in the book of Isaiah, it becomes reasonable to suggest that his death and resurrection were understood, as was the Servant's, to mirror the exile and restoration of Israel. We can represent this as follows:

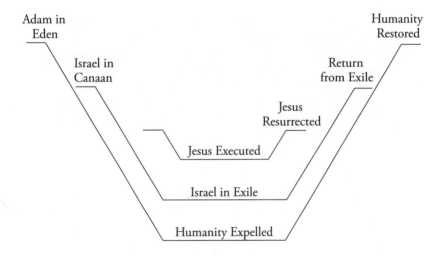

Diagram 3

Jesus as Second Adam

Jesus also plays the role of the new Adam, the fountainhead of a renewed humanity. The diagram above should make it clear that such a role is intimately connected with his role as Israel's Messiah. In this context we can explore the important Pauline text of Romans 5:12-21.

> 12 Therefore, just as sin entered the world through one man, and death through sin, and in this way death came to all men, because all sinned—

> 13 for before the law was given, sin was in the world. But sin is not taken into account when there is no law. 14 Nevertheless, death reigned from the time of Adam to the time of Moses, even over those who did not sin by breaking a command, as did Adam, who was a pattern of the one to come. 15 But the gift is not like the trespass. For if the many died by the trespass of the one man, how much more did God's grace and the gift that came by the grace of the one man, Jesus Christ, overflow to the many! 16 Again, the gift of God is not like the result of the one man's sin: The judgment followed one sin and brought condemnation, but the gift followed many trespasses and brought justification. 17 For if, by the trespass of the one man, death reigned through that one man, how much more will those who receive God's abundant provision of grace and of the gift of righteousness reign in life through the one man, Jesus Christ.

> 18 Consequently, just as the result of one trespass was condemnation for all men, so also the result of one act of righteousness was justification that brings life for all men. 19 For just as through the disobedience of the one man the many were made sinners, so also through the obedience of the one man the many will be made righteous. 20 The law was added so that the trespass might increase. But where sin increased, grace increased all the more, 21 so that, just as sin reigned in death, so also grace might reign through righteousness to bring eternal life through Jesus Christ our Lord.

The key verses for our purposes are 5:18-19, which are part of the section 5:12-21. Verses 13-17 are a digression from a train of thought Paul begins in v. 12 but does not complete until v. 18. Verse 18 repeats the protasis from v. 12 but finally completes it with a long anticipated apodosis. To understand vv. 18-19 in context, then, one needs to see how v. 12 connects into the preceding argument of Romans. Verse 12 begins with "therefore" (*dia touto*), which suggests a connection with what precedes. Richard Bell argues that v.

12 is not a conclusion drawn from 5:1-11[7] but rather looks back further in Romans.[8] Romans 3:23-24 is of critical importance: "for *all* have sinned and fall short of the glory of God, and are justified freely by his grace through the redemption that came by Christ Jesus."1:18-3:20 has already established the universal nature of sin, and 3:23 sums that argument up and introduces the idea that all are justified freely by his grace. But that point has not yet been established, and it is that that Paul seeks to do in 5:12-21. In other words, 5:12-21 aim to show that Christ's redemption is as wide as sin's corruption in that it reaches everyone. We could set out the contrasts Paul draws between Adam and Christ as follows:

Text	First Adam	Second Adam
v. 15	The many died	God's grace and gift overflow to the many
v. 16	The judgment followed one sin and brought condemnation	The gift followed many trespasses and brought justification.
v. 17	Death reigned through one man	Life and righteousness reign through one man
v. 18	One trespass brought condemnation for *all people*	One act of righteousness brought justification and life for *all people*
v. 19	Through the disobedience of one man the many were made sinners	Through the obedience of the one man the many will be made righteous.[9]

Christ's act of righteous obedience on the cross totally reverses the results of Adam's act of disobedience in Eden. What is of special note for our purposes is the universal results of both the disobedience of Adam and the obedience

---

[7] In part, because the "us" of 5:1-11 is a smaller group than the "all" of 5:12ff. and so 5:12ff. could not be seen as a conclusion drawn from vv. 1-11.

[8] Richard H. Bell, "Rom 5:18-19 and Universal Salvation," *NTS* 48 (2002) 417–32. James Dunn maintains that Rom 5:12-21 acts as a summary of the whole epistle to that point (1:18—5:11) and not merely as a summary of 5:1-11 (James D. G. Dunn, *Romans 1–8*, WBC 38A [Waco, Tex.: Word, 1988] 271–72).

[9] Bell finds an allusion to the Servant of Yahweh in Isa 53:11c here. Isaiah says "my (perfectly) righteous servant will make many righteous." This may explain why Paul used the expression "the many" in v. 19 rather than "all people" (Bell, "Universal Salvation," 427–28). What is of interest for our purposes is that Paul seems able to link the Servant with his Adam Christology, which reinforces the connections we have drawn in the previous chapter and this chapter between Adam, Israel, and Christ.

of Christ. Adam's sin brought condemnation and death to *all* people (compare 3:23). Christ's righteous act brings justification and eternal life to *all* people. Indeed Paul is at pains to make clear that the "all people" who were "made sinners" and "condemned" are the *very same* "all people" who will be "made righteous" and who, in Christ, are justified and have life. This is clear from the way he uses parallelism in v. 18 and v. 19.

There have been numerous strategies to avoid the universalist conclusion that seems to be present in Romans 5:18-19. Some argue that the second group in each pair is a more restricted group than the first group. The "all" in the first group means "all who are in Adam," which is literally every human being, whilst the second "all" refers to "all who are in Christ," which is only Christian believers. Several arguments, of varying degrees of merit, can be mustered in defense of this view. First, one can easily show that Paul was clear that justification and life only belong to those who believe in Christ. Second, v. 17 speaks of those who "receive God's abundant provision of grace and of the gift of righteousness," seemingly restricting salvation to those who receive it. Third, Paul only says that "the *many* will be made righteous" (5:19), not that "all" will be.

Let us consider these arguments one at a time. It is true that Paul taught that justification and life come only to believers and also that he taught that not all are believers. However, this should not be thought to undermine the universalism in vv. 18-19. Paul needs only to believe that one day all will believe (and I shall argue later that he did), and his statements are easily fitted together. This enables him to maintain that salvation is only for believers, that not all are currently believers, *and also* that "the many will be made righteous." On the level of logic, there is no contradiction here at all. Consequently, demonstrating that salvation only comes by faith is no objection to universalism in Romans 5:18-19 *unless* one can show that Paul did not think that all would one day believe.[10]

The second argument is that the participle *lambanontes* ('receive') in v. 17 places limits on those who inherit salvation—only those who take it for themselves by faith obtain it. However, *lambanō* here is being used in the passive sense of "receive" and not in the active sense of "take."[11] The reference in v. 17 is not to anything people do to get saved. It refers to God's making us recipients of grace and it places no limits on the universal statements in vv. 18-

---

[10] I will deal with the hell texts in chap. 6.

[11] M. Eugene Boring, "The Language of Universal Salvation in Paul," *JBL* 105 (1986) 287. So too Talbott, "Reply to my Critics," in Parry and Partridge, eds., *Universal Salvation?*, 247–73.; Bell, "Universal Salvation," 429; John Murray, *The Epistle of St Paul to the Romans,* vol. 1 (Grand Rapids: Eerdmans, 1960).

19, for those who receive God's abundant provision of grace could eventually be everyone.

The third argument concerns the expression "the many," suggesting that it is less than "all." However, the term "the many" was a common Hebraic way of saying "all,"[12] a fact that is confirmed when one reads v. 19 parallel with v. 18. "The many" of. v. 19 are the same group as "all people" of v. 18. This conclusion is made certain when one considers 5:15, which says that "the many" died because of Adam's sin. There it is clear that "all people" are referred to by the term.

So I think that we can safely conclude that the people who suffer from Adam's sin are the same people who benefit from Christ's atonement. However, this is not enough to establish that 5:18-19 teaches universalism. Some argue that, although the same group is referred to throughout vv. 18-19, that group is simply all kinds of people—Jews and Gentiles.[13] This claim has considerable plausibility. Throughout Romans Paul is concerned with the Jew–Gentile issue, and that is lurking in the background in 5:12-21. First, Paul shows that "all have sinned," which is to say, not merely Gentiles, *but Jews as well.* Then he goes on to argue that all will be justified, which is to say, not merely Jews *but also Gentiles.* Paul is intent on establishing the equality of Jew and Gentile in both sin and salvation. From this it is inferred by many scholars that when Paul says that there will be "justification and life for all people" he means "for Jews *and Gentiles*" and not "for every individual person." This view is correct in what it affirms but wrong in what it denies. Paul is indeed primarily concerned with establishing the equality of Jew and Gentile in condemnation and in salvation. When Paul says, "for *all* have sinned and fall short of the glory of God, and are justified freely by his grace through the redemption that came by Christ Jesus" (3:23-24), he *does* mean "both Jews and Gentiles." However, one cannot infer from this that he does not mean "all individual Jews and Gentiles." Indeed, I suggest that this is precisely what he does mean. This is clearest in Romans 3:9b-12:

> We have already made the charge that Jews and Gentiles alike are all under sin. As it is written: "There is no one righteous, not even one"; there is no one who understands, no one who seeks God. All have turned away, they have together become worthless; there is no one who does good, not even one.

The point Paul wishes to establish is that both Jews and Gentiles are under sin. He does this by arguing that "all are sinners," and by this he clearly

---

[12] Joachim Jeremias, "*polloi*," in *TDNT* 6:540–45 [536–45].

[13] For instance, N. T. Wright, "Towards a Biblical View of Universalism," *Themelios* 4.2 (1979) 54–61.

means "all individuals." The logic of his argument is that if all individuals are sinners, then, of course, both Gentiles *and Jews* are sinners. In just the same way, 5:18-19 establish that all will be justified; so, of course, both Jews *and Gentiles* will be. In fact, in 5:12-21 the Jew-Gentile issue is not present on the surface of the text and must be inferred contextually. Paul's focus is on the universality of Christ's saving work. The salvation of all individuals is suggested by the wording of 5:18, which clearly speaks of "*all* people." There has been tremendous confusion amongst biblical scholars over the term "all," so it is worth spending a little time clarifying it. It is commonplace to find scholars suggesting that "all" can sometimes mean "all without distinction" rather than "all without exception," and thus "all people" can mean "all *types* of people" (i.e., Jew and Gentile) and does not necessarily mean "all individual people." However, the distinction between two uses of the word "all" is simply bogus. The word "all" only has one meaning in Greek, as in English, and that is "all without exception." Philosopher Keith DeRose asks us to consider the following example:

> Suppose some slippery character is being investigated, and hands over to investigators several files relating to the case under consideration. The slippery character then says that he's handed over all the files about the case. It later turns out that, as the slippery character knew full well at the time of his statement, he's held on to over half of the files. Suppose his reaction to this revelation is: "Well, I handed over several files from each of the 10 major categories into which they fell. And I didn't just pick the least damaging files to hand over. Rather, I picked in a random fashion the files I would hand over from each category, so that each file, regardless of its category, and regardless of how damaging it was to my case, had a chance to be handed over. So, you see, I really did hand over *all* the files—all without distinction, that is; not, of course, all without exception." This won't fly, precisely because "all" just can't mean anything like what the "all without distinction crowd" says it sometimes means. My reaction, at least, is not that this fellow was being deceitful merely in using one sense of "all" while it has another good sense. He's worse than that: There's *no* good sense of "all" that would make true his miserable lie. No, "all," when it's used properly, always means all without exception. Quite simply "all" means all.[14]

So "all people" means "all people without exception." This observation needs two qualifications. First, "the quantifier phrases of natural language ("all," "most," "some," etc.) are to be understood, on an occasion of use, relative

───────────

[14] Keith DeRose, "Universalism and the Bible," http://pantheon.yale.edu/%7Ekd47/univ. htm.

to a contextually determined domain."[15] Thus, suppose I am at a party and complain that all the heaters are broken. Clearly, I do not mean all the heaters in the world without exception are broken! I mean all the heaters *in the party* without exception are broken. This limitation is unstated but clearly understood by those listening. The implication of this is that "all people" in Romans 5 may be understood to mean "*all kinds of people* without exception" *if the immediate context suggests such a qualification.* This is the root of the common misunderstanding amongst biblical scholars that "all" can sometimes mean "all without distinction." However, nothing in the near context suggests such a limitation, so the reader would be misreading Paul to impose such a limitation on the phrase here. If Paul had meant to imply "all kinds of people without exception," then he would have had to indicate contextually that this is what he had in mind. He did no such thing. The second qualification is that "all" can sometimes be used in a hyperbolic way. For instance, all Americans love burgers. What is important to understand here is that "all" still means "all without exception," but the statement is an exaggeration done for effect to emphasize just how many Americans love burgers. It is literally false and both speaker and hearer understand this. Translated into more mundane language, the sentence could be expressed as, "*most* Americans love burgers." The Bible does use "all" in a hyperbolic way at times, but this should not be used, as it often mistakenly is, as an argument to undermine the correct claim that "all" means "all without exception." As far as Romans 5 goes, we can ask, did Paul mean "*most* people are condemned in Adam and *most* people will receive justification and life"? Apart from the fact that very few non-universalists would be happy with the claim that most people will be saved, I don't think that this is what Paul is doing. As I have already argued, Paul is clear that all individuals are sinners (not simply most of them) and that Paul refers to the same group throughout vv. 18-19. In that case, if he means to say that all individuals are condemned in Adam, he also means to say that all individuals are saved in Christ.

Finally, some try to avoid the universalist implications of Romans 5:18-19 by arguing that the verses speak only of the salvation *bought* for all people and *offered* to all people, and it cannot be inferred from this that all people will avail themselves of the offer. This position acknowledges that Romans 5:18-19 speaks of the salvation of all individuals but maintains that Paul simply cannot have expected this universal deliverance to happen, because elsewhere he clearly expects some to be saved and others to be condemned at the judgment. Consequently, 5:18-19 speaks of Christ's universal atonement and his desire to save all, but no more. The problem with this interpretation is that Romans 5 says nothing about an *offer* of salvation for all but of a salva-

---

[15] Ibid.

tion *achieved* for all, which all *will* receive. The objectors are correct in drawing attention to the judgment texts in Paul, and the universalist will need to
have something to say about them. We shall deal with them in Chapter 6. If
we are able to deal sensibly with the hell texts, then there remain no objections to taking Romans 5:18-19 at face value as teaching universalism.

What Paul is keen to communicate in Rom 5:12-21 is the overwhelming power of grace, which far exceeds the power of sin and death. Käsemann
writes, ". . . all powerful grace is unthinkable without eschatological universalism."[16] And de Boer adds that

> Unless the universalism of vv. 18-19 is taken strictly, as I think it
> should and must be, "how much more" is turned into "how much
> less," for death is then given the last word over the vast majority of
> human beings and God's regrasping of the world for His sovereignty
> becomes a limited affair.[17]

The universalist conclusions we have reached on Romans 5 are sometimes
thought to be undermined by another important Pauline text that compares
Christ and Adam, 1 Corinthians 15:20-28.

> But Christ has indeed been raised from the dead, the firstfruits of
> those who have fallen asleep. For since death came through a man, the
> resurrection of the dead comes also through a man. For as in Adam
> all die, so in Christ all will be made alive. But each in his own turn:
> Christ, the firstfruits; then, when he comes, those who belong to him,
> then the end, when he hands over the kingdom to God the Father af-
> ter he has destroyed all dominion, authority, and power. For he must
> reign until he has put all his enemies under his feet. The last enemy to
> be destroyed is death. For he "has put everything under his feet." Now
> when it says that "everything" has been put under him, it is clear that
> this does not include God himself, who put everything under Christ.
> When he has done this, then the Son himself will be made subject to
> him who put everything under him, so that God may be all in all.

Here we have a similar parallel to that found in Romans 5, "as in Adam all
die, so in Christ all will be made alive." The reason that this is thought to

---

[16] Cited in Martinus C. de Boer, *The Defeat of Death: Apocalyptic Eschatology in 1 Corinthians
15 and Romans 5*, JSNTSup 23 (Sheffield: Sheffield Academic, 1988) chap. 5, n.89.

[17] De Boer, *Defeat*, 175. Howard Marshall responds to de Boer by pointing out that the
judgment followed one sin whilst the life followed many and that is why Paul can say "how
much more" (I. H. Marshall, "The New Testament Does Not Teach Universal Salvation," in
Parry and Partridge, eds., *Universal Salvation?*, 76, n.35.) However, although that is one of
the reasons Paul can marvel at the greater power of the grace, others include, as de Boer says,
that the grace undoes all that the transgression did and this does require it to reach as wide as
the sin.

undermine universalist interpretations of Romans 5 is that Paul then expands on the phrase "in Christ all will be made alive" with the following words: "But each in his own turn: Christ, the firstfruits, then, when he comes, those who belong to him, then the end . . . ." This seems to limit the "all" in "all will be made alive" to Christians—those who belong to him. There can be no doubt that Paul uses the expression "those who belong to him" as one that applies only to Christians.

Interpreters with universalist sympathies have adopted different strategies to handle this apparent problem.

> (a) Bell maintains that in 1 Corinthians 15:22 Paul really is
> only speaking of Christians when he says "all will be made
> alive," and that universalism is not in sight. However, says Bell,
> Romans 5 does not place such contextual limitations on the
> range of Christ's salvation, and so it must still be understood in a
> universalist way.[18]

> (b) De Boer thinks that the "all" of 15:22 does refer to all
> humans and that the Christians in v. 23 are to be construed as a
> representative group rather than an exclusive group.[19]

> (c) Hillert concurs with De Boer that the "all" of 15:22 means
> "all humans" and not simply Christians. However, he points out
> that Paul's only real focus in the chapter is with the death of, and
> future hope for, *Christians*. Non-Christians are simply not the
> issue, so he speaks in this passage as if they did not even exist.
> The fate of those who are presently outside Christ is simply *never
> discussed*.[20]

> (d) Talbott argues that Paul envisages three stages to the
> resurrection and not two. He understands 15:22b-24 as follows:
> "in Christ all will be made alive. But each in his own order: (i)
> Christ the first fruits, after that (ii) those who are Christ's at His
> coming, then (iii) the rest, when he hands over the kingdom
> to the God and Father, when he has abolished all rule and all
> authority and power." This interpretation depends on translating
> *to telos* as "the rest" rather than, as is usually done, "the end."
> Talbott thinks that Paul's scheme is as follows: (i) Christ is
> resurrected; (ii) Christ returns, at which point Christians are

---

[18] So Bell, "Universal Salvation," 428.

[19] De Boer, *Defeat*, 112.

[20] Sven Hillert, *Limited and Universal Salvation: A Text-oriented and Historical Study of Two Perspectives in Paul,*, ConBNT 31 (Stockholm: Almqvist & Wiksell, 1999) 207–20.

resurrected; (iii) some unspecified time later Christ will raise the
rest of humanity (who will have become believers) and at that
point his victory will be complete.[21]

Is 1 Corinthians 15:20-28 a problem for universalists or a passage that can be
used to support universalist theology and, if so, how?

The first matter to discuss is whether 15:22 is best understood as refer-
ring to Christians or all humans.

> For as in Adam all die,
> so in Christ all will be made alive.

Does Paul mean that "all in Christ (i.e., Christians) will be made alive"? The
first problem with this interpretation is that it is an unnatural way to read
the Greek. "In Christ" does not modify "all" (i.e., "all in Christ") but is an
adverbial phrase modifying "will be made alive." Thus, it is most naturally
understood to mean that "everyone will be made alive in Christ." This observation is reinforced by the parallelism between v. 22a and v. 22b above.
All die in Adam just as all will live in Christ. De Boer observes that, "One
can scarcely translate . . . 'all who are in Adam die,' if such a translation is
meant to imply that some people are not 'in Adam.'"[22] The parallelism clearly
indicates that the same group is referred to in each half of the verse, and this
supports the universalist understanding of v. 22b. So there is a *prima facie*
case for disagreeing with non-universalists (and Bell).

The next issue that needs some discussion is Paul's elaboration on v. 22b
in vv. 23-24. Should we side with Talbott in reading *to telos* as "the remainder" or with the majority of commentators, translating it as "the end"? It
needs to be said that Talbott does not insist on this point but only suggests it
tentatively. He believes that a universalist interpretation can go through even
if he is wrong on this matter. Although I shall dispute Talbott's view, his interpretation cannot be ruled out as impossible. He makes the following points:

> 1. "The rest" or "the remainder" is listed as an alternative
> translation of *to telos* in various older authorities (and is
> footnoted in the NRSV).

> 2. Paul has a threefold order that must not be compressed into
> two stages. Paul speaks of Christ first, then (*eita*) those who are
> believers at the time he comes, then (*eita*) the remainder/end. He

---

[21] Paul speaks of Christ's return and "then" the end. He makes no comment on whether the
end follows on immediately or after some period. That issue is simply irrelevant in this context,
and we cannot say one way or the other.

[22] De Boer, *Defeat*, 112.

sees the image of a procession of resurrections ("each in his own *order*")[23] with Christ at the front, followed by those who belong to Christ at his coming, and behind them comes the remainder who are there when Christ hands the kingdom to his Father. Even if we prefer to translate *to telos* as "the end," it can refer to the end of the procession and thus remain a reference to people.

3. Even if we wish to translate *to telos* as "the end," this should not be thought to rule out an indirect reference to those who are not believers at the time of the Parousia, as the reference would be to the third and final stage of the cosmic drama, which must, given the claim in 15:22b that "*all* would be made alive in Christ," include the raising to life of those who had not been previously resurrected.

What should we make of such arguments? The linguistic arguments leave open the possibility that *to telos* means "the rest," but it is far more likely that it means "the end."[24]

The argument about the end of the procession is possibly correct but undemonstrable. There is no clear and direct reference to a procession that *to telos* modifies. Left unqualified, *to telos* seems better taken as a reference to the end of God's conflict with the powers when all submit to Christ.

Talbott's final point will be taken up below, but it does not support a translation of "the rest" or even a direct reference to any people. It refers instead to the end of God's purposes. It may be possible to see universalism *implied* by such an end (point 3 above), but that is a different matter.

So it seems to me that Talbott is right not to pin hopes for a universalist interpretation on this suggestion; we should retain the traditional understanding of *to telos* as a reference to God's completed purposes. Does this rule out universalism? Not at all. After v. 22 Paul simply makes no reference to those who are currently non-believers. This is probably not because the Christians are seen as representative of all humans (*pace* de Boer), but rather because in 1 Corinthians 15 it is clear that Paul is only addressing the issue of Christians who have died and the future of Christians (so Hillert). The fate of

---

[23] The Greek *tagma* refers to "that which has been arranged" or "placed in its proper order." In a military context it refers to a corps, a troop, or a division. It seems to be this term that brings the image of a procession to Talbott's mind.

[24] Amongst the minority who have defended the same view as Talbott are Lietzmann and Weiss (Anthony C. Thistleton, *First Epistle to the Corinthians*, NIGTC [Grand Rapids: Eerdmans; Carlisle: Paternoster, 2000] 1231). However, C. E. Hill ("Paul's Understanding of Christ's Kingdom in 1 Corinthians 15:20-28," *NovT* 30 [1988] 297–320) has argued at length that, from a linguistic standpoint, *to telos* cannot mean "the rest." Thiselton says that the majority view is that the lexicographical scope of *to telos* does not include "the remainder" (1231).

those who do not yet believe is simply not an issue that interests him here in this context, and thus it goes unmentioned. We need not look for "the rest" behind *to telos,* because in this pragmatic context there simply are *no* "rest." Even in the universalist text of 15:22 Paul only makes the point that "all will be made alive" to bring out its implications for Christians. We should not infer from this that 15:22 is only about Christians (it *really* is a universalist claim) but that Paul is only interested in using that claim to make specific points about believers. So whilst Paul was not interested in the universalist implications of 1 Corinthians 15:22 *in the context of that particular discussion,* it is perfectly appropriate for readers to draw them out of the text *when the topic under consideration is universalism.*

Why??

The final matter concerns the nature of God's eschatological victory in 15:20-28. Is it suggestive of universal salvation even if universalism is not the main topic of attention? Many universalists have thought so,[25] and I shall argue that they are not wrong to do so. Paul writes that Christ must reign until all his enemies are "put in subjection under his feet." The enemies Paul has in mind are the Principalities and Powers as well as sin and death. Once the enemies are subjected to Christ, he will subject himself to the Father who will then be "all in all." This is "the end" that Paul speaks of as the climax of God's work in history, and the connections with the eschatology of Ephesians discussed in Appendix 2 should be clear.[26] Now many commentators suggest that Christ is said to destroy his enemies (vv. 24, 26), and this is hardly the kind of cosmic universalism that those such as myself find in the text. Several comments are in order. First, no mention is made of the destruction of any humans. The only enemies that are in view are the Powers, sin, and death. So even if God destroys his enemies, it is in order to deliver humanity. Second, there are good reasons for suggesting that the Powers are not actually *destroyed* here. The verb Paul uses in 15:24 is *katargeō* which literally means "to nullify, to render powerless," and the context determines what that means. It certainly can mean "to annihilate," but such an interpretation is not required. We read that Christ's enemies are "put under his feet" (v. 25) and "put in subjection under his feet" (v. 27). Does this mean annihilation

---

[25] Interestingly 1 Corinthians 15 was a favorite text among the patristic universalists.

[26] De Boer explains them: "In both Eph 1:20-23 and 1 Cor 15:20-28, then, we find the following correspondences: (1) In 1 Cor 15:24 and Eph. 1:21 the same three terms for powers occur and in the same sequence. In both cases the modifier 'every' occurs before the first one listed: 'every principality and authority and power.' (2) There is an exact agreement in the citation of Ps 8:7b, which diverges from the LXX text . . . in exactly the same way . . . : 'all things He subordinated under his feet.' (3) Both passages conclude with the phrase 'all in all,' though in Ephesians that phrase is used in connection with Christ, not God as 1 Cor 15:28" (*Defeat,* 119). To this we ought to say that both passages connect the resurrection of Christ to his Lordship over the Powers by citing Ps 110:1 and Ps 8:7b.

for the Powers? Not necessarily. We read that it is not merely Christ's enemies but "all things" that are subjected to Christ (vv. 27-28). This includes the redeemed, and they are certainly not annihilated. Secondly, after the enemies are subjected (*hypotagē*) to Christ, he subjects himself (*hypotagēsetai*) to the Father (v. 28), clearly indicating that the subjection is simply a restoration of the order of creation and not annihilation. Fourth, Colossians 1:15-20, as we saw in Chapter 2, clearly anticipates the redemption of the Powers, and this inclines us to understand their subjection to Christ redemptively here also. Fifth, Ephesians 1:21-22 speaks of the subjection of the Powers in the age to come, which suggests their continued existence. Finally, as Hendrikus Berkhof points out, if the Powers were created good, as Colossians 1 suggests, then for Christ to annihilate them would mark a defeat for God rather than a victory.[27] Thus Christ does not annihilate them but renders them powerless to harm humanity. The main objection to this interpretation is that Paul also speaks of the *katargeitai* of the last enemy, death (v. 26), and surely death is not redeemed! If *katargeitai* means "annihilation" when applied to death in v. 26, then, the critic argues, it must mean "annihilation" when applied to the other enemies in v. 24. Universal salvation *for humans* certainly does not depend on how one answers this objection.[28] However, it seems to me that it is better to understand the term to mean "render powerless" or, as Walter Wink suggests, "neutralize,"[29] in both v. 24 and v. 26. Death, of course, is rendered powerless in the resurrection. In the case of death there really is nothing left once it is nullified by eternal life. It is indeed annihilated. But then death is merely the absence of life in the same way that dark is the absence of light. God turns on the resurrection light and the dark of death is made void—necessarily there is nothing left of it. So too with sin. Although Paul personifies sin and death in 1 Corinthians 15, they are not actual beings. This is not so with the Powers. To render them harmless is *not* equivalent to annihilating them. So it does not seem to me problematic to maintain that Paul could speak of the annihilation of sin and death and the deliverance of the Powers in the same language. The subjection of all things under God through Christ is "so that God may be all in all" (v. 28). The Greek phrase here (*panta en pasin*) is a little ambiguous but translates as either (i) "God may be everything to *everyone*" (taking *pasin* as masculine), or (ii) "all in *all things*," which is to

Wardus thos the point of the conceal work is.

---

[27] Hendrikus Berkhof, *Christ and the Powers* (Scottdale: Herald, 1962) 32–35.

[28] De Boer, who defends a universalist interpretation of 1 Corinthians 15, argues that *katargēsē* does indeed mean" annihilation" throughout this section (*Defeat*, 121).

[29] Walter Wink, *Naming the Powers: The Language of Power in the New Testament* (Philadelphia: Fortress, 1984) 51.

say that all things (taking *pasin* as neuter) will depend upon him, or (iii) "all things among all people."[30]

The Church as Eschatological Israel and New Humanity

The New Testament teaches that Jesus is true and faithful Israel and that those who are incorporated into him by faith are the transformed, end-time Israel in him. This is not to say that the church is a *new* Israel to replace ethnic Israel.[31] Rather, the church is in organic continuity with Old Covenant Israel—the church is the true inheritor of the promises to Israel. This theme is so ubiquitous in the New Testament that there is no need to offer much by way of defense of it. Paul offers perhaps the most helpful illustration to guide our conceptualizing of the relation between the church and Israel. In Rom 11:13-24 he pictures Israel as an olive tree rooted in the Abrahamic promises. Individual Jews who reject the messiah Jesus are like branches cut off from the tree (though always with the possibility of being rejoined should they believe). Gentile believers are like wild branches that are grafted into the tree. The church, according to this image, is not a tree running parallel to Israel's tree nor a replacement for Israel. The church *is* Israel once it has been reconfigured around the messiah Jesus. Abraham is still the root, and the olive tree is the same tree. There is a continuity of identity in spite of some severe chopping off of unbelieving branches and grafting in of Gentile branches. It was a theological picture like this one that enabled the early Christians (Jewish and Gentile) to see themselves as the heirs of the ancient promises to Israel. But, of course, the illustration does not reveal the fact that the number of branches cut off was vast. Most of Israel in Paul's day rejected the gospel message, and this created a very awkward theological difficulty for the early Christians.

The Future Salvation of "All Israel"

Paul's problem was this: Israel was undoubtedly the covenant people of Yahweh commissioned to bring light to the nations. They had been hindered in this task by their sin, but now that Messiah Jesus had come, one would have expected Israel to experience eschatological renewal. Yet the vast majority of Jews in his day had rejected the gospel. This raised serious questions about God's covenant faithfulness to his people, and it is such matters that come under the microscope in Romans 9–11.

> I speak the truth in Christ—I am not lying, my conscience confirms
> it in the Holy Spirit—I have great sorrow and unceasing anguish in

---

[30] See the discussion in Thiselton (*First Epistle*) who, following de Boer, prefers (iii).

[31] A. Andrew Das, *Paul and the Jews,* LPS (Peabody, Mass.: Hendrickson, 2003) 119.

my heart. For I could wish that I myself were cursed and cut off from Christ for the sake of my brothers, those of my own race, the people of Israel. Theirs is the adoption as sons; theirs the divine glory, the covenants, the receiving of the law, the temple worship and the promises. Theirs are the patriarchs, and from them is traced the human ancestry of Christ, who is God over all, forever praised! Amen.

Israel's current status before God is ambiguous and two-sided. On the one hand, they are in a state of alienation from Yahweh because of their unbelief, and Paul is deeply wounded by this thought. On the other, they remain God's covenant people (notice the present tenses, e.g., "theirs *is* the adoption . . ." and see 11:28-29). Is it possible to believe that God has been faithful to his covenant with Israel in this situation? Paul's answer is an emphatic "Yes!" First of all, he argues that not all Abraham's physical descendants inherit the promise. Not all who are descended from Israel are Israel (9:6). Paul's point is that there is more to being Israel than mere physical descent from Abraham (9:7), a claim illustrated by the fact that Ishmael and Esau are also physical descendants but are not heirs of the promise (9:8-14). What matters is divine election—Isaac was elect, but Ishmael was not; Jacob was elect, Esau was not, even though *all* were physical descendants of Abraham. Such election is in God's hands (9:11-18), and it is entirely up to him who he has mercy on and who he hardens. Paul then drives home the shocking relevance of this: God is the potter and has made out of the one lump of clay that is Israel two pots (9:21). One pot is an object of mercy and election (9:23) and is composed of Christian Jews (and Gentiles) (9:23-26). The other pot, composed of unbelieving Jews, is an object of wrath prepared for destruction (9:22). After all, Scripture says that only a remnant of Israel will be saved (9:27-29). The stunning thing about the present situation is that the people of Israel, who pursue Yahweh's covenant righteousness, have failed to attain it and instead stumble (9:31-33), whilst the Gentiles, who do not pursue righteousness, have found it in Christ (9:30). Paul is clearly drawing a very sharp distinction between believing Jews, who are elect heirs to the promises to Israel, and unbelieving Jews, who are not. Paul's heart's desire is that Israel be saved (10:1) through faith in Christ (10:2-11). Yet Israel is an obstinate and disobedient people (10:21), and the Gentiles are inheriting their blessings while they are not. So far, all of this is quite consistent with what we saw in the last section—that the church is the true Israel and many who are physically Israel are not spiritually Israel.

Paul then asks, "Did God reject his people?" and replies, "By no means!" (11:1) First, a remnant of the Jews, himself included, is chosen by grace at the present time (11:1b-5).[32] The rest (i.e., the non-elect Jews) have had their hearts hardened by God so that they do not believe (11:7-10). One could be forgiven, if Paul had stopped here, for thinking that he imagines that God's covenant fidelity to Israel is satisfied so long as a few Jews are Christians— indeed some New Testament scholars believe that this is exactly what Paul thought. It certainly looks like the majority of Jews reject the gospel because God hardened them, rather than electing them as he has the sovereign right to do (9:14ff.), and that this situation is irreversible. But at this point the plot twists.

> Again I ask: Did they stumble so as to fall beyond recovery? Not at all! Rather, because of their transgression, salvation has come to the Gentiles to make Israel envious. But if their transgression means riches for the world, and their loss means riches for the Gentiles, how much greater riches will their fullness bring! (11:11-12)

Here is an astonishing insight. Israel may have been hardened and thus stumbled over the gospel, but this does not place them beyond recovery. Indeed, their very rejection of the gospel has all along been part of God's plan for getting the message to the Gentiles and blessing them! Israel has transgressed and experienced loss, but their fullness is coming. Paul then warns the Gentile Christians not to look down on unbelieving Jews:

> I am talking to you Gentiles. Inasmuch as I am the apostle to the Gentiles, I make much of my ministry in the hope that I may some-how arouse my own people to envy and save some of them. For if their rejection is the reconciliation of the world, what will their acceptance be but life from the dead? If the part of the dough offered as firstfruits is holy, then the whole batch is holy; if the root is holy, so are the branches. If some of the branches have been broken off, and you, though a wild olive shoot, have been grafted in among the others and now share in the nourishing sap from the olive root, do not boast over those branches. If you do, consider this: You do not support the root, but the root supports you. You will say then, "Branches were broken off so that I could be grafted in." Granted. But they were broken off because of unbelief, and you stand by faith. Do not be arrogant, but be afraid. For if God did not spare the natural branches, he will not spare you either. Consider therefore the kindness and sternness of God: sternness to those who fell, but kindness to you, provided that you continue in his kindness. Otherwise, you also will be cut off. And if they do not persist in unbelief, they will be grafted in, for God is able to graft them in again. After all, if you were cut out of an olive

---

[32] It will turn out that this remnant are a firstfruits that function as a promise on behalf of "the rest" (compare 11:16).

> tree that is wild by nature, and contrary to nature were grafted into
> a cultivated olive tree, how much more readily will these, the natural
> branches, be grafted into their own olive tree! (11:13-24)

Israel is like an olive tree. Jews who have not believed the gospel have been
broken off. This is a way of picturing what Paul means when he says that not
all Israel are Israel (9:5). God has been stern with them (11:22) and rejected
them (11:15). Is such a state permanent? Not necessarily: "if they do not persist in unbelief, they will be grafted in, for God is able to graft them in again"
(11:23). What is interesting is that Paul envisages non-elect Jews becoming
elect Jews (i.e, sharing in the election of Israel again in Christ), and this
clearly indicates that the category of the elect is not a rigidly fixed category,
as it is in dogmatic Calvinism. Sven Hillert argues at length that for Paul the
distinction between the elect and the rest need only be seen as a *temporary*
category, dividing believers from non-believers *in the present age*.[33]

So the present state of unbelieving Israel is not irreversible. If they do
not persist in unbelief, they will be re-grafted into the olive tree. But will this
condition be satisfied? Yes.

> I do not want you to be ignorant of this mystery, brothers, so that you
> may not be conceited: Israel has experienced a hardening in part until
> the full number of the Gentiles has come in. And so[34] all Israel will
> be saved, as it is written: "The deliverer will come from Zion; he will
> turn godlessness away from Jacob. And this is my covenant with them
> when I take away their sins." As far as the gospel is concerned, they
> are enemies on your account; but as far as election is concerned, they
> are loved on account of the patriarchs, for God's gifts and his call are
> irrevocable. (11:25-29)

A large part of Israel has been hardened in unbelief to enable the gospel to
reach the Gentiles. Once the "fullness of the Gentiles has come in," (v. 25)
the period of hardening will end, and then "all Israel will be saved" (11:26).
All the branches that have been broken off, the rejected vessels of wrath,
the non-elect, will become objects of mercy (11:31). This will happen when
the deliverer (Jesus)[35] comes from Zion to restore Israel, according to the

---

[33] Hillert, *Limited and Universal Salvation*, chap. 3.

[34] There has been much discussion about what *kai houtōs* ("and so") means here. Does it mean
(a) "and then"? (b) "and in this way" ? (c) "and in the following way" ? or (d) "and so it follows
that"? The two most plausible linguistically are (b) and (d). I suggest that (d) is preferable
because, although (b) is linguistically possible, it only makes sense if "all Israel" does not refer
to ethnic Israel and, as I show in the main text, this is implausible.

[35] Paul quotes Isaiah 59:20-21 (and 27:9), and it is most likely he refers to Christ when he
speaks of "the deliverer." He distinguishes the one who takes away sins (i.e., God) from the
deliverer; in 1 Thessalonians 1:10 he refers to Christ at the Parousia as the deliverer, and Isaiah

Scriptures. Most biblical scholars see this as a reference to the return of Christ and suggest that when the Messiah returns unbelieving Israel will believe. What is the reason God saves all Israel? Because they are *still elect* on account of the patriarchs even if they are currently enemies on account of the gospel (11:28).[36] God's gifts to Israel and his calling to them are *irrevocable* (11:29), so it is simply not conceivable that God would forsake his covenant people Israel. This is Paul's final answer to the problem he has been addressing throughout Romans 9–11. God is faithful to his covenant with Israel; at the present time he has preserved a remnant of Jewish believers, and when Messiah comes "all Israel will be saved." God, in his sovereign wisdom, has chosen to make use of Israel's temporary state of unbelief, but it has all been with the purpose of saving all people.

> Just as you who were at one time disobedient to God have now received mercy as a result of their disobedience, so they too have now become disobedient in order that they too may now receive mercy as a result of God's mercy to you. For God has bound all men over to disobedience so that he may have mercy on them all.

Although Romans 9 may have given the impression that the non-elect who were hardened as objects of wrath were doomed to destruction by irreversible divine predestination, we now see that even God's severity was part of a strategy to show mercy to all—including those to whom he had been severe.[37] This causes Paul to exclaim:

> Oh, the depth of the riches of the wisdom and knowledge of God! How unsearchable his judgments, and his paths beyond tracing out! "Who has known the mind of the Lord? Or who has been his counselor?" "Who has ever given to God, that God should repay him?" For from him and through him and to him are all things. To him be the glory for ever! Amen. (11:33-36)

Indeed. How wise! How glorious! All things have their origin and, in God's wise providence, will find their destiny in God (11:36).

59:20-21 was used messianically by the rabbis. This, according to Richard Bell, all suggests that Paul has the return of Christ in mind.

[36] This suggests a bifurcation of the notion of election. On the one hand, unbelieving Jews are not "elect according to grace" and are "cut off" from the root of Abraham whilst, on the other hand, they are elect and beloved on account of the patriarchs. This election of Abraham and his descendants is the ground for the ultimate salvation of all Israel and the basis on which Paul believes that all Israel will eventually share in the election of grace, ending the temporary bifurcation of unbelieving Israel's election.

[37] Commenting on 11:11, Dunn says, "what was important in 9:14-24 becomes clear at last: that God's outreach in wrath is bound up within his purpose of mercy" (*Romans 9–16*, WBC 38B [Waco, Tex.: Word, 1988] 668).

In light of Romans 9–11 we can see that the remnant of believing Jews found in the church is only a firstfruits of a fuller harvest of all Israel yet to come. As Andrew Das notes, "Throughout the Hebrew Bible the remnant within Israel has always been a sign of hope for Israel as a whole (Gen 7:23; 2 Kgs 19:30-31; Isa 11:11-12, 16; 37:31-32; Mic 2:12; 4:7; 5:7-8; Zech 8:12)."[38] This is exactly what we should have expected.

This brief summary of Romans 9–11 is necessarily simplifying a complex text. It is necessary to defend at greater length some of our crucial interpretative decisions, especially the ones regarding 11:25-27.

First, what does Paul mean by "all Israel" in v. 26? There are four possibilities that have been suggested.

(a) The church as the spiritual Israel of God (Calvin, N. T. Wright).

(b) Elect Jews (i.e., the remnant of Israel) (J. Bengel)

(c) The whole nation of Israel but not every individual member (C. K. Barrett, C. E. Cranfield, A. Das)

(d) The whole nation of Israel including every member (R. Bell)

The first view is very much a minority view in contemporary New Testament studies and for good reason. First, every other use of the term "Israel" in Romans 9–11 clearly refers to national Israel, so a sudden and unannounced switch in the use of the word would serve only to confuse readers. Indeed, in the immediate context "Israel" (11:25), "Jacob" (11:27) and "they" (11:28-32) all refer to national Israel. Second, Paul is clear that God's covenant with national Israel is irrevocable (11:29), that they are still beloved on behalf of the patriarchs (11:28), that after the fullness of the Gentiles has come in they will experience fullness (11:12). This supports the claim that the "all Israel" that is saved is national Israel. Third, the Scripture quoted in support of the claim that "all Israel will be saved" says that the Redeemer will banish iniquity in *Jacob* (11:26b). Fourth, as Chae points out, Paul's point in explaining the mystery in 11:25 ff. is to stop Gentile Christians from being arrogant in the face of Israel's current hardening. It makes sense that he would speak of a brighter future for national Israel to restrain such attitudes.[39]

Richard Bell notes that the second option has the disadvantage of making "all Israel will be saved" an anticlimax. The mention of "the fullness" of

[38] Das, *Paul and the Jews*, 108.

[39] Daniel Jong-Sang Chae, *Paul as Apostle to the Gentiles: His Apostolic Self-Awareness and Its Influence on the Soteriological Argument in Romans*, PBTM (Carlisle: Paternoster, 1997) 274.

national Israel (11:12), their "acceptance" (11:15) and the grafting in of the broken off branches (11:23-24) leads us to expect some good future for national Israel. 11:26 would not provide that if Paul were merely saying that all Christian Jews will be saved. Another serious objection is that "all Israel" in 11:26 is a *contrast* with the present "remnant" mentioned earlier. Presently, only a remnant will be saved (9:27); but then "*all* Israel will be saved" (11:26). The "all Israel" contrasts the current remnant and is thus not identical with it.[40]

So we can conclude that "all Israel" means the nation of Israel as a whole. However, does this refer to every individual Jew or simply the majority of Jews? It is not possible to answer this question with certainty, as Paul does not expand the point. It is certainly the case that one could speak hyperbolically of the salvation of "all Israel" whilst still allowing that some individual Israelites would not be saved (e.g., *Mishnah Sanhedrin* 10). On grounds of contemporary linguistic usage of the expression "all Israel," it is possible Paul meant most Jews, though whether it is possible on *theological* grounds is another matter. Arguably, for Paul, it would be "unthinkable that an Israelite could be excluded from final salvation."[41]

A related question is whether Paul had in mind all Israel that is living at the time of the Parousia (a synchronic understanding) or all Israel throughout history (a diachronic understanding). Bell has argued for a diachronic understanding, and I think that he is right to do so.[42] However, even *if* Paul were merely thinking synchronically, there are still good theological grounds for us to extend this into a diachronic interpretation. The reasoning is simple: Paul is showing how God is indeed faithful to his covenant with national Israel by saving them all. However, if this promise only applies to the final generation, then it remains the case that the vast majority of Jews who have lived are not saved, and the very problem Paul was seeking to solve remains with us. It is solved in a Pauline way if, and only if, all (most?) Jews, past, present, and future, are resurrected and accept the Messiah at the Parousia.

The Future Salvation of All Nations

If what I have suggested so far is correct, then we ought to expect the New Testament to anticipate a greater pilgrimage of the nations than is found in the presence of its Gentile members. We should expect to find that the Gentile Christians are a mere foretaste of the age to come. There may be hints

---

[40] Das, *Paul and the Jews,* 108.

[41] See Richard H. Bell, *The Irrevocable Call of God: An Inquiry into Paul's Theology of Israel,* WUNT 184 (Tübingen: Mohr/Siebek, 2005).

[42] Ibid.

of this in Romans 9–11, which seems to embody the following plot line: (a) Some Jews accept Christ, but others reject him; (b) this causes the gospel to reach the Gentiles, some of whom accept Christ whilst others reject him; (c) the Jews and Gentiles in the church experience God's blessings for Israel, causing unbelieving Israel to be jealous; (d) the fullness of Gentiles comes in; (e) then the Messiah returns, and all Israel is saved; (f) Israel's salvation/fullness brings about "greater riches" for the world (11:12) and "life from the dead" (11:15). These phrases are ambiguous, but they may hint at a fuller salvation for the Gentile world after "the fullness of the Gentiles has come in."[43] However, we cannot speak with certainty about whether Romans 9–11 clearly anticipates the salvation of all the nations in the way that it anticipates the salvation of all Israel. It may or it may not.[44] However, I think that the book of Revelation does teach a future salvation of the nations of exactly the kind we are considering. As I will defend this claim at some length in the next chapter, I shall simply note at this point that Revelation consistently pictures the nations and the kings of the earth as enemies of God and the church as a multi-ethnic community *drawn out from* every tribe, nation, and language. The motif of the pilgrimage of the nations only occurs at the very end of the book in the vision of the new creation. There we read, in terms drawn from Isaiah 60, that the nations and the kings of the earth come into the New Jerusalem to worship. I shall argue that these are the very same nations and kings that had previously been condemned to the lake of fire. Thus it is that Revelation can speak of the "church of the firstfruits" (Rev 14:4), indicating that the multi-national community of the church is a foretaste and guarantee of the full pilgrimage of the nations, which is yet to come. In the new creation the sharp distinction between the church and the nations maintained throughout Revelation collapses under the weight of God's wide mercy.[45]

Every Knee Shall Bow

It is appropriate at this point to consider Paul's amazing picture of Christ's exaltation in Philippians 2:5-12:

---

[43] Does this expression refer to "the full number of Gentiles," indicating a predestined amount or to some kind of fullness of blessing? If the former, are we to understand this predetermined number to refer to all the Gentiles that will ever be saved or to all the Gentiles that will be saved prior to the salvation of "all Israel," after which more Gentiles are saved as Israel fulfils its calling as a light to the Gentiles? It is impossible to be certain.

[44] Jan Bonda argues that it does (*The One Purpose of God* [Grand Rapids: Eerdmans, 1998] chap. 6) while Richard Bell argues that it does not.

[45] This theology is wonderfully captured in Matt Redman's 1996 song, "There's a Louder Shout to Come."

Your attitude should be the same as that of Christ Jesus:
Who, being in very nature God,
>   did not consider equality with God something to be grasped,
but made himself nothing, taking the very nature of a servant,
>   being made in human likeness.
And being found in appearance as a man,
>   he humbled himself and became obedient to death—even death on
>   a cross!
Therefore God exalted him to the highest place
>   and gave him the name that is above every name,
that at the name of Jesus every knee should bow,
>   in heaven and on earth and under the earth,
and every tongue confess that Jesus Christ is Lord,
>   to the glory of God the Father.

The climax of the hymn is an image of the universal Lordship of Christ. The background is the divine oath of Isaiah 45 that every knee will and bow and every tongue confess before Yahweh. Paul daringly applies this to Jesus. Every knee will bow to *him* and every tongue will confess *his* Lordship. I simply wish to make two points.

First, this acknowledgement of Christ is universal. Paul emphasizes that there are no exceptions by expanding the Old Testament text "every knee will bow" with the words "*in heaven and on earth and under the earth.*" This is going considerably further than the Isaiah text. In Isaiah only the living were in mind. All the survivors of the nations would bow, but the dead were dead. Not so here. Even those "under the earth," that is to say, the dead, will bow. So the picture is of every single individual who has ever lived acknowledging the rule of Christ. This much is not terribly controversial amongst commentators. Not so my next point.

Second, this vision is of universal salvation. It is common to suggest that, although all creatures here will bow the knee, some will be forced to do so against their will prior to being damned. In support of that claim it is argued that (a) Paul is not a universalist, so he cannot mean what he seems to mean; (b) The Isaiah text goes on to speak of those who are shamed before him and thus envisages some not accepting the offer of salvation; (c) Paul quotes the Isaianic divine oath in Romans 14:11 in the context of a discussion of the judgment seat of Christ, and that would indicate that he does not imagine a salvific submission to Christ.

I suggest that all three arguments are weak and, further, that there are good reasons to accept the universalist interpretation. Let us briefly consider

the three objections. The first one is somewhat question-begging. I am arguing in this book that Paul could well have legitimately developed his theology
in universalist directions. If my arguments are in any way plausible, then we
are making some headway in undermining this objection. The second objection was dealt with in the previous chapter, so I shall not revisit it here.[46] This
leaves only the third objection. In Romans 14:11 Paul quotes Isaiah 45 in a
judgment context. However, we need to set 14:10-12 within the broader context of 14:1-12. Paul is dealing with an issue that was causing division within
the church at Rome. Some Christians (Paul refers to them as "the weak")
thought that both Jewish and Gentile Christians ought to keep the Mosaic
torah. This meant keeping Jewish food laws and observing the Sabbath. Many
of the Christians in Rome felt, with Paul, that this was not so (Paul refers to
them as "the strong"). The weak were in danger of judging and condemning
their brothers, whilst the strong were in danger of looking with disdain upon
the weak.[47] Paul is keen to stress that on this issue each believer is accountable
to God for her or his conduct, and they must not stand in judgment over
each other and so divide the body. In this context Paul quotes the divine oath
from Isaiah 45, and it serves two functions: (a) it stresses that Christians are
accountable to God (their master) for their own behavior in this matter, and
they must not usurp his role by standing in judgment over each other; and (b)
it is a text about the conversion of the Gentiles in which all the Gentiles are
shown to be bowing and praising (*exomologēsetai*) God alongside Israel, and
this reinforces Paul's point that God accepts them all equally so they must accept each other. There is no hint of condemnation in the context.[48]

There are positive reasons to support a universalist reading of Philippians
2. We argued in the previous chapter that Isaiah 45 envisages all humans that
survive the destruction coming to worship Yahweh. This is indicated by the
call to the nations to come to Yahweh and be saved and in the terms used to
describe their bowing and swearing oaths in his name. So the words of Paul's
source text clearly envisage a universal salvation. What Paul does is expand
the scope of the universalism in truly breathtaking directions to include not
just the living but the dead, and not just humans but angelic creatures as
well. Second, the terminology Paul uses is suggestive of salvation rather than
forced submission. All creatures confess that Jesus Christ is Lord. Elsewhere
in Paul's letters when he speaks of confessing Jesus as Lord it is always in a

---

[46] See Bonda, *One Purpose*, chap. 7, for a good discussion of it.

[47] See Dunn, *Romans 9–16* for an defense of this interpretation.

[48] Paul is quite right to pick up the judgment overtones in the passage because the original
oracle itself comes in the context of one of Deutero-Isaiah's great trial scenes in which God
puts the nations on trial. However, this trial issues in life for them and nothing in Romans 14
suggests otherwise.

context of salvation. No one can say that "Jesus is Lord" except by the Holy Spirit (1 Cor 12:3). If someone confesses with their mouth and believes in the heart that Jesus is Lord, then they will be saved (Rom 10:9). There are no examples in Paul of an involuntary confession of Christ's Lordship. The word translated as "confess" (*exomologeomai*) is a word almost always meaning "praise." Throughout the LXX version of the Psalms it is used of the joyful and voluntary praise of God, and that is how it is used in the LXX source text of Isaiah 45:23. There is no good linguistic reason to think Paul was using it in any other way here.

It is interesting to note that the New Testament re-reading of Isaiah to include the dead has a dual effect on the New Testament literature. In terms of judgment, the picture of the decaying corpses of God's enemies in Isaiah 66:24 is seen to refer to a *post-mortem* punishment and quite possibly one in which the punished ones are conscious (Mark 9:45-48). At the same time, as we have seen above, the universal salvation that Isaiah extended only to the living is now extended to the dead. This creates something of a tension that was not present in Isaiah; for we have some punished in the fires of Gehenna after death, and we also have *all* creatures being saved. We shall argue in the next two chapters that a resolution to this tension is found in reconceiving hell as a purifying fire with an exit.

The Inescapable Love of God

We are finally in a position to consider briefly how we should think of God's love. The love of God is very important for the universalist. Indeed, it would not be an exaggeration to say that it is a strong belief in God's love that often drives people towards universalism. Critics of universal salvation often claim that its proponents focus too much on God's love, to the exclusion of such equally biblical themes as God's justice or his wrath. Universalists are sometimes accused of having a sentimental notion of love rather than a biblical one. People claim that they end up with a God so nice he wouldn't hurt a fly. The accusation is that universalists start off by supposing that God's love must be exactly like human love and that if we would never allow a person to go to hell, then neither would a loving God. But this procedure is flawed, it is said, for we must be careful not to read our notions of love into the Bible. Rather, we must allow our understanding of divine love to arise from the text. We see what it means to say that God is love by observing his love in action. James Packer makes the point very well:

> Basic to Christianity is the conviction that we learn what love is from watching God in action—supremely, from watching God in the person of the Father's incarnate Son, Jesus Christ, as he loves, gives, suf-

fers, and dies to achieve our redemption. We do the watching through
Bible study, following the narratives of the Gospels and the explanations of the Epistles . . . We must never let ourselves think of *agape* in
any term not validated by the redemptive work of Jesus.[49]

How is the universalist to reply? Simply by arguing that Packer is correct, but
also, that if one undertakes his project of considering God's love in terms of
its manifestation in the biblical story, one is led towards a universalist understanding of that love.

To get some understanding of the love of God one must begin with
some prior notion of human love or one could not even get into the hermeneutical circle. If we are to speak in any meaningful way of God's love, it must
bear, at the very least, an analogical relationship to human love. But then a
Christian understanding of God's love will be nuanced by its revelation in
salvation history. We stretch our concept of God's love across the poles of creation, covenant, and redemption. We drape it over the shape of the cross to
follow its contours and wrap it around the stone rolled away from the tomb.
Only thus can we begin to see the shape of God's heart.

In the Old Testament, the object of Yahweh's love is usually the nation of Israel rather than individuals within it, although at times his love
for individuals is mentioned. The word "love" is a covenant concept, often
occurring in the contexts of political treaties, where it refers to "a solemn,
public commitment of fidelity that covenant partners make to each other
. . . Yahweh in covenanting love chooses Israel to be covenant partner whom
Yahweh will protect."[50] *Hesed*, often translated "steadfast love," "loving-kind-
ness," or "mercy," refers to "the fulfillment of covenant obligations, based on a
previously made pledge, to a partner in covenant by acting in ways consistent
with loyalty and solidarity."[51] When God acts with love towards Israel, he is
acting in faithfulness towards his covenant with them. In his love he rescues
them and delivers them, as he promised he would. But we should not think
of God's relationship with Israel as simply a passionless keeping of one's word.
The prophet Hosea, in particular, highlights the depth of affection God has
for Israel (Hosea 11).

One thing that is important to notice about God's love for Israel is that
this love is quite compatible with his anger at their disobedience and his just
punishment of them. When God acts to judge his people, one should not
infer that he is no longer being faithful to his covenant or that he no longer

---

[49] J. I. Packer, "The Love of God: Universal and Particular," in idem, *Celebrating the Saving Work of God* (Carlisle: Paternoster, 1998) 147.

[50] Walter Brueggemann, "Love," in idem, *Reverberations of Faith: A Theological Handbook of Old Testament Themes* (Louisville: Westminster John Knox, 2002) 126.

[51] Ibid., 127.

loves them. He punishes them *because* he loves them, and he will not allow
wrath the final word *because* he loves them. God's love is no guarantee that
one will not experience wrath, but it is a guarantee that, as Stephen Sykes
commented when writing about the collapse of the Berlin Wall, "there is
grace in history in the end."[52] God's love for Israel is compatible with their
punishment but is not compatible with their *eternal* punishment. Covenant
love is not a soft, sentimental love, but it does guarantee grace *in the end*.

We have already seen that God's election of Israel was for the sake of the
nations and that their covenant is grounded on the primeval covenant God
made with creation itself (Chapter 3). God's love for Israel thus becomes the
means by which his love for the nations and the whole of creation can work
for salvation. Although the Old Testament says little explicitly about God's
love for the nations, the theological structure highlighted in chapter 3 un-
covers it, and the New Testament makes it clear. As John's gospel famously
declares, the reason that God sent his Son was because he loved the *world* so
much (John 3:16). And we must remember that the world God loved is, in
John's linguistic universe, the rebellious human society that rejects him and
crucifies his Son. *This rebel* world in its entirety is the object of divine love.
Paul too marvels that it was not for his friends but his enemies that Christ
died, for sinners far from God (Rom 5:6-9). If you want to understand love,
then don't think about our love for God, says the first epistle of John, but
ponder his love for us in sending his Son to die to take away our sin (1 John
4:9-10).

And for whom did Christ die? The Calvinist answer is that Christ did
not die for all people but only for those whom God, before creation, predetermined to save. The New Testament is indeed clear that Christ died for the
church (Eph 5:25), but we should not infer from that that he died *only* for
the church. We might just as well infer from Paul's claim that Christ died for
him (Gal 2:20) that he died *only* for Paul. Christ did die for Paul, and he did
die for the church. He also died for the whole world (John 1:29; Rom 5:18;
1 Cor 15:22; 2 Cor 5:14; Heb 2:9-10; 1 Tim 2:4-6; Tit 2:11; 1 John 2:2).[53]
God's saving, cross-shaped love excludes nobody. It wants all people to come
to repentance and find salvation (2 Pet 3:9).

God loved those who did not reciprocate his love, and God's love was a
suffering love that placed the other above itself. For the New Testament writ-

---

[52] Stephen Sykes, "The Truth Has Set Eastern Europe Free," *The Independent* (Dec. 28,
1989).

[53] For an excellent defense of a universal rather than a limited atonement see I. Howard
Marshall, "For All, For All My Saviour Died," in *Semper Reformandum: Studies in Honor of
Clark H. Pinnock*, ed. Stanley E. Porter and Andrew R. Cross (Carlisle: Paternoster, 2003)
322–46.

ers, the Christian understanding of God is reconfigured around the cross.[54] This God's love is cruciform. This God's love is a redemptive love; a patient, kind love that never gives up (1 Corinthians 13). This Father is a shepherd who, as Jesus taught, does not give up seeking his beloved, wayward sheep, but looks for it *until he finds it* (Luke 15:4). His covenant with creation will not allow him to abandon it to its own darkness, but commits him to redeeming it in its entirety.

The love of God in the New Testament, as in the Old, is perfectly compatible with divine wrath and punishment (Heb 12:7-11). However, such punishment is always a means to an end, and such wrath is never the last word. The last word is always grace. This is the kind of love presupposed by evangelical universalism, and it is neither soft nor sentimental.

John says, "God is love" (1 John 4:8, 16). I want to conclude this reflection on God's love by briefly suggesting that traditional theology has a difficult time accounting for this claim.[55] John's declaration that "God is love" seems to be a claim about God's very essence. It is part of what it is for God to be God that he is love. This can be seen by the grammatical parallel with John's claims elsewhere that "God is spirit" (1 John 4:24) and that "God is light" (1 John 1:5). All three seem to be claims about the nature of God. As Talbott says, the claim that "God is light and in him there is no darkness at all"

> is not a declaration to the effect that, by happy accident, God *happens* to be free from all darkness, all impurity, all unrighteousness; nor is it a declaration that God has *chosen* to remain free from all darkness in his relationship to some fortunate people only. It is instead a declaration about the very essence (or nature) of God.[56]

So too with the claim that "God is love." God does not just *happen* to be love, nor is it true that he *chooses* to be love to certain individuals, as if he could just as easily have chosen not to love them. Rather, it is impossible for God to be God and to act in an unloving way towards anyone.[57] If God is love,

---

[54] See especially Michael J. Gorman, *Cruciformity: Paul's Narrative Spirituality of the Cross* (Grand Rapids: Eerdmans, 2001).

[55] See especially Thomas Talbott, *Inescapable*, chap. 7, for an especially good critique of past and present Calvinist interpretations of 1 John 4.

[56] Talbott, *Inescapable*, 115.

[57] One response to this claim is to appeal to the trinity. God can be love whether or not he loves his creatures, because the members of the trinity exist in pure mutual love. Loving his creatures is something God can choose to do *or not to do* without it having any implications for his being love. This is nonsense. It is correct to say that the trinity does allow it to be true that God be love even if he never chooses to create a universe (thus God can be love even on his own), but once God creates other persons his being love also means that he will love

then *all* God's actions must be compatible with his love. This means that his holiness is loving, his justice is loving, and his wrath is loving. The traditional theologian often sets love up *in contrast to* justice and wrath. We are told that "God may be loving, *but he is also* just," as if the universalist has somehow forgotten about God's justice! But ironically, this objection to universalism actually exposes the weakness of more traditional accounts. The universalist has an integrated account of the divine nature in which all God's actions are manifestations of his "holy love."[58] More traditional theology often seems less concerned about God's holy love than about God's holiness and God's love. Certain actions are seen as loving actions (saving the lost) whilst other actions are manifestations of God's holiness but most certainly not manifestations of his love (sending the lost to hell). But 1 John 4 will not allow us to conceive of any of God's actions being incompatible with his love. Consequently, any account of hell must see hell as a manifestation of divine love and mercy even if it is a severe side of that mercy. The traditional theologian will not allow that it is possible for those in hell to find salvation; but, I ask, how is that teaching compatible with the kind of divine love revealed in the biblical story? How could God be love if he draws a line at death and says, "Beyond this point I will look for the lost sheep no more; and even if they try to return, I shall turn them away." It seems to me that such a God would not be behaving in a loving way. In conclusion, I suggest that the problem is not that the universalist sentimentalizes God's love and forgets his wrath but, rather, that the traditional theologians underestimate God's love and unhelpfully disconnect it from his justice.

Conclusion

In conclusion, we have argued that in Jesus Christ God has acted to save Israel and, thus, to save the world. On the cross he takes upon himself Israel's exile and Humanity's expulsion, both conceived in terms of a divine curse. His resurrection anticipates the return from exile the Jews longed for and the restoration of humanity and creation. Christ is thus, on the one hand, the Messiah representing the nation of Israel and, on the other, the second Adam representing the whole of humanity. In his representative role nobody is ex-

---

them. John brings up the claim that God is love in the context of the love of "the other." For John, God shows his love by sending Christ. He would be most perplexed to think that some people had interpreted his claim that "God is love" so as to make it logically compatible with the counterfactual claim that "God loves nobody apart from himself." To say that God must love all his creatures if he is love is an expression of his perfection and should not be seen as a limitation on his Sovereignty. It is no more theologically problematic than maintaining that God cannot sin or God cannot act in an unholy way.

[58] The phrase is that of P. T. Forsyth.

cluded. Christ does not merely represent a limited group of people within Israel and the nations. Christ's death is not merely on behalf of some elect grouping within the wider family of humanity. He represented all, and his death was for all without any exceptions. In his resurrection, the whole of creation is reconciled, and the whole of humanity is redeemed. None of this makes participation in redemption automatic—repentance and faith are necessary responses to grace. Paul still urges his hearers to be reconciled to God immediately after declaring that God was in Christ reconciling the world to himself (2 Cor 5:18-20).

We argued that the church is to be understood as an anticipation of the future salvation of all humanity. Some Jews and some Gentiles have, in Christ, tasted this future salvation. Jewish believers anticipate the return from exile, and Gentile believers anticipate the fuller pilgrimage of the nations at the end of the age. The present age is one in which humanity, both Jew and Gentile, is divided into elect and non-elect, saved and perishing. However, the church is a sign in the present of the future day when all Israel will be saved and all the nations will come in pilgrimage to worship Yahweh and his Messiah. The final diagram summarizes the argument of chapters 3 and 4. It is identical to diagram 3, with the addition of a dotted line coming up from exiled Israel representing Jewish Christians and a dotted line coming up from expelled humanity representing Gentile Christians. The rectangle behind them is intended to indicate that they are united into the single body of the church. Thus, the church is seen as an anticipation in the present age of a future salvation for Israel and the nations in the new age. This, in a nutshell, is the evangelical universalist vision I defend.

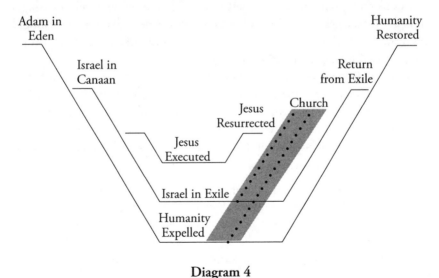

Diagram 4

CHAPTER FIVE

A Universalist Interpretation of the Book of Revelation

On each side of the river stood the tree of life, bearing twelve
crops of fruit, yielding its fruit every month. And the leaves of
the tree are for the healing of the nations.
—Revelation 22:2

T HIS CHAPTER will serve a threefold function. First, it will provide the opportunity to give a more rigorous exegetical defense of the claim made in the last chapter that the Old Testament motif of the pilgrimage of the nations is not exhausted in the church but awaits a future fulfillment. Second, it allows us to demonstrate how the biblical theological web spun out in the previous three chapters can help us interpret a particular biblical book. Third, it gives us the opportunity to suggest a way of handling the biblical passages on hell. This suggestion will be followed up in the next chapter. So it should not be imagined that this chapter is a mere excursus; rather, it is an important bridge between chapter 4 and chapter 6.

The traditional view of the Christian Churches on the nature of hell is that those who are sent there will suffer everlasting conscious torment without hope of redemption. The two clearest biblical supports for this view are found within the book of Revelation, and these texts alone are often thought to be enough to sink both annihilationist and universalist views of hell without a trace.[1] Our texts read as follows:

> A third angel followed them and said in a loud voice: "If anyone worships the Beast and his image and receives his mark on the forehead or on the hand, he, too, will drink of the wine of God's fury, which has been poured full strength into the cup of his wrath. He will be

---

[1] See, for instance, D. A. Carson, *The Gagging of God: Christianity Confronts Pluralism* (Grand Rapids: Zondervan; Leicester: Apollos, 1996) chap. 13.

106

tormented with burning sulphur in the presence of the holy angels and of the Lamb." And the smoke of their torment rises forever and ever. There is no rest day or night for those who worship the Beast and his image, or for anyone who receives the mark of his name. (Rev 14:9-11)

And the devil, who deceived them, was thrown into the lake of burning sulphur, where the Beast and the false prophet had been thrown. They will be tormented day and night forever and ever. Then I saw a great white throne and him who was seated on it. Earth and sky fled from his presence, and there was no place for them. And I saw the dead, great and small, standing before the throne, and books were opened. Another book was opened, which is the book of life. The dead were judged according to what they had done as recorded in the books. The sea gave up the dead that were in it, and death and Hades gave up the dead that were in them, and each person was judged according to what he had done. Then death and Hades were thrown into the lake of fire. The lake of fire is the second death. If anyone's name was not found written in the book of life, he was thrown into the lake of fire. (Rev 20:10-15).

Setting the Hell Texts in Their Contexts

The structure of Revelation is a subject fraught with controversy, but the observations that we shall make are largely straightforward. We may see the structure of the book as follows:[2]

Super-Structure[3]	Sub-Structure[4]	Sub-Sub-Structure[5]	Content
1:1-19	1:1-19	1:1-19 (20)	Prologue
1:20—3:22	1:20—3:22	2:1 (1:20)—3:22	Messages from Christ to the Seven Churches

---

[2] G. K. Beale, *The Book of Revelation: A Commentary on the Greek Text,* NIGTC (Grand Rapids: Eerdmans; Carlisle: Paternoster, 1999); the discussion on structure is found on 108–51.

[3] Ibid., 111. These divisions are based on the "what must come to pass" and the "what must come to pass quickly" formulas in 1:1, 19; 4:1; and 22:6.

[4] Ibid., 111. These divisions are based on the "I was in the Spirit" and the "he bore me away in the Spirit" formulas in 1:10; 4:2; 17:3; and 21:10.

[5] Ibid., ix–xvi.

4:1—22:5	4:1—16:21	4:1—5:14	Heavenly Vision of the Sovereign God and the Lamb
		6:1—8:5	Seven Seals of Judgment
		8:6—11:19	Seven Trumpets of judgment
		12:1—15:4	Deeper Conflict - Seven Visions
		15:5—16:21	Seven Bowls of Judgment
	17:1—21:8	17:1—19:21	Final Judgment on Babylon and the Beast
		20:1-15	The Millennium and Final Judgment
		21:1-8	The New Creation
	21:9—22:5	21:9—22:5	The New Jerusalem
22:6-21		22:6-21	Conclusion

Let us try to locate our hell texts within the structure. Chapter 14 marks the end of a cycle of visions that began in chapter 12. If we divide that section according to the "and I saw" and the "I beheld," formulas we can observe seven signs:[6]

1. the woman and the serpent (12)

2. the persecution by the Beast from the sea (13:1-10)

3. the persecution by the Beast from the land (13:11-18)

4. the Lamb and the 144,000 on Mount Zion (14:1-5)

5. the proclamation of the gospel and of judgment by three angels (14:6-13)

6. the Son of Man's harvest of the earth (14:14-20)

7. the Victory Song of the Saints (15:2-4)

The two visions in 14:6-20 both refer to the climax of God's judgments and 15:2-4 to the eschatological salvation consequent upon those judgments. So our first hell text is set within one of the "final-judgment-followed-by-salvation" sections that Beale notes:

---

[6] Ibid., 730.

Judgment	Salvation
6:12-17	7:9-17
11:18a	11:18b
14:6-20	*15:2-4*
16:17-18:24	19:1-10
20:7-15	21:1-22:5

This observation will later be seen to be of considerable hermeneutical significance.

Section (5) above is structured as follows:

a) First Angel—Proclamation of the Gospel to Rebellious Nations (14:6-7).

b) Second Angel—The Fall of Babylon (14:8).

c) Third Angel—The Final Punishment of the Beast's Followers (14:9-11).

d) Encouragement for the saints (14:12-13).

It is *this* judgment that 15:2-4 celebrates. Thus, no interpretation of the judgments of 14:9-11 can isolate itself from 15:2-4, which is set chronologically later.

The same can be said of 20:7-15, which quite possibly[7] records the same final judgment as 14:9-11 and is also followed by a vision of salvation for the saints (21–22). Any interpretation of the lake of fire in 20:7-15 must be compatible with the vision in 21-22. I shall argue that the salvation climaxes of the two sections are suggestive of universalism and invite a universalist re-reading of the hell texts that precede them.

15:2-4 as the Universalist Postscript to 14:9-11

Revelation 15:2-4 is the salvific climax of the seven visions.

> And I saw what looked like a sea of glass mixed with fire and, standing beside the sea, those who had been victorious over the Beast and his image and over the number of his name. They held harps given them by God and sang the song of Moses the servant of God and the song of the Lamb: "Great and marvelous are your deeds, Lord God Almighty. Just and true are your ways, King of the Nations. Who will not fear you, O Lord, and bring glory to your name? For you alone are

---

[7] See later for a discussion.

> holy. All nations will come and worship before you, for your righteous
> acts have been revealed."

Some have argued that the vision here is a part of the Seven Plagues sequence rather than the climax of the preceding section because it follows on from an introduction to the new section in 15:1. This claim is to be resisted. Collins draws attention to a literary technique she refers to as "interlocking," in which a section of the book both concludes one section and introduces the next.[8] 15:2-4 is one such section (other sections may include 8:2-5; 11:19; 17:1-3; 19:9-10; and 22:9-10): it concludes what precedes, but also anticipates what follows.[9] 15:2-4 serves to tie the seven visions section and the seven plagues section together, and that explains why the plagues are introduced in 15:1 and then continued in 15:5 ff.

The Beast's defeat is completed by 15:2-4, and the saints rejoice in the eschatological, final victory of God. Building upon Old Testament imagery (Isa 51:9-11; Ps 74:12-15; Ezek 32:2), the sea upon which they stand symbolizes the cosmic evil and chaos represented by the Beast (13:1; 21:1). The fire symbolizes God's judgment, which destroys the Beast in his own watery lair.[10] Those who stand on/beside the sea are clearly the resurrected saints[11] who refused to worship the Beast and escaped the fate described in 14:9-13. These are they who share in the Lamb's victory and are to be identified with the 144,000 in 14:1-5 who are sealed and protected against God's judgments. They sing an eschatological hymn of praise that is referred to as the Song of Moses. When Moses led Israel through the Red Sea, the people of Israel sang a song in praise of Yahweh for delivering them by judging Pharaoh and his people (Exod 15:1-18). Here the church praises God for delivering them from the Beast and his followers. The Song of the Sea is sung again, although this time it is also the Lamb's song.

The content of the Song does not come from Exodus 15 but from later Old Testament texts that reflect on the first exodus. John sees these words as finding their greater fulfillment in the final exodus of the church.

---

[8] Adeala Yarbro Collins, *The Combat Myth in the Book of Revelation*, HDR 9 (Missoula, Mont.: Scholars, 1976) 15–16.

[9] Beale, *Revelation*, 113.

[10] Ibid., 789–90 on the symbolism.

[11] Beale argues that there are several reasons to see the redeemed here as resurrected: (a) The expression that the saints were "standing" on the sea of glass is similar to the portrayal of the resurrected Lamb as "standing" on the sea of glass in 5:6. (b) The "conquering" of the saints here (15:2), as that of the Lamb in 5:5, implies resurrection. (c) Some Jewish writings of this period link the Song of the Sea in Exodus 15:1 ff. to the new song the saints will sing in the resurrection. (d) The scene is set after the judgment of the lake of fire which, according to 20:11-15, follows the resurrection (ibid., 792–93).

"Great and marvelous are your deeds, Lord God Almighty." This is an allusion to the LXX version of Psalm 110 (111):2-4 in which God's great works and marvelous deeds in redeeming Israel through judgment of Pharaoh at the Red Sea are praised. In the same way, the divine wrath on the Beast and his followers is also a great act of deliverance for the church.

"Just and true are your ways, King of the Nations." The justice of the punishment of the enemies of God is here stressed (cf. 16:7; 19:2). Christ/ God is King, not only of the church, but of the whole world (cf. 11:15-18; 1:5; 17:14; 19:16). God exercises his kingship over the nations, first of all, by judging them (as these contexts suggest. See especially 19:15-16).

"Who will not fear you, O Lord, and bring glory to your name? For you alone are holy. All nations will come and worship before you, for your righteous acts have been revealed." The rhetorical question alludes to Jeremiah 10:7: "Who would not fear you, O King of the nations?" In both Jeremiah and Revelation the answer is, of course, "no one." All will acknowledge the Lordship of God. All nations will come and worship God. To see the universalist implications of this we need to clarify the referent of "all nations" in v. 4. In the book of Revelation, the nations are created by God and ought to worship him (4:11); instead, they rebel against him. The Beast is given authority over them (13:7b). They partake in the sins of the world-city Babylon and thus also in her judgment (14:8; 17:15; 18:3, 23; 16:19). John is called to prophesy against the nations (10:11), and, just prior to Babylon's final destruction, a final gospel call to repentance goes out to the nations (14:6)—a call they do not heed. Under the deceptive influence of Satan and the Beast, the nations persecute God's people (11:12). When Satan is bound in the millennium, he can no longer deceive the nations (20:3). But afterwards, he raises them for the final battle against the saints (20:8). Consequently, they are the objects of God's eschatological wrath (11:8; 12:5; 19:15).

The saints are never identified with the nations. For John, the nations are the apostate ethno-political groupings that make up God's rebellious world. The saints are distinguished from them as those who have been redeemed from among the nations[12] to form a new kingdom and who are the objects of the nations' rage. There can be no doubt that the nations referred to in 15:4 are the same apostate nations the smoke of whose torment rises forever and ever. So what does the victory song of the saints tell us about

---

[12] Revelation 5:9—"They sing a new song: 'You are worthy to take the scroll and to open its seals, for you were slaughtered and by your blood you ransomed for God saints *from* every tribe and language and people and nation." Revelation 7:9—"After this I looked, and there was a great multitude that no one could count, *from* every nation, from all tribes and peoples and languages, standing before the throne and before the Lamb, robed in white, with palm branches in their hands."

them? That although they are now subject to God's wrath, they will[13] come and worship before God. Notice that John does not say that people *from* all nations (a description which would fit the church, 5:9; 7:9) will come and worship, but that all nations will come and worship.

G. K. Beale, in order to avoid the universalist implications of this, says that

> "All the nations" is a figure of speech . . . by which the *whole* world is substituted for a *part* of it in order to emphasise that many will worship, which is in line with 5:9; 7:9ff.; and 14:3. The whole for the part is clearly the meaning where *pas* ("all") occurs with *ethnos* ("nations") elsewhere (5:9; 7:9; 13:7; 14:8; 18:3, 23). The sense in these verse is not "all" without exception but "all" without distinction. Otherwise some of these verses would affirm that all without exception are redeemed and others that all without exception are deceived or judged, which is clearly not the case (cf. Rom 10:18; Col 1:6; 1 Thess 1:8).[14]

What are we to make of this argument? 5:9 and 7:9 designate the saints as those who have been redeemed *from* the nations. It is very clear in both texts that the saints are composed of *some from every nation,* and thus we do not have an example of synecdoche in these texts. If we look at how the seer uses the word "all" in 5:9 and 7:9, there is no reason to think that he does not mean "all without exception" (there are saints from *every single* nation) rather than merely "all without distinction" (some from *a representative sample of* nations). Similarly, there is no reason not to see the Beast in 13:7 as being given authority over "every tribe and people and language and nation" without exception. Literally every people-group came under the power of the Beast. Exactly the same could be said about 14:8; 18:3 and 23. "All" always means "all without exception." So the claim that *pas* ("all") means "all without distinction" when combined with *ethnos* (nations) is false (or, at least, it begs the question). However, Beale's point seems to be that, even if every nation without exception is included in these referents, we should not imagine that *every person* within every nation is included. "Nation" designates most, but not necessarily all, of the citizens. A nation could be said to be deceived by the Beast, for example, even if some of its citizens are not. This is correct, but it is not much help to Beale's case. This is because he wants to take the word "nations" in 15:4 as a reference to the citizens who were redeemed from the nations. These, in Revelation, amount to a minority from each nation, and it does not seem plausible that a reference to such *relatively* small samples from

---

[13] Note the future tense, which quite likely implies that they are not worshipping God yet but that they will.

[14] Beale, *Revelation,* 797–98.

each nation would warrant the term "nations." This, combined with the fact that the apocalypse seems to distinguish the saints (a kingdom composed of some from every nation) from the nations and consistently uses the latter term to refer to the apostate nations, makes Beale's claim that 15:4 refers to a Christian remnant of the nations implausible. If John had intended what Beale suggests, one would have expected him to write something like, "*those redeemed from every nation* will come and worship."

Beale has a fall-back strategy for those who continue to claim that all nations refers to all the non-redeemed nations cast into the lake of fire. He says that we could read 15:4 as suggesting that "at the consummation of history all will acknowledge God's glory, either willingly *or forcibly*."[15] But there is no suggestion of *forcible* worship in this text. Indeed, as Beale acknowledges in another context, in the Apocalypse *proskunēsousin* (worship) is used only of *voluntary* worship of God or of the Beast[16] and to see this worship as anything other than voluntary adoration is unwarranted. A positive interpretation of this worship is also suggested by the allusion to Psalm 86:9-10, which underlies it: "All nations that you have made will come and worship before you, O LORD, and they will glorify your name, because you are great and you do marvelous things; you alone are God." It is most unlikely that the Psalmist intended to include *the dead* from among the nations, but the eschatological frame within which John has situated the allusion clearly requires a reference to the dead.

So it seems that 15:4 paints a portrait of all the rebellious nations who had followed the Beast and been "tormented with burning sulphur as coming voluntarily to worship God. This, given its structural location, clearly *suggests* that those suffering eschatological punishment will, at some point, exit and be redeemed. This claim is further supported by chapters 21–22. There we read that after the final judgment, in which those whose names were not written in the Lamb's book of life were cast into the Lake of fire (20:10-15), the nations would walk by the light of the New Jerusalem (21:24), would bring their worship into it (21:26) and will be healed by the fruits of the tree of life (22:2). These texts will be considered more carefully next, but once again we can see a hope for the nations post-rebellion and post-damnation. Even if we concede that this may be a case of hyperbole and thus need not mean that literally *every single* individual who is damned will necessarily exit from hell,

---

15 Ibid., 799.

16 Ibid., 753. Beale mentions Philippians 2:9-11 as a case in which the damned are forced to acknowledge Christ's Lordship against their will and this, he suggests, allows for the idea of forced worship. Of course, the universalists will not be impressed by this argument, for they would maintain that Philippians 2:9-11 is a statement about universal *salvation* and has nothing to do with *forced* worship (see chap. 4).

it does mean that the vast majority will; and it certainly sits comfortably with the claim that all will.

The Universalist Follow Up to 20:10-15

We find exactly the same kind of universalist climax after our second most explicit hell text in Revelation.[17] It is clear that the division of humanity into saved and damned continues into the New Creation, for Revelation 21 clearly contrasts the resurrected overcomers in vv. 6-7 with the wicked in v. 8, those who inhabit the lake of fire. This rules out any kind of universalism that does not allow for some to be condemned to hell.

However, John moves on to a vision of the New Jerusalem in 21:9ff., and it is here that we find what looks very much like a universalist hope. 21:12-21 give a very elaborate description of the walls of the City. In the ancient world the walls of a city were essential for the protection of the inhabitants, but that this is not the function of these walls is clear from the fact that the wicked are no longer in a position to attack the city, and thus the gates are left open perpetually (21:25). So what is the wall for? Rissi maintains that it serves as a boundary marker between those inside the City (the redeemed) and those outside the City (who inhabit the lake of fire). This interpretation is supported by 22:14-15, in which the risen Jesus says: "Blessed are those who wash their robes, that they may have the right to the tree of life and may go through the gates into the city. Outside are the dogs, those who practice magic arts, the sexually immoral, the murderers, the idolaters and everyone who loves and practices falsehood."[18] To be outside the city walls is to be in the lake of fire (21:8); and nothing and nobody unclean can enter the city, but only those written in the Lamb's book of life (21:27). It is the City wall that marks the boundary between the two: "a sign of separation."[19] So far, this hardly seems encouraging for the universalist; but then we read in 21:23-27:

> The city does not need the sun or the moon to shine on it, for the glory of God gives it light, and the Lamb is its lamp. The nations will walk by its light, and the kings of the earth will bring their splendor

---

[17] In what follows I have been inspired especially by Mathias Rissi, *The Future of the World*, SBT 2/23 (London: SCM, 1972). A very similar case is made by Vernard Eller in *The Most Revealing Book in the Bible: Making Sense out of Revelation* (Grand Rapids: Eerdmans, 1974).

[18] I think that we should not take the tenses here to imply that people in the lake of fire commit these sins. It is hard to make sense of the image of people managing to muster up the motivation to practice sexual immorality or murder *while being tormented* in the lake. Better to suppose that John means that those who, *at present*, practice such things will be in the lake of fire.

[19] Rissi, *Future*, 71.

> into it. On no day will its gates ever be shut (indeed,[20] there will be no night there). The glory and honor of the nations will be brought into it. Nothing impure will ever enter it, nor will anyone who does what is shameful or deceitful, but only those whose names are written in the Lamb's book of life.

Now we have a vision in which the nations, whom we have already established have been thrown into the lake of fire, enter the New Jerusalem via the permanently open gates! There is a continuous flow from outside of the City (clearly the lake of fire in the light of 21:8; 21:27; 22:15) into the City.[21] In John's visionary geography there are only two places one can be located—within the city enclosed in its walls of salvation (Isa 60:18) or outside the city in the lake of fire.[22] The gates of this New Jerusalem are never closed. Given that those in the city would have no reason to leave it to enter the lake of fire, why are the doors always open? "In John's interpretation of the prophetic message [of Isa 60] by means of the Jerusalem vision the motif of *the open gates* is given a quite new, and positively decisive significance for his entire hope for the future. . . . John announces nothing less than that even for this world of the lost the doors remain open!"[23] In the oracle of Isaiah 60 on which this vision is based we read that the gates were left open for the purpose of allowing the nations to enter (60:11), and that is the case here too: the open doors are not just a symbol of security but primarily a symbol of the God who excludes no one from his presence forever.

Not only do the gates offer the opportunity for the lost to enter salvation from the lake of fire, but in John's vision the lost actually avail themselves of this opportunity. To confirm our earlier observations that the nations are indeed those rebellious nations who suffer eschatological judgment, we read that they are accompanied into the New Jerusalem by the kings of the earth.

---

[20] On this translation see Beale, *Revelation*, 1096.

[21] This interpretation was defended also by Jeffrey Marshall Vogelgesang, "The Interpretation of Ezekiel in the Book of Revelation" (Ph.D. diss., Harvard University, 1985).

[22] Roloff thinks that "it should not be inferred from [21:24] that in John's opinion on the renewed earth there will still be pagans and tribes outside the new Jerusalem. For him there can no longer be an 'outside' the city because the city—or, stated more precisely, the salvation community represented by it metaphorically—is fully and completely identical with the new creation. The fulfillment of the promise of the end-time pilgrimage of nations serves him merely as a symbol of the universal unity, free from distance and fear, of human beings in the presence of God"; *Revelation*, ConComm (Minneapolis: Fortress, 1993) 245 (italics mine). But this is to resist the clear meaning of the text. The text *clearly* does present an inside (salvation) and an outside (the lake of fire) to the city. The damned are still in existence (21:8) so given that they cannot be within the city John has to locate them somewhere else—outside.

[23] Rissi, *Future*, 73–74.

It would be worth our while to examine the sordid history of these characters in the Apocalypse to see more clearly the implications of 21:23-27.[24]

These kings of the earth have committed fornication with the economic whore-city Babylon, and she rules over them. When she is burned up in the fiery judgment of God, they stand appalled. Indeed, the lake of fire is the way in which those who join themselves with Babylon share in the same fate as her (17:2, 18; 18:3, 9). These same kings hide in fear from the end-time wrath of God (6:15) but still join with the Beast to make war on Christ (19:19). But the Christ they attack is the King of kings (19:16) and the ruler of the kings of the earth (1:5), and he defeats them (19:21). There can be no doubt that these kings of the earth find themselves in the lake of fire. Yet it is *the very same* kings of the earth of whom we read that they enter the New Jerusalem via the open gates in order to bring their splendor into it (a contrast with 18:4-19, in which they bring their splendor into Babylon). John has actually changed the "kings" of his source text (Isa 60:3, 11) to "kings of the earth"[25] so as to ensure we understand just who he has in mind. They come, "not as captives or second class citizens,"[26] but as worshippers on an equal standing with the other redeemed.

Beale has resisted this conclusion by advancing several considerations. First, "Nations" is a term sometimes used of the community of the redeemed (5:9; 7:9), and so those mentioned here are presumably that group. But this is simply false. 5:9 and 7:9 do *not* refer to the saints as "the nations," but as a kingdom redeemed from among the nations. In both texts the term "nations" refers to the bigger, non-redeemed group from which the saints come. Elsewhere in Revelation the titles "the nations" and "the kings of the earth" are *always* reserved for the enemies of Christ and the saints, and we have no grounds for thinking that the referent is any different here. For John to change the referent now without warning nor explanation would only lead to confusion.

Second, "There is no basis for seeing the entrance of the nations and kings into the city as suggesting a kind of universalism wherein non-elect peoples not "written in the book of the Lamb" will enter the new Jerusalem. Only the elect will come into the city, which is indicated by 21:27b, where "those written in the book of life" clearly has its antecedent in the nations and

---

[24] Vernard Eller, "How the Kings of the Earth Land in the New Jerusalem: The World in the Book of Revelation," *Katallagete/Be Reconciled* 5 (1975) 21–27.

[25] Rissi suggests that the change was made in light of Ps 89:27.

[26] J. P. M. Sweet, *Revelation* (London: SCM; Philadelphia: Westminster, 1979) 310. Here we see how the New Testament interprets the Old Testament motif of the submission of the nations to Israel (see chap. 3) in an egalitarian way.

kings who enter the city in vv. 24-26 . . . ."[27] To this the universalist would reply that, of course "nothing impure will enter [the city], nor will anyone who
does what is shameful or deceitful, but only those whose names are written
in the Lamb's book of life" (21:27). As 22:14 says, those who have the right
to go through the gates of the city and eat the tree of life are those who "wash
their robes." The universalist simply need maintain that someone in the lake
of fire could wash their robes in the blood of the Lamb and thus be added
into the book of life. What 21:27 and 22:14 do demonstrate, then, is that the
nations and kings can only exit from the lake of fire through repentance and
faith in the atoning work of Christ. Then they are *no longer* unclean, and their
names are thus written in the Lamb's book of life (see Appendix 3 for more
on the Book of Life). Thus, John's vision is of the ultimate defeat of Christ's
enemies by reconciling them.[28] This is the kind of victory most fitting for the
Lamb who triumphs through sacrificial love. Thus, Christ indeed becomes
the "Ruler of the kings of the earth" (1:5).[29]

Third, vv. 24-26 cannot "refer to a universal election and salvation from
the 'lake of fire,' since the Apocalypse elsewhere views some people as suffering that punishment and not temporarily (cf. 14:10-11 and 20:10 with 21:8,
27; 22:14-15)."[30] Beale rightly draws attention here to a tension between
the damnation texts and this vision. He takes his fixed point as the damnation texts and re-reads Revelation 21 to fit in with them. Universalists will
take their interpretation of Revelation 21 as the starting point and attempt a
re-interpretation of the damnation texts. I shall attempt just such a re-interpretation later. Prior to considering the results of such attempts one cannot
say that either is *obviously* the correct approach. I would, though, remind the
reader of the hermeneutical principle governing this book, in which the dice
is loaded in favor of the universalist should an impasse be reached.

The point of the image of the pilgrimage of the nations in Revelation
21, says Beale, has nothing to do with salvation after damnation but aims,
rather, to convey the point that "the Gentiles will never be separated from

---

[27] Beale, *Revelation*, 1097–98.

[28] Sweet sees Revelation 20–22 presenting contradictory images, which exist in an unresolved
tension—all the nations are damned and all the nations are saved. Universalism offers perhaps
the best way to resolve any such tensions.

[29] Rissi also sees significance in the fact that the twelve gates symbolize the twelve tribes
of Israel because he perceives a biblical meta-narrative in which all Israel is restored (Rom
11:25ff.) and then the nations follow on (Rom 11:12). He suggests that Christ will redeem all
Israel *after* the *parousia* (the telos event of 1 Cor 15:23ff.) and then they become the means by
which the rest of nations enter into salvation—the gates through which the gentiles enter. See
also Jan Bonda, *The One Purpose of God: An Answer to the Doctrine of Eternal Punishment*, trans.
Reinder Bruinsma (Grand Rapids: Eerdmans, 1998).

[30] Beale, *Revelation*, 1098.

118   THE EVANGELICAL UNIVERSALIST

open, eternal access to God's presence and that nothing evil can threaten such access."[31] It seems to me that this is an unlikely interpretation of the image. The city that the nations enter is the bride of Christ—the church. It has twelve foundation stones upon which were written the names of the apostles of the Lamb (Rev 21:14) and twelve gates over which are written the names of the twelve tribes of Israel (21:12). The city *already* represents the totality of the church in its Old and New Testament phases. It is already clear that the 144,000 (7:1-8; 14:1-5) is the same as the great multitude that nobody can number drawn out from every nation (7:9-10), which, in turn, is the bride (19:7-8; 21:2) and the city (21:2). The multi-national composition of the community is clear before we read of the pilgrimage of nations. The arrival of the nations here, within the symbolic structures of the book, makes much better sense as the repentance of the previously unredeemed nations. The redeemed, multi-ethnic community was a first-fruits (14:4), and this is the rest of the harvest coming in.

This leads us to another clue within Revelation to support the universalist interpretation of 21:24-27: the fact that the 144,000 are described as being offered as "first-fruits to God and the Lamb" (14:4). The 144,000 represent the redeemed multitude drawn from every nation—i.e., the church.[32] They are said to be the first-fruits. This is an agricultural metaphor. The first-fruits was the first sheaf of the harvest, which was offered to God and which functioned as a guarantee that the rest of the harvest was on the way. Paul speaks of Christ's resurrection as the first-fruits (1 Cor 15:20), but here the church *itself* is offered as a first-fruits. This is best interpreted to imply that the nations are the rest of the harvest, which will be harvested at the right time. The church is a guarantee that they will come in. This observation helps us set the universalist interpretation within the broader theological context of inaugurated eschatology.[33] The church is made up of those who experience the blessings of the new age in the present (to some extent). The conversion of the Gentiles is a taste of the fulness to come in the New Age, when we will see the conversion of all the nations. So those redeemed from each nation are just the first installment—a sign that the rest will follow in the new age.

A further observation to strengthen our interpretation is in 22:14-17.

> Blessed are those who wash their robes, so that they will have the right to the tree of life and may enter the city by the gates. Outside are the dogs and sorcerers and fornicators and murderers and idolaters, and everyone who loves and practices falsehood. "It is I, Jesus, who sent

[31] Ibid., 1099.

[32] Ibid., 416–23 for a detailed defense.

[33] It also fits perfectly with our proposed universalist ecclesiology in Colossians (chap. 2) and Ephesians (Appendix 2).

my angel to you with this testimony for the churches. I am the root and the descendant of David, the bright morning star." The Spirit and the bride say, "Come." And let everyone who hears say, "Come." And let everyone who is thirsty come. Let anyone who wishes take the water of life as a gift.

Here is a description of those who wash their robes[34] contrasted with those who are in the lake of fire. But notice v. 17. The Spirit and the bride issue three invitations to come. Now the metaphor of a bride has only been used in Revelation of the church in its state of eschatological glory (19:7; 21:2). This bride, then, is the glorified church-prophetic. But to whom does she speak? One plausible audience is those in the lake of fire (after all, who else is there?). The promise of the water of life is made by Christ to the church in 21:6. In 22:17 it seems that the bride of Christ, the glorified church, offers this life to those in the lake of fire. If they wash their robes, they can enter the city and drink from the river.

Rissi argues that 22:1-5 is a structurally separate vision that moves beyond the temporary separation between saved and damned to a vision of paradise in which all are saved. There is no longer an "in" and an "out," for *every* curse is now removed (22:3), which, he thinks, includes the curse of the lake of fire. *Everything* is also now made new (22:5).[35] John here alludes to Isaiah 43:19, though he makes the significant addition of "all"—God makes "*all* things" new! By the time we reach 22:1-5, all the lost have entered into salvation. This is possible, though I must confess to remaining unconvinced by Rissi here. 21:1-8 clearly see the existence of the lake of fire (21:8) as compatible with the claim that God makes everything new (21:5) and the claim that death is no more (21:4). Presumably we are intended to take the promises and blessings of 22:1-5 as applying to the City and not as necessarily ruling out the existence of the lake of fire. Nevertheless, we see the tree of life and read that "the leaves of the tree are for the healing of the nations" (22:2b). John had added "the nations" to Ezek 47:12 here and again brings out his own special emphasis. The nations of Revelation certainly need such healing, and the fact that it is promised *after* their condemnation in the Lake of Fire can only encourage a universalist reading of the whole book.

This universal vision of salvation is confirmed again by the proleptic vision in 5:13, in which we see "every creature in heaven and on earth and under the earth and on the sea, and all that is in them, singing: 'To him who

---

[34] Just possibly those who "wash their robes" here are to be distinguished from the saints in this age who "*have washed* their robes" (7:14). This would lend a little support to the interpretation offered above, but I concede that it is only weak support.

[35] Sweet connects the notion of new creation with reconciliation in Revelation 22 as it is similarly connected in 2 Cor 5:14-19 (*Revelation*, 309).

sits on the throne and to the Lamb be praise and honor and glory and power, for ever and ever!'" Here we see an anticipation of the universal worship, which marks the fulfillment of God's purposes.

Another Look at 14:9–11 and 20:10–15

Traditional uses of 14:9-11 and 20:10-15 in discussions of hell almost invariably fail to perceive the significance of their structural location vis à vis the universalist passages we have noted. Attempts to change the referents of the terms "nations" and "kings of the earth" are unpersuasive. The universalist texts do seem to indicate clearly that the damned of 14:9-11 and 20:10-15 will be redeemed at some point and enter the New Jerusalem. This insight should govern our examination of the damnation texts. Do they rule out such a post-damnation salvation as the majority tradition thinks? I shall argue that they do not. First of all, we need to set our "problem texts" within two further contexts: first, the broader understanding of divine punishment found in the Apocalypse and, second, the Old Testament background to these "problem texts."

First of all, let us set the texts in the context of Revelation's understanding of divine judgment. It seems to me that divine judgment in the Apocalypse is multi-functional. Three distinct, though not unrelated, dimensions of judgment stand out:

> a) divine judgment is retributive—the punishment is deserved, and will fit the crime (e.g., 11:18; 16:8; 18:3, 6-7; 22:18-19).

> b) divine judgment is the means by which God delivers his suffering people from their oppressors (e.g., 15:2-4; 19:1-10). This theme is drawn from the exodus and return from exile motifs in the Old Testament.

> c) divine judgment has a warning and educative dimension.

It is the last of these I wish to focus on. It is a common theme in the Old Testament that God's judgments are designed, in part, to lead his people to repentance. Prophetic oracles sometimes express astonishment that the people fail to repent even in the face of God's loving but severe discipline. We find just such sentiments in 9:20, in which we read that "the rest of humankind, who were not killed by these plagues, did not repent of the works of their hands or give up worshiping demons and idols of gold and silver and bronze and stone and wood, which cannot see or hear or walk." Obviously, the judgment did not induce repentance, but that simply highlights how blind and stubborn the nations are and does not indicate that God was not spurring them towards salvation. Similarly, the gospel warning in 14:6-7 uses judgments as a final spur to salvation:

> Then I saw another angel flying in mid heaven, with an eternal gospel to proclaim to those who live on the earth—to every nation and tribe and language and people. He said in a loud voice, "Fear God and give him glory, *for the hour of his judgment has come*; and worship him who made heaven and earth, the sea and the springs of water."

Though such disciplining judgments did not always bring about repentance (9:20; 16:9, 11, 21), when combined with the prophetic witness of the church, they could (11:13). So God's judgments are designed, in part, to spur the nations to stop acting as they are.

We must be very careful not to imagine that the fierce wrath of God experienced by the nations in Revelation means that God does not love them or want their salvation. In 3:19 Jesus tells the saints in Laodicea that he rebukes and disciplines those he loves. They should repent in order to avoid such discipline. Indeed the nature of God's discipline of his people is very similar to his discipline of the unredeemed in that both include a "like-for-like" retribution and both can be fierce (compare 2:20-23 with 18:4-7). The crucial insight of 3:19 is that Christ does this *out of love*. Why could we not see the judgment of the nations in the same way? Indeed, why could we not even interpret the lake of fire as fulfilling these same three functions? After all, it is simply the climax of the escalating punishments and not obviously a *totally different kind* of punishment. The universalist would see the lake of fire as deserved and terrible but also as educative, being aimed at producing a realization of one's sins and thus repentance. Universalist philosopher Thomas Talbott speculates, "I suspect that God has a special way of teaching us the true meaning of our selfish actions. In some cases at least, he may require us to experience the effects of our actions from the perspective of others, almost as if we were the one being affected; in that way, we shall literally reap what we have sown. A vicious child beater may thus be required to experience the beatings he has administered, together with all the fear and terror he has caused, from the perspective of the very child he has beaten. He will be made to see himself as the child sees him."[36] Although this goes beyond anything stated explicitly in the Apocalypse, it seems to be in accord with the rationale for punishment found throughout (see, for instance, 18:5-6).

A second kind of context I would like to sketch out before considering our problem texts is that of John's use of the Old Testament. John does not simply plunder the Old Testament for phrases and images that may be useful

---

[36] Thomas B. Talbott, "Universalism and the Supposed Oddity of our Earthly Life: A Reply to Michael Murray," *F&Ph* 18.1 (2001) 104 [102–9].

to him. He uses his texts according to a set of consistent hermeneutical principles. I suggest that John has appropriated not simply words and images, but a plot line that those words and images would call to mind in the first readers. The basic plot line is set out in the exodus story, was re-appropriated in Isaiah, and now can be found in the Apocalypse. We could outline it as follows:

	Enemy	Crime	Divine Response	Result of Judgment	The New Situation
Exodus	Pharaoh & Egypt	Oppress Israel	Judgment (plagues)	Israel saved from Egypt	The nations witness God's salvation of Israel (Exod 15:14-16)
Isaiah	Babylon (& Edom)	Oppress Israel by destruction of Jerusalem and exile	Judgment of nations (esp. Babylon & Edom)	Israel saved— Second Exodus from Babylon and restoration of Jerusalem	The nations flood to Jerusalem to worship Yahweh
Revelation	Beast & Babylon	Oppress church	Judgment of Babylon	Church (new Jerusalem) saved	Nations flood to new Jerusalem

John, I suggest, selects and uses Old Testament texts according to this plot line. Now the texts that form the Old Testament background to our problem texts come from Isaiah's descriptions of the judgment of Babylon and the nations (esp. Isaiah 34 and 63). John uses them for this same purpose. To understand his use of them we need to appreciate how Isaiah's oracles of the judgment of the nations relate to his oracles on the salvation of the nations. Given that John uses Isaiah's "salvation of the nations" oracles as well as his "damnation of the nations" oracles, we can hope to shed some light on Revelation by paying attention to Isaiah's plot line here.

To recap Chapter 3: the Isaiah plot line—especially, though not exclusively, in Isaiah 40–66—runs as follows: God has called Israel to be a light to the nations and to bring his instruction to them (2:1-5; 42:1-7). The nations are in the darkness of idolatry and need to turn to Yahweh. However, Israel herself has sold out to idolatry and has become a blind prisoner in darkness (42:18-25; 43:19-24; 43:26-28; 46:8-13; 48). God must restore Israel before he can bring his salvation to the nations through them. God restores his servant-Israel via an individual who takes on the mission of the nation (49:1-13), "absorbs" the curse on the nation (52:13—53:12), and brings a remnant of the nation back to Yahweh (53:10; 50:10; 54:17; 65:8-16). God also judges Babylon and the nations (13–14; 24–26; 34, 47 etc.), thus bringing about a second exodus (27, 35, 40:3-5, 9-11; 60:4-5 etc.) and a new creation (65:17 ff. etc.). Once the nations are judged and destroyed (24–26, 34), Jerusalem is restored, and then the nations flood to Jerusalem to find Yahweh (60; 2:1-4; 66:18-23); and, at last, Israel can fulfill its mission to be a light to the nations (60:1-3). Of particular interest is the way in which all the nations are portrayed as idolaters (esp. in 40–55) and are all destroyed by Yahweh's anger (Isa 34:1-4). Edom is singled out as the nation that represents all the others in their opposition to Israel and, as such, experiences the full destructive power of God (Isa 34:5-17; 63:1-6.)[37] The "destruction of Edom" oracles represent the destruction of *all* the nations[38]—the enemies of Israel. But in the Isaiah plotline this decimation opens the way to the return of Israel to Jerusalem (Isaiah 35) and the restoration of the holy city portrayed in terms of a new creation (Isaiah 35; 65:17—66:24). Then we read that the nations come to Jerusalem to bring the exiles back and rebuild the city. They join with Israel in worshipping Yahweh.[39] Several things need to be made clear at this point. First, these nations that come to Jerusalem have earlier been said to have been destroyed in the eschatological fire of God's anger. Second, the oath of Yahweh is that all people will enter into a saving relationship with him (Isa 45:22-25). Third, it is clear that this universal salvation does not happen in one instant. The picture of new creation in Isaiah portrays some of the nations coming out of destruction to the New Jerusalem (60:1-11, 13ff.) whilst others remain in rebellion and under destructive wrath (60:12; 66:24). However, it is also clear that they cannot remain *forever* in the state of rebellion portrayed in 60:12 if Yahweh is to fulfill his oath of 45:22-25. Either they are annihilated or they are allowed to turn from their rebellion and join the others in Jerusalem. The book of Isaiah does not tell us which but leaves a blank space for the interpreter to fill in.

It is exactly this plot that the Apocalypse follows. We see that John draws on texts in Isaiah that call to mind key moments of the story at just the right moments. John's visions of the New Age are heavily influenced by Isaiah's,[40]

---

[37] Both these texts are crucial in Revelation's judgment scenes (see 14:9-11, 18-20; 18:9-10; 19:13-15).

[38] Note the link between Isaiah 34:1-4 and 5-17; note also the link between 63:12 and 3-6.

[39] On the theme of the pilgrimage of the nations see Isa 2:1-4; 11:10-12; 18:7; 60:1-16; 61:5-6; 66:12, 18, 23; Pss 22:27-29; 47:7-9; 68:29; 72:9-11; 86:9; 102:21-22; 122:3-4; 138:4-5.

[40] Compare Revelation 21:1—22:5 with Isaiah 60 and 65:17ff. See John Fekkes, *Isaiah and Prophetic Traditions in the Book of Revelation: Visionary Antecedents and their Development,*

and his visions of the destruction of the nations and of Babylon are similarly Isaiah-influenced. The order of the plot is also the same in the two texts. This alerts the interpreter to be open to the possibility that John can speak of the destruction of the nations with the powerful, prophetic rhetoric of wrath and yet still hold open hope for their restoration if and when they submit to Yahweh. Indeed such submission may be some time after destruction and the inauguration of the new creation. With these general comments in mind let us turn to our problem texts.

> A third angel followed them and said in a loud voice: "If anyone worships the Beast and his image and receives his mark on the forehead or on the hand, he, too, will drink of the wine of God's fury, which has been poured full strength into the cup of his wrath. He will be tormented with burning sulphur in the presence of the holy angels and of the Lamb. And the smoke of their torment rises for ever and ever. There is no rest day or night for those who worship the Beast and his image, or for anyone who receives the mark of his name." (14:9-11)

The background to the description is Jeremiah 25:15-16, Isaiah 51:17-23, and Isaiah 34:8-10. The first thing to notice is that these texts are not simply used to describe God's punishment of individuals who worship the Beast *but also his pre-mortem judgment of the new Babylon*. We can bring this out best in the following table:

Old Testament	Fate of New Babylon	Fate of Babylon's Associates
Jeremiah 25:15-16. This is what the LORD, the God of Israel, said to me: "Take from my hand this cup filled with the wine of my wrath and make all the nations to whom I send you drink it. When they drink it, they will stagger and go mad because of the sword I will send among them."[41]	Revelation 16:19. The great city split into three parts, and the cities of the nations collapsed. God remembered Babylon the Great and *gave her the cup filled with the wine of the fury of his wrath.*	Revelation 14:9-10. A third angel followed them and said in a loud voice: "If anyone worships the Beast and his image and receives his mark on the forehead or on the hand, he, too, *will drink of the wine of God's fury, which has been poured full strength into the cup of his wrath.*"

JSNTSup 93 (Sheffield: JSOT Press, 1994).

[41] The nations, areas, and cities Jeremiah has in mind include Judah, Egypt, Uz, Philistia, Edom, Moab, Ammon, Tyre, Sidon, Dedon, Teman, Buz, Arabia, Zimri, Elam, Media etc. and, at the climax, Babylon. All the nations of the earth will "fall to rise no more" (Jer 25:17-26). This comprehensive destruction is well suited to John's purpose.

Isaiah 34:8-10.	Revelation 18:9-10.	Revelation 14:10-11.
For the LORD has a day of vengeance, a year of retribution, to uphold Zion's cause. Edom's streams will be turned into pitch, her dust into burning sulphur; her land will become blazing pitch! It will not be quenched night and day; its smoke will rise forever. From generation to generation it will lie desolate; no one will ever pass through it again.	When the kings of the earth who committed adultery with [Babylon] and shared her luxury see the smoke of her burning, they will weep and mourn over her. Terrified at her torment, they will stand far off and cry: "Woe! Woe, O great city, O Babylon, city of power! In one hour your doom has come!"	He will be tormented with burning sulphur in the presence of the holy angels and of the Lamb. And the smoke of their torment rises for ever and ever. There is no rest day or night for those who worship the Beast and his image, or for anyone who receives the mark of his name.
	Revelation 18:15. The merchants who sold these things and gained their wealth from her will stand far off, terrified at her torment. They will weep and mourn	**Revelation 13:12, 16-17.** [The False Prophet] exercised all the authority of the first Beast on his behalf, and made the earth and its inhabitants worship the first Beast, whose fatal wound had been healed... He also forced everyone, small and great, rich and poor, free and slave, to receive a mark on his right hand or on his forehead, so that no one could buy or sell unless he had the mark, which is the name of the Beast or the number of his name).
	Revelation 19:3. And again they shouted: "Hallelujah! The smoke from [Babylon] goes up for ever and ever."	

One obvious conclusion here is that John wants to use the same kind of judgment language to describe the fate of Babylon and of her associates. The nations shared in the wine of her adulteries, (14:8) so they shall also share the wine of God's wrath with her (14:9-11). Now it is clear that the language is symbolic in the case of Babylon. For instance, it is not literally true that the city was in torment and "the smoke from her goes up forever and ever" (19:5). In just the same way, we should not imagine that it is literally true that "the smoke of their torment rises forever and ever." This is the rhetoric of divine judgment. Indeed, it is not even certain that Revelation 14:9-11 describes a *post-mortem* judgment at all. Immediately prior to it we read, "A second angel followed and said, 'Fallen! Fallen is Babylon the Great, which made all the nations drink the maddening wine of her adulteries'" (14:8). Immediately after this we are into our description of the punishment of the associates of Babylon in the same Old Testament imagery used to describe Babylon's fate. It is entirely possible that this is an apocalyptic description of the historic destruction of the nations and has little or no bearing on the issue of post-mortem punishment.[42] However, given the parallels between 14:9-11 and 20:10-15, I shall assume, for the sake of argument, that 14:9-11 does refer to post-mortem judgment. Do these two texts rule out the possibility of post-mortem salvation?

First, let us consider the imagery of drinking the wine of God's wrath. Jeremiah tells us that Judah drank this wine to "rise no more" (see n. 46). However, in the Isaiah scroll we read that though God's people have suffered at the hands of Babylon, the tables will now be turned.

> Awake, awake! Rise up, O Jerusalem, *you who have drunk from the hand of the LORD the cup of his wrath, you who have drained to its dregs the goblet that makes men stagger.* Of all the sons she bore there was none to guide her; of all the sons she reared there was none to take her by the hand. These double calamities have come upon you—who can comfort you?—ruin and destruction, famine and sword—who can console you? Your sons have fainted; they lie at the head of every street, like antelope caught in a net. They are filled with the wrath of the LORD and the rebuke of your God.
> *Therefore hear this, you afflicted one, made drunk, but not with wine. This is what your Sovereign LORD says, your God, who defends his people: "See, I have taken out of your hand the cup that made you stagger; from that cup, the goblet of my wrath, you will never drink again.* I will put it into the hands of your tormentors, who said to you, Fall prostrate that we may walk over you. And you made your back like the ground, like a street to be walked over." (Isa 51:17-23)

This too is John's message—New Babylon has oppressed the saints and drunk the wine of their blood, but now she will drink God's cup of wrath down to the dregs. This sounds like an irreversible punishment, so it is of some interest to observe that one of the very texts from which John drew the imagery speaks of how Judah, having drained God's wrathful goblet, will have it removed.

---

[42] This is very much in line with N. T. Wright's view of apocalyptic as a symbolic presentation of historical, earthly events in heavenly language. N. T. Wright, *The New Testament and the People of God* (London: SPCK; Minneapolis: Fortress, 1992) 280–99. Wright thinks that NT scholars have seriously misunderstood apocalyptic language by taking it too literally. For a detailed application of this approach to the whole New Testament see especially A. Perriman, *The Coming of the Son of Man: New Testament Eschatology for an Emerging Church* (Milton Keynes: Paternoster, 2005).

It is clear that one can drink God's wrath and move beyond to redemption. Why could it not be the same for the nations as it was for Israel? Nothing in the imagery indicates punishment with no hope of redemption.

Consider also the echoes of Sodom in 14:9-11: destructive fire from heaven, burning sulphur, the land turned to a wasteland, and ascending smoke (Gen 19:24-28; Deut 29:22). This city became paradigmatic of God's eschatological judgment (Jude 7), and it is no surprise to find the allusions here. But it would be wrong to imagine that even a punishment so severe removed all hope of restoration. Yahweh, addressing Jerusalem, says:

> However, I will restore the fortunes of Sodom and her daughters and of Samaria and her daughters, and your fortunes along with them, so that you may bear your disgrace and be ashamed of all you have done in giving them comfort. And your sisters, Sodom with her daughters and Samaria with her daughters, will return to what they were before; and you and your daughters will return to what you were before. (Ezek 16:53-55)

Even a city as paradigmatically sinful as Sodom one which had experienced a punishment from which the imagery of hell was developed, could later experience restoration! In this connection we may also note that Revelation makes much of Exodus imagery, with the nations playing the role of Egypt and the church that of Israel. God rescues his people by punishing his enemies with increasing severity until the final victory at the Sea. Yet the Old Testament also sees a post-judgment restoration of Israel's paradigmatic enemy Egypt—a restoration in which *they become his people* alongside Israel (e.g., Isa 19:16-25). This is summed up in the phrase, "and the LORD will smite Egypt, smiting and healing, and they will return to the LORD, and he will heed their supplications and heal them" (Isa 19:22). Given the typological uses made of the exodus and Sodom texts by Revelation, one should be very careful not to allow the fierce, prophetic rhetoric of punishment to rule out salvation for the damned.[43]

The other main Old Testament background to Revelation 14:10-11 (and, to a lesser extent, 20:10-15) is Isaiah 34. In Isaiah, God punishes Edom (as representative of the nations) for its sins against his people just as God punishes the Beast and its followers in Revelation for their treatment of his people. The rhetoric is powerful, and the image is one of utter desolation. However, as has already been noted, it is clear that the imagery was not intended to be taken literally. The smoke did not literally rise from Edom for-

---

[43] In terms of the reconciliation of paradigmatic enemies of Israel see also Midian (Isa 60:6) and, of interest because of the focus on Edom texts in Revelation, the model reconciliation of the antagonistic Jacob and Esau in Genesis 33.

ever, for the fire burned only until its work was completed. John adopts the same judgment-rhetoric, but again it need not be taken literally.

So far, the Old Testament background of Revelation 14 seems not to require eternal conscious torment. It is clear that the expression 'There is no rest day or night for those who worship the Beast and his image" does seem to refer to conscious sufferings that continue uninterrupted *for as long as the period of suffering lasts.* The consciousness of the suffering is also suggested by the term "torment" (*basanismos*) in vv. 10 and 11. This term is generally used of conscious suffering,[44] though it can be used metaphorically of the city of Babylon personified (18:9-10, 15). "The smoke of their torment" in v. 11 refers to smoke that rises here as a memorial to God's devastating punishment that torments the damned.[45] As far as our argument goes, everything hinges on the duration of this suffering. Revelation 14:11 describes the smoke as rising *eis aiōnas aiōnōn* and 20:10 says, "And the devil, who deceived them, was thrown into the lake of burning sulfur, where the Beast and the false prophet had been thrown. They will be tormented day and night *eis aiōnas aiōnōn.*" This expression literally means "unto the ages of ages" (not "forever and ever") and, strictly speaking, is compatible with a limited, though *very* long, duration.[46] So, *strictly speaking,* nothing in Revelation 14 nor 20 requires an interpretation in which the damned suffer *forever and ever.* However, the strong impression given is of never ending duration. If one considers the other uses of *eis aiōnas aiōnōn* in Revelation (1:6, 8; 4:9-10; 5:13; 7:12; 10:6; 11:15; 15:7; 22:5), most of them do seem to refer to things that last forever and ever, and this is a strong reason to see the phrase as having this meaning in Revelation 14 and 20 when it describes the duration of rising smoke and of the of the punishment of the demonic trinity. So what are we to make of this? We look to see if a universalist reading can be found. Several options spring to mind:

First, argue that John was simply adopting stereotypical descriptions of the post-mortem life of the damned, which formally contradict 21-22 but which are subverted by 21-22 and are thus *not intended to be taken strictly*

[44] Beale, *Revelation*, 762.

[45] Ibid., 761–62.

[46] We may draw attention to the translation of Isaiah 34 v. 10 and v. 11 where we read that its smoke will rise "forever." The Hebrew *le'ôlam*; literally means "for an age" and is not a technical term for "forever." Similarly the LXX *eis geneas* means "unto generations" and not necessarily "forever." Similarly, in v. 11a we read 'from generation to generation it will lie desolate." Neither this nor the LXX *eis chronon polun* (for a long time) necessitate the idea of "*never* ending duration." This desolation of Edom will last for a long time into the future and no restoration is envisaged here *but a restoration would not, strictly speaking, contradict anything here.* Beale concurs that 'in context the phrase refers to an *uninterrupted* memorial of Edom's judgment, which lasts for a long time' (Beale, *Revelation*, 763).

literally. John may be giving traditional language a new twist by putting it within a universalist context. Given the nature of apocalyptic language and John's creative Christian re-appropriation of the tradition, this is a possibility.

Second, argue that 14 and 20 do not envisage the *eternal* damnation of *humans*. 14:9-11 says that the *smoke* rises forever (not literally), but this need not mean that their *torment* lasts forever.[47] David Powys observes that in Revelation 20:10 the devil, the Beast, and the false prophet are "tormented forever and ever" in the lake of fire, but 20:14-15 and 21:8 make no mention of such eternal suffering for the rest who are thrown in there. He concludes, "in terms of the present study the critical finding is that if the lake of fire will constitute literal torment for any, it will be so *only* for the Beast, the false prophet and Satan."[48] Now the Beast is not an individual person but the personification of a totalitarian political kingdom. This is clear from the Danielic background to the image (Dan 7:17) and from 17:7-12, in which the Beast includes, but is itself more than the sum total of, a range of kings.[49] In the same way, the false prophet is not an individual but a false religious/propaganda system. Fudge argues that "the language [in 20:10] is symbolic, and a literal interpretation is impossible. Political power and apostate religious beguilement are not persons who can be tortured in fire."[50] Of course, there are humans who are involved in the Beast and false prophet systems (rightly Beale), and they will enter the lake of fire; but the focus of 20:10 is the utter defeat of the *systems* and not the individuals. These systems will be utterly defeated for all time (this defeat is symbolized in the image of torment "forever and ever," which is a deliberate contrast with 22:5, in which the redeemed "will reign forever and ever"), but the image itself need not rule out the redemption of those who played some role within the systems. To illustrate what I mean, consider how one could imagine speaking of the eternal destruction of the Third Reich at the same time as imagining that all those who played a role in that system may repent and renounce what they once stood for. One could symbolize this defeat by speaking of a personification of the

---

[47] The phrase "the smoke of their torment" *could* be taken to imply that the torment lasts as long as the rising smoke but it *need* not.

[48] David J. Powys, *"Hell"—A Hard Look at a Hard Question: The Fate of the Unrighteous in New Testament Thought* (Carlisle: Paternoster, 1997) 372.

[49] Carson thinks that the Beast is best thought of as recurring individuals that can indeed experience pain (*The Gagging of God*, 527). However, in the image of 17:7-12 the Beast is not simply its heads, as Carson's view would suggest, but the whole creature (the system), which is represented and guided by the heads (the individuals). So I disagree with Carson here.

[50] Fudge, *The Fire That Consumes* (Carlisle: Paternoster) 193. So too John Stott in D. Edwards and J. Stott, *Essentials: A Liberal-Evangelical Dialogue* (London: Hodder & Stoughton, 1988) 318.

system being tormented forever and ever. The universalist *could* maintain that only the demonic trinity will suffer *eternal* conscious torment and that all the humans will eventually be redeemed from the second death.[51] That which is "tormented" forever may not be persons at all, but the personification of evil in its various guises.[52] Certainly the city of Babylon (symbol of a corrupt economic system) can be personified as a whore who is then tormented in her destruction (Revelation 17–19).[53]

To this it could be replied that at the very least, the devil is a personal being who is tormented forever and ever (so Beale and Carson). That is certainly what 20:10 *seems* to say, and it is for this reason that universalists often play it safe and limit universal salvation to humans whilst denying, or remaining agnostic about, the salvation of the devil. This may be enough for the universalist, but Colossians 1:15-22 seems to speak very clearly of the ultimate reconciliation of *all* created things, and this must include the devil (see too Phil 2:9-11). Is there any way of reconciling this text with Revelation 20:10? Let me very tentatively suggest two. One could maintain, as some recent theologians have, that the devil is not a personal being but something more akin to a personification of evil.[54] If this view were acceptable, then *none* of the divine trinity who suffer torment forever and ever are persons but symbols of evil in its general (Satan), its religious (false prophet), and its militaristic and political dimensions (the Beast, along with Babylon, which is evil in its economic dimension). To reinforce the non-personal interpretation we should note that

---

[51] This term occurs in the Palestiniean targums (Tg Isa 22:14; 65:5-6, 15; Tg Jer 51:39, 57; Tg Onkelos Dt 33:6; the Paris MSS on Deut 33:6). See Martin McNamara, *The New Testament and the Palestinian Targum to the Pentateuch*, 2d ed., AnBib 27 (Rome: Pontifical Biblical Institute, 1978) 117–25. The concept is the opposite of "living in the world to come"/ "having eternal life" and is probably linked with Gehenna in Tg Isa 65:5-6 (so McNamara; but see Powys, *Hell*, 392–93 n.107). It need not connote extinction (*pace* Powys).

[52] This is not to suggest that persons will not be tormented for a period of time.

[53] Another alternative is, I suppose, to argue that the damned are indeed justly *sentenced* to suffer eternal conscious torment but that none of them serve out the full term of their sentence as they find forgiveness through Christ. This is possible but runs into the problem that 14:11 says that "the smoke of their torment rises unto the ages of ages," which seems to be a simple statement about what *will* happen and not a hypothetical statement about what would happen were they not to repent. The view could, however, be strengthened if it were successfully argued that the *smoke* will rise forever as a memorial *long after the punishment itself has ceased*.

[54] For some evangelical defenses of this view see N. G. Wright, "Charismatic Interpretation of the Demonic," in *The Unseen World: Christian Reflections on Angels, Demons and the Heavenly Realm*, ed. Anthony N. S. Lane, THS (Carlisle: Paternoster, 1996) 149–63. See also R. Cook, "Devils and Manticores: Plundering Jüng for a Plausible Demonology' in the same volume, 165–85.

death and Hades are also thrown into the lake of fire (20:14), and they are certainly not conscious beings.[55]

If a non-personal devil seems to be a bridge too far, then let me tentatively make another proposal. One could maintain that the devil will be punished forever, but that Lucifer will ultimately be saved. Paul is able to speak of how God saves humans through the putting to death of "the flesh" or the "old person." The human in rebellion against God is "killed" so that there is new creation (2 Cor 5:17). According to the tradition, the devil is a fallen angel. The devil, like the "flesh," must be destroyed forever, because creation has no place for him. But he dies, and Lucifer is reborn as a redeemed angel. It would still be possible to speak of the devil being tormented forever and ever to symbolize this defeat even though no actual being is still in the lake of fire. This goes beyond anything taught in Revelation, but it is one way of trying to reconcile what Revelation teaches with what Colossians 1 teaches and I tentatively commend it to the reader.[56]

> In Revelation's universal perspective, the doctrines of creation, redemption and eschatology are very closely linked. It is God the Creator of all reality who, in faithfulness to his creation, acts in Christ to reclaim and renew his whole creation. Because he is creation's Alpha he will also be its Omega. The scope of his new creation is as universal as the scope of his creation. It is as Creator that he claims his universal kingdom, taking it beyond the threat of evil and nothingness into an eternity of his own presence.[57]

So there are ways of trying to do justice to the lake of fire texts that are compatible with universalism. I do not claim to have disproved traditional interpretations nor to have demonstrated the truth of my suggestions. I do claim to have proposed a range of possible interpretations that are both compatible with universalism and with the text of Revelation. These possibilities gain considerable plausibility from their contexts and, given the legitimate

---

[55] Beale argues that death and Hades are not said to be tormented whilst the Satanic trinity are. He takes this to indicate that the latter are, or include, conscious beings whilst the former are not. All that it need indicate is that death and Hades are not personified whilst Babylon, the Beast, the false prophet (and the devil?) are.

[56] The traditionalist would, no doubt, object that I do not consider the possibility that Rev 20:10 "means what it says" and it is Colossians 1 that needs to be re-interpreted. The traditionalist is perfectly in order to attempt this but I imagine that their proposals for Colossians 1 would sound as far fetched to me as my interpretation of Rev 20:10 probably sounds to them. Nobody obviously has the edge here so I appeal to my legitimate hermeneutical bias in favor of universalism as justification for re-reading Rev 20:10 in the light of Colossians 1.

[57] Richard Bauckham, *The Theology of the Book of Revelation*, NTT (Cambridge: Cambridge University Press, 1993) 163. Bauckham himself, in spite of his comments here, is not a universalist.

hermeneutical bias in favor of universalist readings, I suggest that they have the edge over traditional interpretations.

CHAPTER SIX

To Hell and Back

But as children are punished by their teacher or their father,
so we are punished by Providence. Now God does not exact
vengeance (for vengeance is retribution for evil),[1] *but rather*
he punishes for the good, both public and private, of those who
are being punished.

—Clement of Alexandria[2]

THERE CAN be no doubt that the main argument against the evangelical universalism I have defended thus far is the presence of many texts about final judgment and hell found across the New Testament. Any kind of Christian universalist must have something intelligent to say about such passages if he or she desires to be taken seriously as an orthodox Christian. In this chapter I will propose a way of making sense of such teachings that is consistent with universalism.

It seems to me that there are three possible ways a universalist could handle these passages.

a) A universalist could argue that the hell passages really do teach eternal damnation and that they simply contradict the teaching of more universalist texts. Such universalists are arguing that the New Testament teaches contradictory things about the fate of humanity, and the Christian is left to choose the one that feels like the most Christian. One problem is that damnation texts can be found in the writings of those, such as Paul, who also anticipate a more universalist future. Was Paul so muddled in his thinking as not to perceive

---

[1] Clement means that vengeance is not intended for the good of the one punished but for their harm ("for evil").

[2] *Stromata* 7.16.102.5

a contradiction in his teachings?[3] Another problem is that much of Jesus' teaching is about the judgment. Reisner reckons that 25% of the Synoptic teaching of Jesus is about final punishment.[4] It is clear that an important part of the teaching of the historical Jesus was warning about eschatological judgment. To reject such notions as sub-Christian would be quite an astonishing claim for any Christian to make. A related problem is that the theme of divine punishment is so pervasive across both Old and New Testaments that to suggest that it was not fully Christian would be a dead-end route. On the other hand, to reject the universalist tendencies as unchristian is also a dead end if the arguments in chapters 1–5 carry weight.

b) The universalist could try to find a way to affirm the truth of both the universalist and the hell texts. One could argue with John Robinson that the New Testament sets out two alternative visions for humanity: eternal life and eternal damnation.[5] One vision asserts that all will be saved, the other that many will be damned. These two visions need to be set alongside each other and taken with equal seriousness, but not as two contradictory predictions about the future of the world (this misunderstands the character of myth) nor as alternative *possible* futures (as if all *may* be saved or some *may* be damned). Rather, we should see the vision of damnation as the *truth from the perspective of the persons facing the decision* with which the gospel confronts them. The hell passages set forth the genuinely deserved fate for sinners—a fate that ought to be avoided at all costs. However, the universalist texts set forth the truth as it is for God and faith on the further side of the decision. Robinson writes, "to the man in decision—and that means to all men, always, right up to the last hour—hell is in every way as real a destination as heaven. Only the man who has genuinely been confronted with both alternatives can be saved."[6] However, anything less than full universal salvation could not be seen as anything other than a defeat for the God of love. Both sets of texts are true, but only one set will be realized in the actual future.[7] This existential-

---

[3] It is not that Paul's thought developed across his epistles from a belief in eternal hell to universalism or vice versa, for we find the two teachings in the same letter (e.g., Romans).

[4] Marius Reisner, *Jesus and Judgment: The Eschatological Proclomation in Jewish Context* (Minneapolis: Fortress, 1997) 303–4.

[5] J. A. T. Robinson, *In the End God: A Study of the Christian Doctrine of the Last Things* (London: James Clarke, 1950).

[6] Ibid., 118.

[7] Ibid., 123.

ist approach has much to commend it. It certainly cannot be accused of taking the hell texts as trivial or false, and it provides a theologically suggestive way for holding two different kinds of texts in tension. However, I shall not be taking this route.

c) A universalist could argue that the hell texts do not actually affirm *everlasting* damnation but warn of a terrible but *temporary* fate. This is the classical Christian universalist position found in Origen, Gregory of Nyssa, and many subsequent universalists in Christian history. It is this approach to interpretation that I would like to pursue.

There are some preliminary theological issues that are worth setting out to guide our reflections on hell. The reader needs to understand that what I am doing in this chapter is not a straightforward exegesis of hell texts. Instead, I am offering a way of theologically integrating such texts within the framework of evangelical universalism. The following theological insights can light our way.

Theological Reflections

Divine Wrath

Hell is usually seen as the full manifestation of God's wrath. The theological issue concerns the nature of that wrath. God is not like some pagan deity with a bad temper who may "lose it" at any moment. New Testament scholar Chris Marshall writes that wrath \

> designates God's fervent reaction to human wickedness. God's re-
> fusal to tolerate, compromise with, or indulge evil . . . wrath is not a
> chronic case of ill temper on God's part but a measured commitment
> to act against evil and injustice in order to contain it and destroy it
> . . . it is not so much a matter of direct, individually tailored punitive
> intervention as it is a matter of measured withdrawal of his protective
> influence and control, a refusal to intervene to stem the deleterious
> effects of human rebellion.[8]

A key biblical foundation for the idea that wrath is primarily God's withdrawing his protection is found in Romans 1:18-32, where God's wrath is revealed from heaven when God gives people up to pursue their self-destructive sinful

---

[8] Christopher Marshall, *Beyond Retribution: A New Testament View of Justice, Crime and Punishment* (Grand Rapids: Eerdmans, 2001) 171, 173. See also Stephen H. Travis, "Wrath of God (NT)," in *Anchor Bible Dictionary*, ed. D. N. Freedman (New York: Doubleday, 1992) 6:996–98; idem, *Christ and the Judgment of God* (Baisingstoke: Marshall, Morgan & Scott, 1986).

desires. The wrath *is* God's letting them slide down the path to destruction. In Joel Green's words, "wrath is . . . God . . . handing people over to experience the consequences of the sin they choose (Rom 1:18, 24, 26, 28; cf. Wis 11:11-16; 12:23)."[9]

If we think of hell as the state in which God allows the painful reality of sin to hit home, then we can understand both the terrible imagery used in Scripture to portray such a fate and the urgent warning to avoid the wide road that leads in that direction. It also removes the objection that God is being presented as a cosmic torturer hurting people until they agree to follow him. God does not torture anybody—he simply withdraws his protection that allows people to live under the illusions that sin is not necessarily harmful to a truly human life. The natural (though none the less God-ordained) consequences of sin take their course, and it becomes harder and harder to fool oneself into believing the seductive lies of sin anymore. In this way hell is educative and points us towards our need for divine mercy.

Divine Punishment Now and Not Yet

Divine wrath is experienced now (Rom 1:18-32) and in the future (Rom 2:5, 8; 1 Thess 1:10; 5:9; Col 3:6). It is John's Gospel that really brings out the connections between the two. John writes that "whoever believes in [the Son] is not condemned, but whoever does not believe *is condemned already* . . ." (John 3:18). The eschatological condemnation that stands over those who are not born from above (John 3:1-15) is not only their future destiny but also their present experience. This means that we should not set God's present and his future wrath up as if they were totally different kinds of things. God's wrath in the present is a foretaste of the same phenomena that some will experience in the future. So understanding something of the nature of wrath now will give us some theological orientation for better understanding future wrath.

Well, as far as the church goes, God brings punishment; but it is always to protect them and to rescue the offender.[10] Divine judgments in the present age are usually seen as reformative and educative (Heb 12:5-11; Tit 2:11-12; Rev 3:19; 1 Cor 11:29-32), though they are occasionally destructive (Acts 5:1-11). 1 Corinthians 5:1-5 is an interesting case study. Paul asks the church to hand a consistently sinful church member over to Satan for the destruction of his flesh "so that his spirit may be saved in the day of the Lord." The punishments serve as a call to repentance. Chris Marshall writes that the purpose

---

[9] Joel B. Green and Mark D. Baker, *Recovering the Scandal of the Cross: Atonement in New Testament and Contemporary Contexts* (Downers Grove, Ill.: InterVarsity, 2000) 54.

[10] Marshall, *Beyond Retribution*, 149–62.

of God's punishments is "ultimately redemptive and restorative. The point is not to torment human beings but to enable them to see their moral frailty and their consequent need for God's healing assistance."[11] My suggestion is that we see the punishment of hell as fundamentally the same kind of punishment, albeit in a more intense form.

One text that brings out the perspective on punishment I am commending to readers here is Lamentations 3:22-23, 31-33:

> Because of the LORD's great love we are not consumed, for his compassions never fail. They are new every morning; great is your faithfulness . . . For men are not cast off by the Lord for ever. Though he brings grief, he will show compassion, so great is his unfailing love. For he does not willingly bring affliction or grief to the children of men.

This text of Lamentations reflects on Israel's exilic sufferings and especially the sufferings of those who have been left behind in the ruins of Jerusalem. Right at the heart of the book lies this word of hope. Yes, the Lord has brought us grief and has cast us off but he derives no pleasure from treating us in this way, and *he will not do so forever*. Because of the Lord's faithful, covenant love the final word is Restoration!

Now the obvious response to the discussion above is to maintain that God's punishment of unbelievers is of a different order from his punishment of believers. Believers are punished to correct them, whilst unbelievers are punished for purely retributive reasons. I think that there are good reasons to resist that claim.

We argued in Chapters 3 and 4 that Israel's exile parallels the general human condition of expulsion from Eden. We saw that God's punishment on Israel was a microcosm of his punishment on humanity in Adam. We also maintained that God's covenant with Israel was a parallel to a more general covenant with creation and with humanity grounded in creation. These connections allow us to see that God's punishment of Israel/the church is of the same order as his punishment of humanity in general. Christ's cross *is* Israel's exile *is* humanity's expulsion. Christ's resurrection *is* Israel's return from exile *is* humanity's restoration. Israel's exile is a "type" of hell and her return from exile is a "type" of redemption from hell. Consequently the promise of God's fidelity to faithless Israel in the Lamentations 3 passage quoted above can also be expanded and generalized to include God's faithfulness to the whole of humanity in Christ.

The parallel between God's punishment of his people and of those who are not yet his people is strengthened when we consider the discussions in

---

[11] Ibid., 172.

the last chapter. We saw that in the book of Revelation one function of the punishments on the nations was to drive them to repentance and that the language used to describe possible wrath on faithless believers was the same as that used to describe wrath on the nations. In the case of the believers, this was motivated by divine love; and there is no reason not to think that this was also the case in relation to the nations. The same phenomena can be seem time and time again in the Old Testament when God's wrath on Israel is of the same kind and experienced for the same kinds of reasons as his wrath on the nations. God's punishment of Israel was not radically different from his wrath on the nations. Both were retributive and both were educative, and neither meant the obliteration of the hope for restoration.

Once we see that God's justice is more than mere retribution but is also restorative, and once we see that divine punishments are more than deserved but also corrective, then a way is open to see God's final punishment as another manifestation of this very same justice and not something qualitatively different. It is retributive but also restorative. It is deserved but also corrective. Divine wrath can be seen as the severe side of divine mercy. It is just as much an act of God's love as is his kindness. Granted, it is a side of God's love it would be better not to experience but it is none the less loving for that.[12]

Hell and the Cross

Theologian Jürgen Moltmann notes that any Christian reflection on hell must be a reflection in the light of the cross of Jesus. It is on Golgotha that Christ has suffered the hell of our God-forsakenness for us. It is inconceivable for Moltmann that the cross will not ultimately achieve its intended goal—the complete death of death for the whole of creation. Hence,

> If we follow the method of providing christological answers for eschatological questions, then in trying to measure the breadth of the Christian hope we must not wander off into far-off realms, but must submerge ourselves in the depths of Christ's death on the cross at Golgotha. It is only here that we find the certainty of reconciliation without limits, and the true ground for the hope for "the restoration

---

[12] The notion that the punishment of hell was corrective and purifying is not a new one. It is a strong theme in the thought of Clement of Alexandria, Origen, and Gregory of Nyssa. The way that they picture it is more in terms of purification—the burning away of sinful impurity (based often on 1 Cor 3:15). See especially Steven R. Harmon, *Every Knee Should Bow: Biblical Rationales for Universal Salvation in Early Christian Thought* (Dallas: University Press of America, 2003). I place less emphasis on the purifying power of hell and more on its revelatory power—its ability to expose the reality of sin and its effects.

of all things," for universal salvation, and for the world newly created to become the eternal kingdom.[13]

I think that Moltmann's theology here finds its parallel in that of Paul in Colossians 1 (see Chapter 2). However, it seems to me that he goes too far. Moltmann argues that if Christ has suffered hell for all creation, then it is simply not possible that hell can be the destiny of any of God's creatures.[14] There are two problems here. First, the Bible seems able to affirm *both* that Christ has suffered for all *and* also that some will be sent to hell. Clearly the biblical writers did not detect any contradiction here. Second, the logic of Moltmann's position seems to suggest that after the cross nobody would experience any form of divine wrath, punishment, or the like. Surely, one could argue, if Christ has suffered judgment for us, then there is no place for judgment in human experience any more. Yet it is patently the case that not only people outside the church but also those within can experience divine wrath and judgment. So the cross is no guarantee that in the short and medium term eschatological punishment (now and not yet) will not be our lot. However, I suggest that what the cross does guarantee is that such punishment will not be the last word; that after "crucifixion" God speaks another word—"resurrection." In the end, the cross and resurrection taken together constitute God's final word spoken over creation. Hell is exhausted at Golgotha on Friday, and life triumphs on Sunday! Resurrection, not Golgotha, is the future of creation.

Divine Accomodation

It is the case that biblical writers often appropriate concepts and symbols from their social environments and use them to powerful effect. Indeed, one even finds pagan myths taken up within Scripture. For instance, the Ancient Near Eastern creation myth in which the world comes into being through the slaying of the chaos dragon is taken up in the Old Testament where it is Yahweh rather than Baal who slays the monster (Isa 27:1). There are numerous examples of Old Testament passages that clearly draw on pagan ideas and texts.[15] However, whenever such concepts are adopted they are adapted. The very act of relocating such concepts within a new conceptual framework radically modifies their meaning and function. Concepts and symbols, like

---

[13] Jürgen Moltmann, *The Coming of God: Christian Eschatology*, trans. Margaret Kohl (London: SCM; Minneapolis: Fortress, 1996) 250.

[14] Ibid., 251.

[15] See Frank Moore Cross, *Canaanite Myth and Hebrew Epic* (Cambridge: Harvard University Press, 1973); Jeffrey J. Niehaus, *God at Sinai: Covenant and Theophany in the Bible and the Ancient Near East* (Grand Rapids: Zondervan; Carlisle: Paternoster, 1995) chap. 4.

words, do not have an inherent meaning but draw their meaning from the linguistic and cultural network within which they are situated. When a biblical text draws on some concept or symbol we ought to ask how it should be understood *within the framework in which it has now been placed*. For instance, when the Old Testament takes up echoes of ancient myths, it subverts them to some extent and demythologizes them. When New Testament writers take the language of Imperial Rome to speak of Christ's Kingship and victory, such language is necessarily subverted and reinterpreted when used of Christ. He may be the victor, but what it means to win must be understood in the light of the cross (Rev 5:5-6). The New Testament takes and transforms concepts and symbols from both Jewish and Hellenistic environments.

What I want to suggest is that we ought to ask how the language of eschatological punishment, which was adopted from Second Temple Judaism, should be understood when situated within the theological environment of the New Testament. There was no single concept of hell in Second Temple Judaism but a cluster of images and concepts that held in common the claim that God would bring the wicked to account and punish them. Jesus and his followers took and made use of some of the language and images employed in the discourse of the time without endorsing *every* aspect of Second Temple Jewish beliefs about this fate. In particular, I shall argue that Jesus never explicitly endorsed the claim made by some Jews that the wicked would be tormented *forever* nor the claim of others that they would be *annihilated*. My claim is that although Jesus only once mitigated his claims about hell so as to suggest that it was a temporary fate (Mark 9:47-49), there are good rhetorical reasons why he would not have done so normally. I shall argue further that when the language of hell is located within the framework of New Testament theology a reinterpretation of it that allows for belief in redemption from hell is legitimated. This is simply a canonical expansion of my strategy for interpreting the hell passages in Revelation, explained in the last chapter. Clearly my interpretation is underdetermined by the texts, so I cannot claim that it is obviously *the only* way to interpret the matter. I am not so much exegeting the texts as trying to draw out the logic of New Testament theology as I understand it and its implications for those texts. In the process I may be offering ways of reading the texts that go beyond what their authors had in mind. When that is the case, I am seeking to remain true to what they did have in mind, even if I feel compelled by the wider canon of Scripture to say more.

The Teaching of Jesus

Did Jesus Actually Speak of Hell?

It ought to be noted that a debate has arisen within recent Gospels scholarship about whether Jesus actually spoke of punishment in the afterlife at all. N. T. Wright has argued that the apocalyptic language of the Gospels has been misunderstood by generations of Christian readers. Such language did not refer to the end of the space-time universe, as is commonly thought, but was a powerful way of speaking of the theological dimension of cataclysmic events of divine judgment and vindication *within history*. According to Wright all the passages that warn of the fires of Gehenna speak not of any post-mortem punishment but of the pre-mortem events of AD 70 when Jerusalem was destroyed. The threat of Gehenna was one made to the generation contemporary with Jesus (Matt 12:38-39)—a warning that "all that was left of Israel's hopes and dreams" could become "a heap of rubble, with Jerusalem as a whole turned into a large, smoking extension of Gehenna, her own rubbish dump."[16]

If Wright is correct, then clearly none of the Gospel texts on eschatological judgment count *directly* against the claims of the universalist, because, strictly speaking, Jesus never spoke about post-mortem judgment. Andrew Perriman has recently expanded Wright's basic approach to take in the whole New Testament.[17] On Perriman's reading the only passage in the Bible that is actually about *final* punishment is Rev 21-22 with its teaching on the Lake of Fire. All the other hell texts are actually about divine wrath in the present age—more particularly, in the first century.[18] If this is correct, then the hell passages are not hell passages and our case is made considerably easier. That said, *even if* Wright and Perriman are correct, it seems to me that New Testament teachings could still function as types of post-mortem judgment and would invite a legitimate re-reading as warnings about hell. Of course, in such re-interpretation of the Gehenna texts interpreters would need to be very aware of the nature of the apocalyptic language and beware of trying to infer detailed doctrines about hell.

I am not sure quite what to make of Wright and Perriman's arguments, so I do not wish to build my universalist strategy upon their fascinating but

---

[16] N. T. Wright, *Jesus and the Victory of God* (London: SPCK; Minneapolis: Fortress, 1996) 336.

[17] Andrew Perriman, *The Coming of the Son of Man: New Testament Eschatology for an Emerging Church* (Milton Keynes: Paternoster, 2005).

[18] Randall Gleason takes a very similar approach to the judgment texts in Hebrews in "The Eschatology of the Warning in Hebrews 10:26-31," *TynBul* 53.1 (2002) 97–120. Much of the debate turns on the controversial issue of the proper way to interpret apocalyptic language.

controversial approach to New Testament judgment warnings. The following discussion shall assume, for the sake of argument, that Wright and Perriman are mistaken and that both Jesus and the New Testament authors did indeed speak of hell.

Jesus' Teaching in Context

Jesus often warned his audience about the coming judgment in very striking terms. He spoke of fire (Matt 5:22; 18:8, 9, 45, 47), of "eternal fire" (Matt 18:45, 47; 25:41), an unquenched fire that would not go out (Mark 9:48) accompanied by worms that will not die (Mark 9:48). Jesus refers to the place where the fire burns as Gehenna (Matt 23:33). It is a place of judgment (Matt 12:41-42), condemnation (Matt 23:33), 'eternal punishment' (Matt 25:46), and divine wrath (Matt 3:7, 12; Luke 3:7, 17). Sometimes Jesus spoke in the imagery of expulsion to "outer darkness," where there will be weeping and grinding of teeth (Matt 8:12; 22:13; 25:30; 24:51). The diversity of the images that, if taken strictly literally, would be somewhat contradictory (flames and outer darkness) alerts us to the metaphorical nature of the language employed here. Certain themes stand out when we examine the teachings of Jesus on Gehenna. First, it is a place of *rejection* for those excluded from God's kingdom (Luke 13:22-29; Matt 7:13-14; 25:10b-12; 7:22-23; 8:11-12), a wide road that leads to loss (Matt 7:14) and the outer darkness of the outcasts (Matt 8:12; 22:13; 25:30). The rejection creates a sense of anguish (Luke 13:28; Matt 8:12) with weeping and grinding teeth, although it is uncertain if the reaction described is one of fright or anger. Second, as we have already seen, it is a place of destruction by fire (Luke 3:7-9; Matt 7:19; 10:39; 16:25-27; 13:30, 36-43; 13:50). Third, we are to picture this fate as one of just punishment for the wicked (Matt 24:51; 25:41, 46).

The concept of Gehenna employed by Jesus finds its origins in the associations that the valley of Hinnom (*gehinnom*), south of Jerusalem, had with unrighteousness, burning, and slaughter. It was the site of Ahaz's and Manasseh's idolatrous human sacrifices to Molech. In Isaiah 30:33 it is a funerary pyre for the King of Assyria. Jeremiah describes it as a place where dead bodies were piled up and ashes were thrown (31:40). Indeed, he predicted that it would be so full of the dead that it would be called the valley of slaughter (7:32). Perhaps most importantly for the imagery of the gospels is the vision of Isaiah 66:24, which shows the valleys around Jerusalem filled with dead bodies being consumed by worms and fires. The text reads, "And they will go out and look upon the dead bodies of those who rebelled against me; their worm will not die, nor will their fire be quenched, and they will be loathsome to all mankind." This is clearly the foundation for Jesus' Gehenna imagery, such as is found in Mark 9:45-48:

> And if your foot causes you to sin, cut it off. It is better for you to enter life crippled than to have two feet and be thrown into hell. And if your eye causes you to sin, pluck it out. It is better for you to enter the kingdom of God with one eye than to have two eyes and be thrown into hell, where "their worm does not die, and the fire is not quenched."

In the Isaiah passage the dead are not those in hell suffering eternal, conscious torment but are the corpses of Yahweh's enemies heaped up being consumed by fires and worms.[19] It is not clear whether Jesus' Gehenna imagery makes those in the fire conscious or not.[20] Elsewhere Jesus speaks of weeping and gnashing of teeth in connection with expulsion to outer darkness, but it is not certain that this conscious suffering is thought merely to precede the expulsion or to continue throughout it. Second, we need to be careful about mixing the metaphors, and it is not clear that the conscious suffering motif is intended to accompany the fire imagery or only the outer darkness imagery. That said, it is certainly possible that Jesus did expand on the Isaianic roots of the image in order to generate an image of those in the fires consciously suffering (cf. Judith 16:17). Once the Isaianic image is interpreted in post-mortem terms, then it is possible that Jesus pictures the enemies of Yahweh as being resurrected and then judged by fire; and this opens up ways of re-reading Isaiah such that the enemies are conscious as they burn—a truly terrifying image.[21]

It is these Old Testament echoes rather than the often suggested, although unsubstantiated, claim that the Valley of Hinnom was Jerusalem's rubbish-dump that form the basis of the imagery in the Gospels. When Jesus

---

[19] See E. W. Fudge, *The Fire that Consumes: The Biblical Case for Conditional Immortality* (Carlisle: Paternoster, 1994) 62–66.

[20] They are not conscious in Isaiah 66.

[21] Such an expansion also invites a universalist re-re-reading of the Isaiah passage. As we have seen, Isaiah sees no contradiction between the salvation of all (Isa 45 & 66) and the death of God's enemies (Isa 66:24) because the "all" who are saved are "all those who are still living" (see Chapter 3). We have also seen that Paul in Philippians 2 expands on the divine oath that "every knee would bow" and "every tongue confess" to include the living and the dead (Chapter 4). This makes the "all" who would be saved literally everyone. Now if Jesus is doing the same kind of expansion with Isaiah 66 as Paul is doing with Isaiah 45 we have the theological task of resolving the resultant contradiction. Jesus sees the dead as continuing to exist in hell (expanding on Isaiah 66) and Paul sees them as being saved (expanding on Isaiah 45) creating a tension absent in Isaiah. One way of handling such a tension is to suggest that the fire, although it burns until its task is complete, will not burn forever. Thus the very eschatological expansion Jesus employs on Isaiah legitimates limiting the temporal duration of the fires.

spoke of Gehenna, he referred not to the literal valley and (probably) not to literal fires nor literal darkness; but he most certainly did refer to a state of condemnation to be avoided at all costs.

The strongest argument against a universalist interpretation of Jesus' teaching starts by arguing that any adequate interpretation of Jesus' words about final punishment must begin by reading them against the background of beliefs held by his contemporaries.[22] Second Temple Jewish beliefs on the post-mortem fate of those outside salvation are not at all uniform. Some texts seem to anticipate the annihilation of the wicked (e.g., the Dead Sea Scrolls); others seem to envisage them enduring everlasting, conscious torment (e.g., Judith 16:17); whilst yet more seem to envisage both (e.g., 1 Enoch 23:11; 91:19)! However, none of them expected any kind of universal salvation. Thus, when Jesus spoke about the fires of Gehenna, almost everyone who was listening to him would interpret his words as a reference to the *final* state of the lost. Few, if any, of Jesus contemporary listeners would have understood his words as leaving any room for hope for those who find themselves in Gehenna. There is no indication in the Palestinian Targums of anyone escaping the fires of Gehenna, although early Rabbinic Literature does offer evidence that a few important Jews thought that *some* people (not all) would emerge from them. Shammai certainly taught that some in Gehenna would later emerge into life.[23] So far as we can tell, such beliefs were not common; but the very fact that he held them shows that it was certainly possible for a Jewish teacher in that period to hold out hope for redemption from Gehenna. This is important, not because it provides a strong case for thinking that Jesus followed Shammai in this regard (it does nothing of the sort), but rather because it shows that a belief in salvation from Gehenna was not obviously incoherent. That is, it shows that the concept of Gehenna in Second Temple literature was evocative and commonly employed but was highly ambiguous and somewhat flexible. After surveying all the literature, Powys describes it as "a convenient and largely vacuous concept."[24] Gehenna was a place of punishment and fire but beyond that was generally left unexplained. When we find Jesus drawing on the idea of Gehenna, we must remember that it was not a clearly worked out concept. Beyond its being a place of fiery punishment for

---

[22] On which see Powys, *Hell*; R. Bauckham, "Early Jewish Visions of Hell," *JTS* 41 (1990) 357–85; idem, "Life, Death and the Afterlife in Second Temple Judaism," in *Life in the Face of Death: The Resurrection Message of the New Testament*, ed. R. N. Longenecker (Grand Rapids: Eerdmans 1998) 80–95; Reisner, *Jesus and Judgment*, 19–163.

[23] See Powys, *Hell*, 188–90; Reisner, *Jesus and Judgment*, 136; and Allison, "The Problem of Gehenna," p. 62, n. 28 for several rabbinic texts that limit the duration of Gehenna. See also Numbers Rabbah 18:20 which speaks of the deliverance of the sons of Korah from Gehenna after a period.

[24] Powys, *Hell*, 178. See too Allison, "The Problem of Gehenna," 78–81.

the wicked, the details, if anyone wanted to fill them in, were up for grabs. That said, I think that it is quite clear that Jesus' contemporaries would not have thought that he was a universalist of any variety. To the traditionalist this settles the case, but I think that there is more to be said. I want to argue, first of all, that none of Jesus' recorded teachings about Gehenna explicitly affirm the notion that it was everlasting; and nothing Jesus is recorded to have said rules out the possibility that some or all of its inhabitants may at some point come to salvation. I am *not* trying to show that Jesus taught universalism nor that he taught that those in Gehenna could or would be saved, for he did neither.[25] My aim is the much more modest one of showing that what he did teach does not formally contradict universalist claims. This, of course, does not provide any reason to suppose that a universalist interpretation of Gehenna is biblical without substantive additional reasons for embracing such an interpretation. My second task is to show that we do have such reasons.

Did Jesus Affirm the Everlastingness of Gehenna?

Even if I am right about the theological hermeneutic, if Jesus explicitly affirmed the everlasting nature of final punishment found in the traditional views, then my case would be considerably weakened. So, did Jesus explicitly teach that hell is everlasting? There are two main Gospel passages that have often been used to suggest that he did. I suggest that neither passage explicitly teaches an everlasting punishment.

The Rich Man and Lazarus

The parable of the rich man and Lazarus in Luke 16 speaks of a gulf fixed after death between Hades and Abraham's side, and no one can cross over (16:26). At first blush, this seems to spell the end for universalism. Let me simply note that it is not at all clear that it actually does. First, nowhere else does Jesus ever suggest that the coming judgment precedes the end of the age, and the teaching of this parable, consequently, seems somewhat out of joint with Jesus' teachings elsewhere in the gospels. This makes us suspect that Jesus is not representing his own views on the afterlife here so much as using the story to make some other point (on which see later). Second, if we are to suppose that Jesus is talking about what happens after death, then, assuming the parable is consistent with the rest of his teaching, it cannot be about the *final* fate of the damned, for the parable describes the fate of the lost in *Hades* (= *sheol*) and not in *Gehenna*. This parable may, then, describe some inter-

---

[25] With the exception of Mark 9:47-49.

mediate period between death and final judgment.[26] If that is so, then the chasm *may* be fixed up to the Day of Judgment but not *necessarily* afterwards. Third, it has been common amongst Christian commentators in recent years to play down what information about post-mortem existence can be gleaned from this parable in light of its apparent adaptation of a pagan post-mortem story. The story is about wealth and poverty not the afterlife.[27] It is commonly suggested that Jesus made use of a folk myth to make his point without actually endorsing the myth itself. This is brought out in the Evangelical Alliance (UK) report on Hell:

> From a literary critical perspective, most now recognise that it is based on a well-established Near Eastern folk tale, of which several versions had been produced in Jewish Literature at the time, and in which the central concerns were avarice, stewardship and pride rather than the mechanics of heaven and hell.[28]

Giving some detail about one recent interpretation will show that we need to be very cautious about using this parable in constructing doctrine about the fate of the unsaved. David Powys begins by noting that the parable is the climax of a sustained attack on Pharisaic life and thought that runs throughout chapter 16. Indeed the Pharisaic connection reaches back to chapter 14, which is set in the house of a Pharisee. Chapter 15 has three salvation parables given as a response to "the mutterings of the Pharisees." Chapter 16 then engages in direct attack on Pharisaic piety. Part of that critique is the claim that the Pharisees were lovers of money (*philaguroi*) (16:14). Powys suggests that the story of the Rich man and Lazarus continues this critique by challenging the very foundations of Pharisaic piety—the belief that piety would guarantee entrance to paradise. The rich man is a *philaguroi* (a lover of money) as the Pharisees were earlier described. This, given the context, strongly suggests that the rich man is a Pharisee. Indeed "the whole scenario conformed to Pharisaic expectation, save in one respect: the Pharisee was standing in the place meant for the unrighteous, and the unclean and presumably unrighteous beggar was in the place meant for the righteous."[29] Contrary to his expectations the rich man finds himself not in paradise but in torment in Hades.[30] The eschatology

---

[26] "Hades . . . comes increasingly to include the idea of a preliminary experience of what is to be the individual's ultimate fate at the final judgment (2 Esd 7:80; 1 Enoch 22:11; cf. Jude 6-7; 1 Pet 3:19)." John Nolland, *Luke 9:21—18:34*, WBC 35B (Dallas: Word, 1993) 829.

[27] On this see Bauckham, "The Rich Man and Lazarus: The Parable and the Parallels," *New Testament Studies* 37 (1991) 225–46. So too C. F. Evans, *Saint Luke* (London: SCM; Philadelphia: Trinity, 1990) 614.

[28] *The Nature of Hell*, 81.

[29] Powys, *Hell*, 224.

[30] Powys sees Hades here as a synonym for Gehenna used for satirical understatement.

of the parable is one of "immediate, automated post-mortem compensation, a commonplace in Pharisaic teaching, but foreign to the teachings of Jesus as reported elsewhere."[31]

> The purpose of the story was not to affirm the reality of Gehenna, but rather to demonstrate the inadequacy of Pharisaic piety, and to do this by means of the system of concepts which gave that piety its rationale. "Gehenna," "reward and punishment" and "the world to come" were paraded not to affirm them as true, but to lampoon them as incapable of promoting true faithfulness. . . . If this interpretation of the rich man and Lazarus is accepted, it must be concluded that the story has no bearing on the question of the fate of the unrighteous, save as a protest against the Pharisaic treatment of the question with its concepts of "the World to Come," automated judgment, reward and punishment and "Gehenna." Its purpose was to call the Pharisees to repentance.[32]

To Powys, the parable is an *ad hominem* argument by Jesus against the Pharisees. Jesus adopts the eschatology of the Pharisees in order to lampoon their pseudo piety.[33] If this is so, then we learn nothing about the afterlife from the parable.

The Sheep and the Goats

Matthew 25:31-46 is the classic text, as far as establishing the eternality of hell goes. Jesus sets two fates in parallel: "eternal life" (*zōēn aiōnion*) and "eternal punishment" (*kolasin aiōnion*) (25:46). If the "*eternal* life" is everlasting, then, it is argued, so is the "*eternal* punishment." "Eternal" cannot mean one thing when applied to life and another when applied to punishment. Case closed. Or is it?

The question is, What does *aiōnios* mean in this context? Does it mean "everlasting"? The translation of *aiōnios* has been the subject of numerous studies in recent years, but there seems to be a strong case for maintaining that it means "pertaining to an age" and often refers not just to any age but to "the age to come" (cf. Heb 6:2; 9:12). Thus "eternal life" may be better translated as "the life of the age to come" and "eternal punishment" as "the

---

Distinctively Pharisaic terminology ("world to come," "reward and punishment," "Gehenna," "Gan Eden," "judgment") are missing from the parable but this, according to Powys, is masterly understatement as the *concepts* are clearly present.

[31] Powys, *Hell*, 225.

[32] Ibid., 227.

[33] Powys, *Hell*, 218–28.

punishment of the age to come."[34] But if this is so, then it is no longer obvious that the punishment is everlasting. True, the age to come is everlasting, but that does not necessitate that the punishment of the age to come lasts for the duration of that age, simply that it occurs during that age and is appropriate for that age. Some reply that if the punishment of the age to come is not everlasting, then neither is the life of the age to come. The reasoning here is clearly fallacious, for one cannot infer from the claim that the punishment of the age to come is not everlasting that the life of the age to come is not everlasting. Chris Marshall claims that "the point is not that the fire will burn forever, or the punishment extend forever, or that the life continue forever, but rather that all three will serve to establish the rule of God."[35] This text does not clarify the duration of either the punishment or the life, but texts like 1 Corinthians 15:42-44 clearly establish the indestructible nature of resurrection life.

So Jesus never explicitly affirmed those aspects of traditional Jewish belief that taught that the final punishment was everlasting. Of course, this cannot be used to show that he denied such claims. He simply never comments one way or the other. Obviously, as the traditionalists maintain, the default assumption should be that he did believe in everlasting punishment (understood as either eternal conscious torment or annihilation) *unless we have good reason to think otherwise*. The traditionalist is correct about that. But we *do* have reason to think otherwise.

My contention is that the arguments of Chapters 1–5 and the theological guidelines at the start of this chapter provide the biblical and theological reasons for rejecting an interpretation of Jesus' teaching that does not allow for redemption from hell. These are the reasons for exploiting the fact that Jesus' claims about Gehenna do not explicitly affirm its identity as a state beyond hope of redemption. Any interpretation of Gehenna must be compatible with the claim that God is love and would never act in a way towards a person that was not ultimately compatible with what is best for that person. Any interpretation of Gehenna as a punishment must be compatible with the claim that divine punishment is more than retributive but has a corrective intention as well (for divine punishment of the sinner must be compatible with, and an expression of, God's love for that sinner). Any interpretation of Gehenna must be compatible with God's ultimate triumph over sin and the fulfilment of his loving purpose of redeeming all his creatures. It is these kinds of teachings found in Scripture, combined with the fact that, as we have seen, the author of Revelation was quite capable of appropriating very strong language and imagery about the destiny of the lost and then portray-

---

[34] See the discussion in Fudge, *Fire,* chap. 2.

[35] Marshall, *Beyond Retribution,* 292.

ing the inhabitants of the lake of fire as entering salvation, that give us very good reasons for understanding Jesus' teaching about Gehenna in such a way as to allow for redemption from that state.

"But," the traditionalist will object, "if Jesus did not believe that Gehenna was everlasting, then we would have expected him to make that clear, because he cannot have expected anyone to guess it. Why would Jesus not clarify matters if he knew his listeners would think he referred to their final destiny?"

The purpose of most of the hell texts is to serve as a warning to avoid it at all costs. That is what God wished to accomplish by means of Jesus' words, and, *in such a communicative context,* to add a "p.s., it'll work out OK in the end" was not only unnecessary but also counter-productive. Consider how often Old Testament prophets warned of God's judgment on Israel to urge the people to avoid it. In such contexts one rarely hears a message of restoration, but such restoration invariably came and was spoken of *when the context required it.* Let us suppose, for argument's sake, that universalism is true. Perhaps God could tolerate certain misunderstandings about hell in certain contexts in which clarification would have undermined the rhetorical force of his message. What God affirms about the accepted views of hell would be appropriated and sanctioned by him. What God does not comment on about the standard view can be presumed to be sanctioned by him *unless we have reason from other biblical texts to think that God would not sanction them.* The universalist would argue that we do indeed have evidence from other parts of God's revelation that would lead us to conclude that he does not endorse the aspect of standard views of hell according to which it is the *final* destiny of the damned. So it should not be too surprising that Jesus did not clear up the confusion at the time. We also need to recall, as Tom Talbott reminds us, that there were many important truths that Jesus did not explicitly teach his disciples during his earthly ministry but which became clearer in the following years—truths they were not ready for at the time (John 16:12). He asks us to consider how difficult it was for the early Christians to come to terms with the grace of God extending to the Gentiles in the way that it did and then points out how much more scandalous the idea of universal salvation may have been. We should not suppose that, because Jesus did not explicitly teach universal salvation or explicitly repudiate the idea that many people would never experience salvation, universalism is an un-Christian idea incompatible with Jesus' ministry. If later revelation leads in universalist directions, as I have argued it does, then we need to understand the ministry of Christ in that light. It is the whole canonical story that we examined in Chapters Two to Four that forms the broader theological context within which we must understand Jesus' teachings about Gehenna, and it is that very context that serves to modify some of the understandings of it common in Jesus' own day.

To this we need to add that there is a hint within the recorded teaching of Jesus that he was modifying the traditional teaching about Gehenna in the kinds of ways I have suggested. In Mark 9:42-50 we read one of Jesus' stern warnings about avoiding the fires of Gehanna. It climaxes with the words, ". . . to be cast into the hell, where 'their worm does not die, and the fire is not quenched.' For (*gar*) everyone will be salted with fire." The words "*for* everyone will be salted with fire" are offered as an explication of the comments about Gehenna. The verse has long perplexed commentators, but it seems to indicate that the fires of Gehenna function as a place of purification. Presumably, if *everyone* must pass through eschatological fire to enter the Kingdom (compare Matt 3:11), then Gehenna is only one mode of such purification and, clearly, the mode to avoid at all costs. Perhaps the alternative to fire is the metaphorical removing of the hand and eye to avoid sinning mentioned in the immediate context. The picture would then be as follows: "one must take the fiery and ruthless road of avoiding sin or one will find oneself in the terrible fires of Gehenna. For everyone will be purified by fire one way or the other, whether now or in hell. The better route is clear." However, if it is the case that Gehenna functions as a *purifying* fire, then, although it is best not to go that route, the route itself will lead to the kingdom eventually. Craig Evans says that the purifying fire mentioned in 9:49 is a different fire from that mentioned in the previous verses.[36] The reasoning for this is that Gehenna could not be purifying, as there is no escape from it. However, apart from begging the question, this interpretation stumbles over two matters. First, Jesus says that "*everyone* will be salted with fire." On Evans' interpretation, only the believers are *salted* with fire, whilst the rest are destroyed by fire. Second, Jesus clearly indicates by the use of the word "for" (*gar*) that the comments about being salted with fire are intended as a fuller comment about verses 42-48, which clearly refer to the fires of Gehenna. It is very hard not to see the purifying fire in v. 49 as, at least in part, a reference to Gehenna in v. 48. However, I am willing to admit that this saying is not entirely unambiguous, and I do not want to suggest that it alone can carry the burden of driving us to a universalist reading of hell.

Paul on Hell

We cannot deal with every New Testament text about final punishment, but it will be advantageous to deal with a few crucial passages. Paul clearly sees humanity as divided into two groups, those who are being saved and those

---

[36] Craig A. Evans, *Mark 8:27—16:20*, WBC 34B (Nashville: Nelson, 2001) 73.

who are perishing (2 Cor 2:14-17; 1 Cor 1:18), and sees eternal life and wrath as the alternative eschatological destinies laid before such groups (Rom 2:7-8).

It is important to see that often Paul does not mitigate his warnings of final judgment and that this could lead his interpreters to suppose that the division between lost and saved is final and eternal. However, as Sven Hillert points out, such comments often come in passages in which Paul is seeking to persuade his readers of his position and to mitigate the warnings might weaken his argument. In other words, Paul *may*, and Hillert is very cautious here, often have strategic contextual reasons rather than theological ones for not limiting his comments on the division between lost and saved.[37] What is interesting is that in other contexts Paul does mitigate his warnings of final division. For instance, the incestuous man in 1 Corinthians 5:1-5 is handed over to Satan for the destruction of his flesh, a threat that sounds final; but this is immediately limited by the words, "so that his spirit may be saved in the day of the Lord." Again, in 1 Corinthians 6:9 ff. the ungodly fail to inherit the kingdom of God, but Paul then adds that the readers themselves once fell into this category, indicating that one can move from being someone who will not inherit the kingdom to someone who will. In Romans 9 we saw the division within Israel between those "elect according to grace" and those who are "objects of his wrath fitted for destruction." This division looks very final, but Romans 11 demonstrates it to be temporary. This serves as a warning to those who move too quickly from Paul's claims about an *apparently* final division between lost and saved to a traditional doctrine of hell. The fact that he may have envisaged the division as temporary is hinted at by (a) the fact that he has rhetorical reasons not to limit the division is certain contexts; (b) the fact that in contexts in which such strategic reasons are not present he does sometimes limit the division; and (c) as already discussed, in other contexts Paul can make apparently universalist claims, which further suggest that he saw the division as one that would eventually be overcome.

There is only one passage in Paul that, at first sight, really does seem to teach that the damnation of sinners is irreversible: 2 Thessalonians 1:6-10.

> God is just: He will pay back trouble to those who trouble you and give relief to you who are troubled, and to us as well. This will happen when the Lord Jesus is revealed from heaven in blazing fire with his powerful angels. He will punish those who do not know God and do not obey the gospel of our Lord Jesus. *They will be punished with everlasting destruction and shut out from the presence of the Lord and from the majesty of his power* on the day he comes to be glorified in his holy

---

[37] Hillert, *Limited and Universal Salvation,* chap. 4.

people and to be marveled at among all those who have believed. This
includes you, because you believed our testimony to you.

The key verse is v. 9, italicized above. I will set aside, for the sake of argument,
Perriman's approach to the text, according to which it is not about *future*
(from our perspective) judgment at all but, instead, is about an anticipated
historical judgment on those who persecuted the church in the first century.[38] Taking the majority view that this does refer to a still-future Coming
of Christ, I can do no better here than simply to note two things.

First, the Greek text is probably better translated, "They will be punished with eternal destruction *that comes from* the presence of the Lord" rather than "eternal destruction *and shut out from* the presence of the Lord," as
most translations have. The Greek simply says, "they will be punished with
eternal destruction *from* (*apo*) the presence of the Lord." The word *apo* could
be translated as "away from" (which is how many translations take it—as the
NIV quoted above)[39] or "coming from," depending on the context. Following
Gene Green[40] and Tom Talbott, I suggest that the context favors the translation "coming from"—the destruction comes from the presence of Jesus.[41]
Talbott sums up: "The presence of the Lord in flaming fire, the glory of his
power, is *the source of,* or that which brings about, the destruction of the wicked."[42] So this passage does not envisage any eternal *separation* from God.

Second, the punishment is "eternal destruction" (*olethron aiōnion*). How
are we to understand this expression? Well, we note first that the adjective
aiōnion suggests that the destruction referred to is the "destruction of the age
to come" (not *everlasting* destruction), and thus the phrase need not carry any
connotations of eternal conscious suffering. Second, the word *olethron* can
mean "ruin" or "destruction," depending on the context. If the phrase is best
translated as "the ruin of the coming age," one could suggest that we understand it in much the same way as the "punishment of the coming age" was
interpreted in our discussion of parable of the sheep and the goats. So Paul
affirms that they will experience the ruin of the age to come, but this need
not be their *perpetual* fate. In the context Paul is simply pointing out that
those who have persecuted the Christians will not get away with it but will be

[38] Perriman, *The Coming of the Son of Man.*

[39] See Abraham J. Malherbe, *The Letters to the Thessalonians,* AB 32B (New York: Doubleday, 2000) 403 for a defense.

[40] G.L. Green, *The Letter to the Thessalonians* (Leicester: Apollos; Grand Rapids: Eerdmans, 2002) 292.

[41] Another possibility is that *apo* is causal—the Lord bringing ruin "*by* his presence and glory" (C. G. Findlay, *A Critical and Exegetical Commentary on St Paul's Epistles to the Thessalonians* [Boston: Gould & Lincoln, 1891] 150).

[42] Talbott, *Inescapable,* 94.

punished at the appearing of the Lord. He has no interest in this context in discussing whether a future salvation is available for them or not. Such questions cannot be settled by the exegesis of this verse. However, the arguments of some commentators that the phrase refers to "eternal ruin" rather than "eternal destruction" are less than convincing and leave the issue somewhat open. The word *olethron*[43] is found in the New Testament only in Paul. Apart from the passage under consideration, Paul uses the word in a passage in 1 Thessalonians 5:3 about the return of Christ. He says, "While people are saying, 'Peace and safety,' destruction (*olethros*) will come on them suddenly, as labor pains on a pregnant woman, and they will not escape." In v. 9 this fate is described as "wrath" and opposed to "salvation." This is the clearest parallel use to 2 Thessalonians 1:9, but it is equally ambiguous. Similarly ambiguous is 1 Timothy 6:9, which warns, "People who want to get rich fall into temptation and a trap and into many foolish and harmful desires that plunge men into ruin and destruction (*olethron*)." The final use of *olethron*, in 1 Corinthians 5:5, seems to refer to annihilation rather than mere ruin, but it is in a particularly interesting context. Paul writes to the Corinthians to direct them in how they should discipline a member of the church who has been involved in an immoral sexual relationship and, presumably, is unrepentant. He says that they are to "hand this man over to Satan, so that the sinful nature may be destroyed (*olethron*) and his spirit saved on the day of the Lord." Paul is urging them to hand the man over to a very harsh punishment that would destroy his sinful nature (probably some sort of exclusion from the community, but it is not totally clear what he had in mind). The destruction experienced by the man was an annihilation of his sinful nature, not of his humanity or his existence. *The destruction was intended for his own good and salvation.* Now I do not want to suggest that one can simply suppose that the destruction of the sinful believer in 1 Corinthians 5 was of the same kind as that experienced by the persecutors of the church in 2 Thessalonians 1:9 simply because Paul uses the same word. Clearly, there are differences in the context. For a start, we are speaking of a believer in Corinthians and non-believers in Thessalonians. We are speaking of a destruction of the sinful nature in 1 Corinthians, whilst in Thessalonians no such qualification is offered. In 1 Corinthians the destruction is so that the man may be saved when the Lord returns, whilst in 2 Thessalonians the destruction occurs when the Lord returns. However, we should note that Paul could conceive of a destruction that was ultimately good for the person concerned, even if it was painful at

---

[43] *olethros* occurs four times and only in Paul (1 Cor 5:5; 1 Thess 5:3; 2 Thess 1:9; 1 Tim 6:9), *olethreuōn* and *olethreutou* are found in Heb 11:28 and 1 Cor 10:10, and *exolethreuthēsetai* is found in Acts 3:23. The words are used only of persons.

the time.[44] Is it conceivable that 2 Thessalonians 1:9 leaves a space for understanding the "eternal destruction" as a similar kind of annihilation, even in light of the discontinuities between the two cases? Tom Talbott argues that it does, and he proposes that we think of 2 Thessalonians 1:9 in terms of a destruction of the sinful nature that brings about its complete annihilation and thus ultimately serves as an agent of redemption.[45] He concedes that nothing in the passage requires such an interpretation but thinks that nothing precludes it either. I have to say that there is nothing in the immediate context to suggest his interpretation. In context, Paul is not interested in redemptive destruction/ruin but retributive destruction/ruin. It is most unlikely, to my mind, that Paul was thinking of this ruin as a means of grace when he wrote. However, that is not to say that Talbott is wrong to interpret it in such a way, so long as he does not claim to be excavating the unspoken thoughts running through Paul's head. It seems to me that Talbott is saying that in the broader contours of Paul's theology *we readers* could understand his comments here with the kinds of qualifications Talbott mentions. Perhaps all that Paul had in mind when he wrote was the retributive punishment of the enemies of the church, and perhaps he expressed this in pretty final-looking terms. However, Talbott could still legitimately claim to have an authentically Pauline interpretation of the text if it were such that, were one able to sit down with Paul and discuss the issue with him, he would agree that the qualifications did bring out the fuller dimensions of his theology, even though he never had them in mind when he wrote. Talbott could answer the question, "Would Paul agree with your interpretation?" with the reply, "He would if I had an hour to discuss it with him." The question then becomes whether Paul would agree with Talbott's interpretation or with the suggestion that I tentatively made earlier about "the ruin of the age to come." I believe that he would side with me, for the kinds of reasons set out in chapters 2–4; but it is here, in the broader arena of Pauline theology, that the debate would need to be settled. Second Thessalonians 1:9 remains a problem text for universalists, but it is not so unambiguous and overwhelming that it seriously undermines the case for universalism. As I explained in chapter 1, every theological system has its problem texts; and, in this respect, universalism is no different from Calvinism, Arminianism, or any other "ism."

---

[44] We ought also to note that in Pauline theology salvation from sin comes through identification with Christ's death—the believer is one whose old self has been crucified with Christ, has died and been buried in baptism (Rom 6:1-13). A Christian is, to Paul, a person who has died and been reborn. The new life of the resurrection is not possible without the *destruction* of the old nature.

[45] Thomas Talbott, *The Inescapable Love of God*, (Boca Raton, La.: Universal, 1999) 92–98.

Conclusion

I have argued that, within a canonical context and a broader biblical theology, it is possible to interpret the biblical passages about hell as references to a terrible *but temporary* fate. I believe that New Testament writers took pre-existing language and ideas about everlasting damnation; but, by using them within a Christian theological framework, they reshaped such language by connecting it with a set of ideas that serve to starve traditional interpretations of oxygen. It is my belief that, by not allowing the Christian theological context within which such language was co-opted to reshape its meaning, traditional Christian theology has had to tolerate excruciating tensions and inner contradictions. If we recognize that the Bible writers could take up categories and language from host cultures and reshape them by using them in new theological contexts, then we have a way of making sense of the apparent tensions between the hell texts and other texts.[46]

---

[46] While one could always turn the tables and use the hell texts to subvert the grace texts such a hermeneutic seems clearly inferior from the perspective of Christian theology.

CHAPTER SEVEN

The Advantages of Christian Universalism & Replies to Remaining Objections

I am not pessimistic because I believe that the history of the human race, no matter how tragic, will ultimately lead to the Kingdom of God. I am convinced that all the works of humankind will be reintegrated in the work of God, and that each one of us, no matter how sinful, will ultimately be saved.

—Jacques Ellul[1]

IN THIS final chapter I aim to clarify some of the advantages that I think Christian universalism has. I shall cover the following points.

(a) Christian Universalism makes the problem of evil less difficult.

(b) Christian Universalism enables us to hold together important biblical teachings that pull apart when one holds to a traditional view of hell.

(c) Christian Universalism adds an inspirational dimension to our ecclesiology, worship, and mission.

(d) Christian Universalism has significant pastoral benefits.

In the process of discussing such benefits we shall also try to respond to common objections to Christian universalism.

---

[1] Jacques Ellul, *Perspectives on Our Age: Jacques Ellul Speaks on his Life and Work* (Toronto: Canadian Broadcasting Corporation, 1981) 104.

Advantage 1: Universalism and the Problem of Evil

The Problem of Recompense

It is often a thought of some considerable comfort to those suffering that if the injustices they suffer are not rectified in the present age, they will be in the life to come. The sufferings of the present will be more than made up for in the glories of the new age. A deep worry about the traditional Christian views on hell is that the implication of them is that very many people who suffer terrible injustices in this life, indeed perhaps most of them, will *not* actually have those wrongs righted in the life to come. In fact they will find that, as far as their suffering goes, they will leap out of the frying pan into the fire. Instead of finding any compensation they will find divine condemnation. Universalism avoids this problem and allows us to expect ultimate divine comfort for all the victims of this world.

Irenaean Theodicies: John Hick

One of the ways Christians have tried to deal with the problem of evil is by appeal to what is often referred to as Irenaean theodicies. According to this family of responses to evil, at least part of God's reason for allowing evil is that it can play a constructive role in shaping human character. Suffering presents opportunities for growth and can, in part, be justified, because it leads to a greater good. There are countless stories of people who can testify to having learned much from the sufferings that they have endured and, in retrospect, can see God's hand in allowing them to go through it. However, it is clear that without universalism such theodicies are often problematic. Consider the following example: a mother is driving her thirteen year old daughter to a friend's party when a truck coming towards them loses control and smashes into their car, injuring both the mother and the girl. After some weeks in intensive care the daughter dies. Although the mother escapes, she suffers terrible depression as a result of the trauma and loss she has experienced. In her despair she turns to God and, through the friendship of some Christians, becomes a believer in Christ. Clearly God has used her suffering to bring her to salvation, and this is certainly a great good that has come of the suffering. But what of her daughter? Her suffering and death was part of a chain of events that God used to bring her mother to salvation, but does this serve to justify her suffering if she herself receives no benefit? Her sufferings do not help shape *her* character and contributes nothing to the making of *her* soul. Indeed, on traditional modes of thinking, her suffering and death take away from her any further opportunities for salvation. If the mother says that God allowed her daughter to die because it was the key to her turning to the Lord,

it looks very much like God is not treating her daughter as a person valuable
in her own right, but merely as a means to someone else's good. Now this
problem is easily removed on universalism, because the daughter's suffering
and death can also be used by God for her own salvation after death. Thus,
God can use the suffering of any person to contribute not simply to the good
of others but also to their own good. It is no coincidence that John Hick, one
of the chief contemporary exponents of Irenaean theodicies, is a universalist.[2]
For Hick, universalism is an essential component of the "soul making" theodicy. Without it, the theodicy becomes considerably more awkward. This is
not to suggest that the "soul making" theodicy is without problems or that it
can do all of the work necessary to explain evil. Clearly it has its limits, but it
is still a resource Christians may well want to have recourse to; and universalism makes such appeals considerably easier.

Horrendous Evils and the Goodness of God: Marilyn Adams

Another leading Christian philosopher to write creatively on evil and suffering is Marilyn Adams; and, as with Hick, universalism is essential to her
approach. Adams is especially concerned with what she called horrendous
evils—that is,

> evils the participation in which . . . constitutes prima facie reason to
> doubt whether the participant's life could . . . be a great good to him/
> her on the whole . . . . What makes horrendous evils so pernicious
> is their life-ruining potential, their power prima facie to degrade the
> individual by devouring the possibility of positive personal meaning
> in one swift gulp.[3]

Such evils, which seem to rip the heart of meaning from a life, provide reason
to doubt God's goodness towards any individual whom he allows to experience them. It may be that one could argue that by allowing such evils, God
does create a better world overall and that those who suffer horrendous evils
may be a necessary sacrifice for the benefit of the whole system. However,
Adams responds:

> A cosmic creator and/or governor who operated with such reasons
> alone would not thereby be one who placed a high value on human
> personhood in general or individual persons in particular. On the
> contrary, such government would thereby show itself to be at best
> indifferent, at worst cruel. Rather, I contend that God could be said

---

[2] John Hick, *Evil and the God of Love* (London: Macmillan; New York: Harper & Row,
1966).

[3] Marilyn M. Adams, *Horrendous Evils and the Goodness of God* (Ithaca: Cornell University
Press, 1999) 26, 27–28.

to value human personhood in general, and to love individual humans persons in particular, only if God were *good* to each and every
human person God created. And Divine *goodness* to created persons
involves the distribution of harms and benefits, not merely globally,
but also within the context of the individual person's life. At a mini-
mum, God's goodness to human individuals would require that God
guarantee each a life that was a great good to him/her on the whole by
balancing off serious evils. To value the individual qua person, God
would have to go further to defeat any horrendous evil in which s/he
participated by giving it a positive meaning through organic unity
with a great enough good *within the context of his/her life.*[4]

Sacrificing some individuals for the benefit of the system is not the action of
a God who values individuals. If God values individual persons, he will act
with goodness towards them; and this requires, first, that he brings about, a
better balance of good over evil for every individual and, further, that any
horrendous evils experienced by an individual would have to be defeated.
When Adams speaks of horrendous evils being defeated within the context
of the life of an individual, she means that God would ensure that the evil is
situated in the context of, and organically related to, a life that, when looked
at *as a whole*, is a accepted as a good life.[5] That is to say that evil must be re-
seen in a context that alters the way we make sense of it such that our understanding of its significance changes. Adams also insists that each individual
must come to recognize at least some of the positive meanings for their lives
to be considered a great good *to them* on the whole. Evil has not been defeated in the life of an individual if she or he cannot see that it has been. God
is the meaning-maker, who enables each person to heal and helps him or her
see meaning in life when considered as a whole.[6] Indeed, some horrors are so
ruinous that only the infinite goodness of God offers any hope for the reversal
and defeat of such evils.[7] God knows how to defeat evil by weaving it into
many good and creative plots. Ultimately it is only in relationship with God
that horrendous evil is overcome. So by integrating horrendous evil into one's
relationship with God, one confers a positive aspect upon such experiences.[8]

---

[4] Ibid., 30–31.

[5] This does not mean that the unjust act is transformed into a just one or the evil act into a
good one. The horror remains forever a horror.

[6] Ibid., 82.

[7] Ibid., 82–83.

[8] Human response when confronting evil ought to be, first of all, to take measures to prevent
it when it threatens and to try to stop it when in the midst of it. When it is *fait accompli* we can
try to make good on it or balance it off or, most profoundly, we can try to defeat it by turning
it to good (ibid., 181–82).

> Retrospectively, I believe, from the vantage point of heavenly beati-
> tude, human victims of horrors will recognize those experiences as
> points of identification with the crucified God, and not wish them
> away from their life histories. God's becoming a blasphemy and a
> curse for us will enable human perpetrators of horrors to accept and
> forgive themselves. For they will see, first of all, that these acts did not
> separate them from the love of God who thus identified with them
> on the cross . . . They will also be reassured by the knowledge that
> God has compensated their victims (once again through Divine iden-
> tification and beatific relationship). Finally, they will be amazed and
> comforted by Divine resourcefulness, not only to engulf and defeat,
> but to force horrors to make positive contributions to God's redemp-
> tive plan.[9]

Clearly punishing the perpetrators of horrendous evils in hell forever and ever
is not going to overcome horrendous evils in the lives of the victims, and it
would certainly not be a display of God's goodness to the criminals. Eternal
conscious torment contributes *nothing* to God's purposes of redeeming creation. In fact, it would "only multiply evil's victories."[10]

God, in Adams' view, has no obligations at all to creatures.[11] However,
divine goodness and love do require that God not assign creatures vocations
that *permanently* crush them. Hell, as traditionally conceived, removes any
possibility of God's overcoming the evils participated in by any individuals
sent there and must surely represent the eternal frustration of his loving purposes for them. Divine goodness requires universalism.

> My criterion is universalist in insisting that God be good to each cre-
> ated person. Given the ruinous power of horrors, I think . . . that it
> would be cruel for God to create . . . human beings with such radical

---

[9] Ibid., 167. It is important to note that Adams does not envision "postmortem cries of
'*felix culpa!*' or [imagine that] participants in horrors would ever think it reasonable to have
consented to them in advance as constituent and/or instrumental means to the goods God
brings from them. We are too small and horrors too great for that!" (ibid., 203). Her point is
that *looking back* from their beatific state of enlightenment, participants would be brought to
the point of accepting the horrors they have experienced and no longer wishing to erase them
from their lives for they now perceive a positive meaning in them. For an excellent discussion
of "irredeemable evil" and the place of heaven in theodicy see Jerry Walls, *Heaven: The Logic of
Eternal Joy* (New York: Oxford University Press, 2002) chap. 5.

[10] Adams, *Horrendous Evils*, 43.

[11] Unusually Adams does not engage in any attempt to justify God's allowing evil. In her
estimation horrors are too big to be rectified by justice and God is too big to be networked
into our systems of rights and obligations (ibid., 188)—God has no obligations to us and
thus does not need a moral justification for allowing evil. Thus she seeks no morally sufficient
reason why God permits evil.

> vulnerability to horrors, unless Divine power stood able, and Divine
> love willing, to redeem.[12]

I do not wish to endorse every element of Adams' approach, but it seems
to me that she is essentially right when she says that it is not enough to
show that the horrendous evils experienced by some can bring benefits to the
world *as a whole* or certain other individuals in it. Of course, the sufferings of
Hitler's victims have led to some good things that would not otherwise have
happened; but if that is all that we have to say, then it can look very much
like God allows the irreparable destruction of some people merely as a means
to the blessings of other people. Such behavior is incompatible with God's
loving *all individuals*. It is hard to think how God could be said to love a person he allows to be *irreparably* harmed for the good of some third party. I am
inclined to say with Tom Talbott that if God loves his creatures, he will not
allow them to experience *irreparable* harm. Adams is correct, I think, to argue
that God's goodness requires that he seek the defeat of evil in the lives of all
his individual creatures, and this purpose is clearly frustrated by traditional
view of hell.

   Not all would agree that universalism helps the Christian to handle the
problem of evil less awkwardly. Indeed, Michael Murray has argued that universalism of the kind I have defended accentuates the problem of evil. He
suggests that this earthly life seems to be rather ineffective at bringing people
to salvation. Perhaps the majority of people die without receiving eternal life
through Christ. According to those such as Thomas Talbott, hell seems to be
an excellent environment in which to find salvation, because all the masses of
people who are sent there end up saved. "Obviously the post-mortem state
in which most turn to God is vastly better suited for the conversion of the
unregenerate. But if so, why not create us all *ab initio* in this latter state?"[13]
Whilst Murray admits that this does not undermine universalism as such, it
does suggest that the earthly phase of human existence is something of an
enigma to universalists. The sufferings of this life seem very ineffective at
producing salvific fruit, so why not skip them and go straight to the outer
darkness, where we can all be saved? The worry is that for the universalist the
sufferings of this life seem inexplicable and pointless, making the problem of
evil even more acute.

   In response we must stress that the universalist need not concede the
point that this life is ineffective at bringing people to salvation. It is perfectly
intelligible for a universalist to suggest that this life makes an important,
perhaps essential, contribution towards salvation for most people, perhaps

---

[12] Ibid., 157.

[13] M. Murray, "Three Versions of Universalism," *F&Ph* 16.1 (1999) 62 [55–68].

even all people. That the majority of people do not embrace salvation in this life does not mean that their experiences now do not lay a foundation for a later acceptance of it. It could well be that without the experiences in this life salvation would take much longer to be attained in the post-mortem state. Indeed, there is something rather absurd about the proposal that God ought to create people in hell so that they will be saved. Hell is supposed to be a punishment for wrongdoing, but in this supposedly efficient scenario people have not even had the opportunity to act wrongly. I understand hell to be a post-mortem situation in which God brings home to us the terrible consequences of sin, and this makes sense for someone who has lived a sinful life and needs such an education. However, sending people direct to hell makes no sense whatsoever. How would the terrible sufferings educate them in the consequences of a sinful lifestyle they had never even adopted? Indeed, it is not clear how it would lead to salvation; and, even if it did, God would seem to have simply tortured people into heaven. The sufferings of this life, then, may well play a positive contribution towards the salvation of those who so suffer, and the present life is no odder to a universalist than a non-universalist.[14]

Advantage 2: Universalism and the Coherence of Christian Theology

One of the greatest advantages of Christian universalism is that it seems to remove some of the stark tensions between certain widely held Christian beliefs and to produce a more coherent Christian theology. For instance, universalists are able to affirm with many other Christians that God loves all  people and desires to save them and to that end sent his Son and his Spirit to effect this plan. However, they are also able to maintain, along with many other Christians, that God will succeed in achieving all his purposes. Clearly, the only way in which both beliefs can be accepted in any robust form is if everyone is saved in the end. As we saw in Chapter One, accepting the reality of eternal hell requires that one either deny that God does love all and desire to save them (Augustinianism/Calvinism) or that God will achieve *all* his purposes (Freewill theism). The first denial seems to me to be profoundly problematic—the belief that God loves all people, desires to redeem them, and that Christ died to save all people is deeply grounded in a biblical theology and seems to be required by the assertion that God is love. To reject it is not a live option to a great many Christians. The denial that God will achieve all his purposes is less problematic, but one must ask why anyone would want

---

[14] For a detailed response to Murray see Thomas Talbott, "Universalism and the Supposed Oddity of our Earthly Life: Reply to Michael Murray," *F&Ph* 18.1 (2001) 102–9.

to limit the extent of God's power and victory in this way? The answer is that they believe that a strong doctrine of human freedom requires that God allow us to deny him forever; and, thus, God, although he would *like* all people to freely accept him, will not *force* them to do so. Thus, God chooses to limit the exercise of his power to allow people to thwart his purposes for their lives. The Scriptural evidence is a little ambiguous on this issue. At times the Bible seems to speak as if all human choices, for good and evil, are within God's providential control. Human freedom is thus no obstacle to God's achieving his purposes.[15] At other times the Bible speaks as if God's plans are, temporarily at least, hindered by human free choices. It is wise not to be too dogmatic about "the" biblical view on this topic; for, however one tries to construe it, some texts will seem awkward. The matter will need to be settled on theological and philosophical grounds. I argued in Chapter One that one could hold to a non-determinist view of human freedom and still make sense of the claim that God will bring it about that all people freely choose to accept salvation; and, if I am right, this completely removes the grounds for denying that God will achieve his purposes for all people *in the end*. If I am right, there are no good reasons to deny that God wants to save all people *and that he can save all people without violating their freedom*. If this is so, then he will save all people; and that is exactly what I have argued. Universalism thus allows a Christian to affirm coherently and simultaneously two sets of claims that both have strong appeal to those wanting a biblically grounded theology. It allows the best of both theological worlds.

Universalism also allows us to give what seems to me to be a more satisfactory theology of the wrath of God. One constant danger that a traditional doctrine of hell generates is that God's nature is divided up and set in an internal conflict. The theology goes as follows: God loves humanity and wants to save them but at the same time is holy and cannot stand human sin. Being just, he cannot leave such sin unpunished. So God has an internal dilemma: he wants to save us because he is loving, but he also wants to punish us because he is just. God's love and his justice are set in opposition. This analysis produces a conception of divine justice that has no integral link with divine love and a conception of divine love that is disconnected from divine justice. The joy of the redeemed in the new creation is the result of God's love and mercy, whilst the torment of the damned is the result of God's justice (not his love). But surely all God's acts are loving, and surely all his deeds are just. A theology that allowed both heaven and hell to be equally acts of divine love and justice is what we need. Those in hell are experiencing the wrath of God, but such wrath is not the *absence* of divine love but the *severity* of a divine

---

[15] D. A. Carson, *Divine Sovereignty and Human Responsibility: Biblical Perspectives in Tension* (1981; reprinted, Eugene, Ore.: Wipf & Stock, 2002).

has can tell be retributive in a common time framework? If the sinner dies one day before the end do [...]

love that allows the obstinate to experience the consequences of unwise life-
styles with the aim of ultimately redeeming them. God's justice is loving and
his love just, and all the divine attributes cohere without any tension.[16] The
universalism that I have defended in this book promoted this coherence of
the divine nature. God's actions towards humans are at all times just, holy,
wise, loving, and merciful. Hell is a manifestation of divine justice, holiness,
wisdom, love, and mercy. This is not too difficult to see if universalism is true,
but it is very hard to see how one could understand hell in such terms if traditional doctrines of hell are correct. How could tormenting sinners forever
and ever be seen as a loving action?

This observation serves to undercut the common objection that universalists practice *Sachkritik*—criticizing and rejecting one part of the Bible on
the basis of another. Thus, it is said, universalists make much of the biblical
texts about God's love but use them to reject the many texts about God's
justice and fierce punishments. This is a fair criticism of some contemporary
Christian universalists;[17] but, as it stands, this objection does not apply to
the argument in this book. The evangelical universalist has a lot to say about
God's justice and his punishment. She believes in the severity of God, and
she does not shrink from warning of the wrath to come. It is misleading to
suggest that she has some sentimental notion of love that she reads into the
biblical text. She is keen to develop her doctrine of God's love from its revelation in Israel and in Christ mediated via Scripture. She sees that God's love
can manifest itself in blessings but also in curse, for God punishes those he
loves (Heb 12:6; Rev 3:19). To the universalist it is her opponents who err;
for they fail to understand the depth and breadth of God's love revealed in

---

[16] The classical, though now much maligned, doctrine of divine simplicity also suggests such
an analysis. The doctrine of divine simplicity maintains that God cannot be divided into
separate parts. All God's attributes (love, justice, goodness, wisdom and so on) are identical
with each other and with the very being of God (granted, a hard notion to understand!) Thus,
it makes no sense whatsoever to see any of God's actions as manifestations of justice *but not
love* or love *but not justice*. Hell would have to be motivated by divine justice *and love* towards
its inhabitants. To my mind this is very clear so I am somewhat perplexed that those classical
theologians who were the chief defenders of the doctrine (e.g., Aquinas) did not seem to see
the implications it had for their view of hell.

[17] For instance, Ernest Best, after plausibly defending a universalist interpretation of Ephesians
1:10, writes, "as far as early Christianity is concerned it must be allowed that there is also a
strain, a more widely found strain, in Scripture which sees part of creation as finally remaining
outside the love and care of God and Christ, perhaps acknowledging his sovereignty but not
willing to offer any allegiance; where this holds, the stress lies on the defeat of evil and not
its summing up in Christ. The existence of both strains must be accepted, *yet we need to ask
which represents more closely the central drive of the New Testament. Eph 1:10 seems to do so*" (E.
Best, *Ephesians*, ICC [Edinburgh: T. & T. Clark, 1998] 142; italics mine). I find this claim
astonishing in light of the great emphasis placed in the NT on God's judgments.

Scripture, and they fail to see that God's wrath is not the opposite of his love but a manifestation of it. To the universalist, *all* God's acts are acts motivated by holy love.[18]

Objection 1: Universalism Undermines the Severity of Sin and the Righteousness of Judgment

A common concern about universalism is that it would undermine central Christian doctrines. In particular it is often said to undermine the seriousness of sin, of hell, and the righteousness of punishment. We shall briefly consider these concerns in order.

It is not uncommon to hear universalists being criticized for underplaying the power and severity of sin, because they allegedly have too rosy a view of how willingly people will embrace the gospel. The severity of sin is sometimes thought to be underestimated, because they are said to deny that God would be just to punish anyone forever. Let us handle these objections separately.

Must universalists have too rosy a view of how willingly people will embrace the gospel? I see no reason why we should.[19] The universalist could easily believe that sin so corrupts humans that nobody would or could accept the gospel without divine assistance. Indeed, that is what I do believe. All that we need claim is that God will eventually provide such assistance to all.[20]

Must universalists underestimate the severity of sin? Not at all. The suggestion that universalists believe that "people are not really all that bad and that everyone *deserves* to be saved" is absurd. We see sin as utterly offensive to God and harmful to human persons and communities. We do not deny that divine punishment is a fitting response to such behavior. Indeed, I spent much of Chapter 6 arguing that an evangelical universalism *must* have an important place for divine punishment. What makes us universalists is not that we have unusually weak views of sin but unusually strong views of divine love and grace. Where sin abounds grace abounds all the more.

---

[18] Theologian H. H. Farmer complained that theologians traditionally consider God's justice as *absoluta* whilst his mercy is merely *ordinata*. That is to say, whilst God *may* be merciful, he *must* be just. This makes justice and not love the central category for understanding God's relationship with humanity. One needs to ask if Farmer has identified an unscriptural aspect of traditional theology here. Is a more scriptural view one according to which all God's acts are both just and loving?

[19] Even if some of us may, we are certainly not alone in that—plenty of non-universalists err in the same way if error it be.

[20] It also has to be said that arguably some theologians *overplay* human hostility to God. Humanity was made for relationship with God and cannot be complete apart from such a relationship. The spiritual longing this creates is a hunger for the true God even if sin stops us from seeing this clearly. Within all people there is a latent awareness of and hunger for God.

I have argued that eternal conscious torment is not a just response to sin; and, in the eyes of some, this amounts to an underestimate of the severity of sin. I have two responses to that. First, I have already argued that the Anselmian view that all sins incur infinite demerit is terribly problematic. Not only is it hard to justify morally, but one also fails to find it taught in Scripture. Indeed, it seems to run counter to the teaching of Scripture, according to which some sins are worse than others. However, just because I do not think that a sin incurs *infinite* demerit, it does not follow that I deny it incurs *very serious* demerit. Second, even if I am wrong, a universalist could accept the claim that eternal conscious torment is a just punishment for sin—all that they need to argue is that God rescues everyone from such a punishment. In that case, if taking sin seriously requires (as I do *not* think it does) that we accept the justice of everlasting torment, the universalist is just as capable of doing that as the traditionalist.

A related objection is that nothing short of eternal conscious torment counts as taking hell seriously; and, consequently, universalists do not take hell seriously. I mentioned above that a universalist *could* believe that hell is eternal conscious torment, and such a universalist surely does not underestimate hell, even on this severe understanding of it! The critic may reply that a hell that has an exit is not as severe as one with none. Indeed, so perhaps the critic feels that nothing short of eternal conscious torment *with no hope for redemption* amounts to taking hell seriously. If this is so, then we must throw up our hands and confess that we do indeed fail to take hell seriously. But of course, this is absurd. To suppose that one does not take divine punishment seriously unless one construes it in the most maximally awful way possible is just playing games. That is akin to suggesting that the only people who take the dangers of drug-taking seriously are those who suppose that every person who has ever taken drugs will die an inevitable, painful, and lingering death with no hope of deliverance. It is perfectly possible to take hell very seriously without believing that it is as bad as it could possibly be. Clearly one need not construe the consequences of sin or drug taking in a *maximally* bad way to take them seriously. For the universalist, hell is something to be avoided at all costs, just as Jesus warned us. To object by saying, "Well, if hell is not forever, it doesn't really matter if someone has a spell there," is like suggesting that because you will recover from the long and painful illness, it isn't worth taking precautions to avoid it. It is like telling an Old Testament prophet not to bother warning Israel to repent, because God will always restore them after the judgment anyway. The prophet would reply that it is better to avoid the judgment in this first place, and the prophet is surely correct. I wonder if I could pose a counter-question to our critics: "Is it perhaps you who fail to take God's love and grace as seriously as it deserves?"

It seems to me that the only major Christian doctrine threatened by universalism is the teaching that those in hell have passed beyond the point of no return; and, as this belief is quite detachable from the web of Christian belief without doing any damage to the rest of the web, I can only conclude that, although it is a widely held doctrine, it is peripheral in its structural role in Christian theology. It can removed and replaced without doing harm to Christian theology. Indeed, if I am right, once we remove and replace it with a universalist view of hell, we have a much more coherent web of beliefs than we had before.

Advantage 3: Universalism and the Church

The universalist will see the church in much the same ways as the non-universalist. She is Christ's bride, his body, the community of the redeemed, the Temple of the Lord indwelt by his Spirit, the children of God. However, to the universalist, the church is also a microcosm of the age to come. In the church one finds people from every tribe and tongue joined in one body. One day it will not simply be people called out *from* every tribe and nation who love the Lord but the *totality* of every tribe and nation. Our calling is to act as a prophetic sign to the nations representing the destiny of all humanity. When people look at the church, God wants them to see a vision of what redeemed humanity can be—what it will be. This view of the church is a development of the ecclesiology of Colossians, Ephesians, and Revelation. The church is called to be a reconciled humanity that in Christ has transcended all the barriers that fracture human communities. Paul brings out the socio-ethical implications very clearly in his concern that divisions between Jew and Gentile must be transcended in Christ. They are united in Christ. It is a very high calling and both a major challenge and inspiration to our practices. It is a calling rooted in the realized eschatology of the New Testament—the churches experience this reconciliation now as a sign of the fullness in the age to come, when all humanity will be summed up in Christ and reconciled to God and each other. Sadly, we model this reconciliation in very imperfect ways in our churches, and this is both a major failure on our part and an evidence that the fullness is yet to come, even for the church. So this universalist angle on ecclesiology functions as a promise (the church as a prophetic sign to the nations of the future of the world) and a challenge to both the world (be reconciled to God) and the church (live as the reconciled community you already are in Christ).

The vision also connects with the theology and practice of worship. The dream that inspires the universalist is one in which the whole of creation—all creatures great and small—join together in a symphony of worship to their creator. The day when every knee will bow and every tongue will worship is what we long for. To the universalist, the worship of the church in the present age is an eschatological act—a foretaste of the age to come. When we meet together to worship God we are anticipating the day when all creation will love him. So Christian worship is an act of hope and a prophetic sign on the part of those who live by the power of the coming age even in the midst of this present darkness. This universalist doxology is to my mind another advantage to the universalist vision.

The Church embodies in itself God's mission to the world. Just by being itself, it acts as a sign to the world of the salvation achieved in Christ. Mission is not an add-on but is essential to the very identity of the ecclesia. Although mission is much broader than evangelism, it is certainly not narrower; and I would like to reflect briefly on universalism and evangelism. Christian universalists share with non-universalists many of their motivations for gospel proclamation: to obey Christ's command, to save people from the coming wrath, to bring them into living fellowship with the triune God and his church. However, Christian universalists are perhaps more likely to be additionally inspired by a more unusual reason—the vision that in proclaiming the gospel one is playing a part in God's glorious purpose of reconciling the whole of creation (Col 1:20) and summing all things up in Christ (Eph 1:10). Working with the Spirit in bringing about this glorious destiny is a strong motive for evangelism and mission in its broader sense also.

Objection 2: Does Universalism Undermine Evangelism?

A common objection is that universalism undermines the imperative to preach the gospel. This is well expressed by the great Anglican evangelical, J. I. Packer. He writes:

> If all people are, in the title of a 19th century tract, "Doomed to be Saved," then it follows that the decisiveness of decisions made in this life, and the urgency of evangelism here in this life, immediately, are undermined . . . You can see what the missionary implications of this are going to be. What is the main job of the Christian missionary witness? To win men to Christian faith? Or to do something else for them? Universalism prompts the latter view.[21]

A similar objection is made by Jay Wesley Richards. Richards suggests that if we believed in universalism, "it would surely comfort our consciences as Christians. We would not need to worry about the fact that we had not witnessed to our agnostic and unrepentant colleagues at work. We need not

---

[21] J. I. Packer, "The Problem of Universalism Today," in idem, *Celebrating the Saving Work of God* (Carlisle: Paternoster, 1998) 171 [169–78].

fret too much that people are dying in Tibet without ever having heard the name of Jesus Christ."[22] Now, the theme of Christian mission and evangelism is central to the New Testament. If Christian universalism undermines it, then that is a clear indicator that it is incompatible with a biblical theology, and Packer would be right to go on to say that "universalist speculation at the present time is a very great evil, calculated to blight a ministry, and as the older evangelicals used to think, 'guaranteed to ruin souls.'"[23]

But Packer is *not* right. His argument is based on the assumption that the *only* motivation Christians have for evangelism is that if the gospel is not preached, some people will be *eternally* damned. Now, *if* this is the *only* motivation for proclaiming the gospel, then Packer is correct; but surely it is not. Surely, the New Testament provides many other motivations to proclaim the gospel. We believe that people are only saved through faith in the gospel,[24] and how can they believe if they have not been told?—that's one very Pauline reason to proclaim it (Rom 10:13-15). Christ commands it—that's a Matthean reason (Matt 28:18-20). It also serves the glorious purpose of summing up all things in Christ—a very Pauline (or deutero-Pauline) motive (Eph 1:10). In fact, it is a little ironic that Packer, as a five point Calvinist, faces an exactly analogous objection. If God will save the elect anyway, so the objection runs, why bother proclaiming the gospel to them? They will be saved one way or another. Packer's response, and I would agree with him, would be that the way God saves the elect is through the proclamation of the gospel. But if that response saves Calvinism, it will save universalism also; and if the criticism damns universalism it damns Calvinism too.

However, the universalist could have one motivation for evangelism that Packer, as a Calvinist, lacks. Packer believes that all the elect will believe the gospel before they die. The universalist, however, may believe that the people temporally condemned to hell could have been spared that fate had they accepted the gospel.[25] She thus has a possible motivation to proclaim Christ that Packer lacks—to ensure that as few people go to hell as possible. Thus it is wrong to suggest that the Christian universalist need not worry about

---

[22] Richards, "A Pascalian Argument Against Universalism," in *Unapologetic Apologetics*, ed. W. A. Dembski and J. W. Richards (Downers Grove, Ill.: InterVarsity, 2001) 216.

[23] Packer, "Problem," 178.

[24] Unless we are inclusivists. I am open to inclusivism but have opted to defend an exclusivist version of universalism to show how even within such limits universalism can operate.

[25] Anastasia could go one of two ways here. She could take a very strong view of divine sovereignty in which case all whom God's intends to save before they die will be saved before they die and the rest will be saved later. Alternatively, she could take a weaker view of divine sovereignty according to which God's desire is that all accept the gospel before they die but many reject that. If she took this latter view then she would have the additional motive for evangelism.

the unevangelized. They ought to worry, because they can only be spared the coming wrath if they accept the gospel; and they can only do that if they hear it. They also ought to worry, because the church is under a mandate from its Lord; and failure to live up to it is culpable failure of love for God and our neighbor.

A more sophisticated version of this objection has recently been made by Jay Wesley Richards. Richards concedes that if we all believed in universalism, evangelism would continue; but

> if we are honest, we should admit that there would probably be fewer Christians than there are now. This doesn't mean that all missionary activity and evangelism would cease. But it would surely be less common, since its urgency would be diminished. After all, what missionary would be willing to die in his or her own pool of blood at the hands of pagan tribes if the salvation of such tribes were in no way dependent on such risk?[26]

He adds,

> Universalists uniformly deny this connection, but common sense and study of denominational missionary activities clearly confirm a very high correlation between the teaching of universalism and a diluting or redefining of the Great Commission. Universalism does not logically entail a repudiation of a call to repentance and acceptance of Christ's Lordship, but these certainly seem to follow as a historical fact.[27]

He goes on to produce a Pascalian argument against universalism. He begins by designating it a theologically hybrid theology, by which he means that it seems compatible with some parts of Scripture but seems incompatible with other parts (the many hell texts). The choice is between a universalism in which nobody goes to hell[28] and a particularism in which some are saved and others are damned. Richards has no doubts about which one he thinks is most biblical, but for the purposes of his argument he generously considers them as equal candidates for belief. To decide between them he employs a Pascalian wager. The calculation is simple. If we teach particularism and we are wrong, the infinite goods of universalism are realized; so there is infinite

---

[26] Richards, "Pascalian Argument," 216.

[27] Ibid., 217.

[28] It ought to be noted that the kind of universalism Richards considers is one in which nobody is sent to hell (213–14) and thus the hell texts becomes more anomalous for such universalists than they do on my evangelical universalism. By setting up this kind of universalism as the opponent he makes it easier for particularism to win the argument. However, to be fair, he does add at the end of the essay that different kinds of universalism would have to be considered on a case by case basis (218).

gain and no infinite cost. If we teach universalism and we are right, there is infinite gain and no infinite cost. However, if universalism is false and we teach it, the costs are infinite; for we will fail to proclaim the gospel to those who need it, and the number of the saved will be diminished. Clearly, the prudent course of action is to teach particularism, because we have little to lose but much to gain.

I think that we need to take these warnings seriously, and any evangelical universalist will have to pause and consider carefully this objection. Richards is correct that universalism does not entail a denial of the need for faith and repentance nor a reduction of missionary activity. One could be a universalist and a zealous missionary for all the kinds of reasons already explained. However, psychologically speaking, is it not plausible to think that the belief that universalism is false is more likely to motivate missions? Will one not be more willing to die for the gospel if one believes that a failure to respond in this life to the call will place a person in a place of eternal damnation?

Let me offer a few brief reflections. I have not studied the matter, but I would not be surprised if historically the rise in universalism did lead to an erosion of mission. This, I suggest, is because the *kinds* of universalism that have arisen within some liberal Christian churches have not been the kind of evangelical universalism that I have been developing. For instance, the pluralist universalism of John Hick would without doubt undermine Christian mission. We need to be cautious, however, about judging the effects of *evangelical* universalism by the results of other kinds of universalism.

Second, we need to recall that Pascal's original argument in the *Pensées* was offered for those who felt that the evidence for and against God's existence was evenly balanced and that reason could not tip the scales one way or the other. On the question of God's existence much was at stake, and, Pascal argued, fence-sitting was not an option. So how should one proceed? The wager argument offered a rational way of deciding on which side of the fence to jump. But the situation with universalism is *not* like that for the simple reason that, speaking for myself at any rate, the arguments for universalism are much stronger than those against it. I do not need a wager argument to help me decide which way to jump, because the scales are already tipped in favor of universalism.

I have no doubt that a belief in eternal conscious torment has motivated many missionaries to acts of courage for the sake of Christ and his world, and I do not regret their deeds in the slightest. However, as I have already mentioned, there are plenty of other profoundly motivating reasons for mission apart from this (including the belief that hell is temporary conscious torment). Whilst I would not desire to diminish the motive for mission, if the prime motivation is a false one, we should not hang on to it just for its pure pragmatic value.[29] Rather, we should cultivate some of the many other motivations for mission. Indeed, my anecdotal observation is that Western missions and evangelism are less and less motivated by the terror of eternal conscious torment. This is the case even amongst those who believe in such a fate for the lost. To some extent this is due to changes in the larger culture around us in which torment in hell no longer strikes terror into the heart. It is impossible not to be affected to some extent by such changes. However, in spite of the decrease in the role played by this psychological motivator, it has not stopped Christians wanting to obey the Great Commission. The evangelical universalists simply have to ensure that they are actively fostering a mission-focused spirituality and ever be on their guard against the very real dangers Richards warns us against.

Advantage 4: Universalism and Pastoral Issues

Consider the case of a Christian mother at the funeral of a beloved son who had rejected his Christian upbringing and turned away from the Lord. What hope can Christian faith offer to her? Liberal theology offered a feeble promise of eternal life based on little more than the niceness of God. The liberal burial seems to suggest that it does not matter how one lives or how one responds to the Lord, as entry for all to the new creation is guaranteed, irrespective of how they have lived. On the other hand, traditional theology can offer virtually no hope at all, for it is more or less certain that her son will be condemned to hell with no hope of redemption. The best that she can hope for is that perhaps in his dying moments he turned to the Lord in faith; but, to be honest, it is a very slender hope. Alternatively, she may console herself with the thought that you never can be sure what God will do. He is the judge of the earth and he will do what is right. He is sovereign and may act unexpectedly in the case of her son. But again, this vague hope is more slender than the previous one. When the rubber hits the road, she "knows" that her son is lost forever. Those who think that people believe the gospel because it provides them with a comfort blanket would do well to consider such a scenario, for clearly Christian belief is more a source of torment than comfort in this case, and such situations are very frequent.

Christian universalism provides a theology of hope for such a bereaved person. The Christian minister burying her child can offer a genuine and biblically grounded hope that her son will be saved without undermining the importance of how one lives or how one responds to the Lord. Of course, the minister cannot promise that the son will not go to hell, but she can

---

[29] Richards would agree. He thinks, however, that the biblical case for universalism is so hampered by the hell texts that it could not mount a serious case for being true. I disagree.

promise that <u>he has not passed a point of no return, that he is not beyond hope, and even that eventually he will experience the salvation of God.</u> This is profoundly comforting and in no way compromises the integrity of the Christian gospel.

What if I am Wrong?

One common concern is that the orthodox churches worldwide (Orthodox, Catholic, and Protestant) have more or less universally rejected universalism, so there must be something wrong with it.

There is much substance to this objection, and <u>Christians do need to weigh the wisdom of the ages with deep seriousness.</u> Most of the greatest theologians of the church have indeed rejected universalism. As I said in Chapter 1, the tradition needs to be the starting place, the default position, only to be abandoned under extreme pressure. However, there are some qualifications that need to be made to this impression of an overwhelming rejection of universalism.

First, within the early Church, three different views on hell co-existed as generally acceptable orthodox alternatives: eternal conscious torment, annihilation, and universalism.[30] Some of the great orthodox theologians of the Church were universalists. We find universalism, quite possibly, in Clement of Alexandria (160–215 AD), and certainly in Origen (ca. 185–ca. 254 AD) and Gregory of Nyssa (335–ca. 395 AD).[31] Whilst Origen later fell into disfavor with the Church and has only relatively recently experienced something of a restoration of his theological reputation, Gregory has always been considered a crucial orthodox figure in all main branches of the Church.[32]

The situation changed with the writings of Augustine. In 420 Augustine defended the doctrine of eternal conscious torment against "certain tender hearts of our own religion, who think that God, who has justly doomed the condemned into hell fire, will after a certain space, which his goodness shall think fit for the merit of each man's guilt, deliver them from that torment."[33] Augustine's views on a whole range of topics, this one included, became more or less universal in the Western Church. The central concerns that some theologians had with <u>Origin</u> were less to do with his universalism (though clearly

---

[30] Brian E. Daley, *The Hope of the Early Church: A Handbook of Patristic Eschatology* (1991; reprint, Peabody, Mass.: Hendrickson, 2003).

[31] On these three see Steven R. Harmon, *Every Knee Should Bow: Biblical Rationales for Universal Salvation in Early Christian Thought* (Dallas: University Press of America, 2003). On Gregory of Nyssa see especially Morwenna Ludlow, *Universal Salvation: Eschatology in the Thought of Gregory of Nyssa and Karl Rahner*, (Oxford: Oxford University Press, 2000).

[32] Indeed the Second Council of Nicea honored him with the title "Father of the fathers."

[33] *The City of God*, 21.17.

Augustine and his followers did dispute that) than his supposed claim that the Devil and his angels would be saved, that souls pre-existed and were placed into bodies as punishment, that souls went through an eternal cycle of salvation–fall–punishment–salvation–fall–punishment, and that the resurrection was spiritual. Whether or not Origen actually taught all these things,[34] the church was right to resist them as unchristian. The Synod of Alexandria in 400 AD condemned Origen for his supposed belief in the pre-existence of souls but made no mention of his universalism. However, because of the association of universalism with these other, more dubious, claims, universalism began to be thought of by many as guilty by association. In 543 the Emperor Justinian (527–565 AD) anathematized the doctrine of deliverance from hell,[35] and in 553 the Fifth Ecumenical Council in Constantinople issued a series of fifteen condemnations against the teachings of some extreme Origenist monks in Palestine. Their version of the doctrine of *apokatastasis* condemned by the council was a far more radical (and questionable) version than anything found in Origen or Gregory.[36] It is worth noting that Origen's universalism was singled out for condemnation by the council *because* it was associated with the "fall" of pre-existent human souls into bodies and a spiritual resurrection. It is also worth mentioning that, unlike Origen, Gregory of Nyssa, whilst he was a universalist, avoided any back-dated condemnation, perhaps because he was never associated with the heretical doctrines that Origen (rightly or wrongly) was thought to have held. After the Council one can understandably find only a few who seemed to incline in universalist directions. The most obvious candidates include Maximus the Confessor (580–662 AD), John Scotus Eriugena (810–877 AD) and some of the Medieval mystics like Lady Julian of Norwich (ca. 1342–after 1416); but caution must be taken in claiming them as overt and fully fledged universalists.[37] The story of universalism's mini-revival from the sixteenth to the twentieth century can be found in the surveys of Morwenna Ludlow and David Hilborn and Don Horrocks.[38]

---

[34] On Origen's actual thought see Daley, *Hope*, 47–64; Harmon, *Every Knee*, 47–81; Frederick W. Norris, "Universal Salvation in Origen and Maximus," in *Universalism and the Doctrine of Hell*, ed. Nigel M. de S. Cameron (Grand Rapids: Baker; Carlisle: Paternoster, 1992) 35–72.

[35] The relevant curse is: "IX. If anyone says or thinks that the punishment of demons and of impious men is only temporary, and will one day have an end, and that a restoration (*apokatastasis*) will take place of demons and of impious men, let him be anathema."

[36] The text along with Justinian's anathemas can be found at http://www.fordham.edu/halsall/basis/const2.html.

[37] On Maximus see Norris, "Universal Salvation"; and on Maximus and Eriugena see Daley, *Hope*.

[38] In Robin Parry and Christopher H. Partridge, eds., *Universal Salvation? The Current Debate* (Carlisle: Paternoster, 2003; Grand Rapids: Eerdmans, 2004).

Currently, the Orthodox Churches allow belief in universalism as an acceptable personal opinion, though it may not be taught as dogma. To some extent this reflects the very high regard that the Orthodox have for Gregory of Nyssa. Consequently, one can find Orthodox Christians, such as Bishop Kalistos Ware, who hope for universal salvation.[39] The Catholic Church allows the belief that one may hope and pray for the salvation of all but not the belief that one may be certain that God will save all. Some notable Catholic theologians who could be described as hopeful universalists include Karl Rahner (1904–84), Hans Urs von Balthasar (1905–88), Hans Küng (1928–), and, apparently, Pope John Paul II (1920–2005).[40] Protestant Churches have varied greatly. Suffice it to say that, although, as in other churches, universalism has always been a minority position often frowned upon, there has been a constant trickle of Protestants of varying degrees of orthodoxy who have been universalists. Amongst the more notable, mention may be made of Friedrich Schleiermacher (1768–1834), Thomas Erskine (1788–1864), Andrew Jukes (1815–1900), George MacDonald (1824–1905), Hannah Whitall Smith (1832–1911), Archbishop William Temple (1881–1944), Karl Barth[41] (1886–1968), H. H. Farmer (1892–1981), Jacques Ellul (1912–94), Hendrikus Berkhof (1914–95), William Barclay (1907–78), Bishop John A. T. Robinson (1919–83), and Jürgen Moltmann (1926–).

It is important in assessing the orthodoxy of universalism to ask the question, "Does universalism entail the denial of any claims central to orthodox Christian faith?" For instance, does a belief in universal salvation require one to give up belief in the Trinity? Well, granted that many universalists have been Unitarians (and thus "heretics"), there is no necessary connection between universalism and a denial of a Trinitarian view of God. Indeed, a universalist, I would contend, could maintain *all* the central elements of orthodox Christian faith. Universalism, in other words, is quite compatible with belief in the Trinity, in creation, fall, and redemption, in the inspiration of Scripture, in incarnation, in mission, and so on. If it were not, I would be worried. Indeed, I have argued that it helps resolve some tensions between traditional Christian beliefs that are otherwise very awkward to resolve. For instance, the tension between God's love and hell is resolved by universalism in such a way that these important Christian claims are easier to hold

---

[39] Kallistos Ware, *The Inner Kingdom,* Collected Works 1 (New York: St Vladimir's Seminary Press, 2000) 193–215.

[40] For numerous quotes from Pope John Paul II on this topic see http://www.romancatholicism. org/jpii-quotes.htm.

[41] Barth, of course, denied that he was a universalist. My point is that the *logic* of his theology is clearly universalist even if he backed away from its implications. See Oliver Crisp, "On Barth's Denial of Universalism," *Themelios* 29.1 (2003) 18–29.

together than has traditionally been the case. So, until I can be convinced otherwise, I judge that, even though it is not mainstream within Christianity, universalism is no threat to orthodox Christianity.

But what if I am wrong in thinking that God will save everyone? I said right at the start that I am a hopeful dogmatic universalist. That is to say that, although, according to my theological system, God will save all people, I am not 100% certain that my system is correct. So what if I am wrong? Well, if I am wrong, then I will have inspired some false hope in the hearts of some people; but I do not think that I will have done any serious damage. I have not produced a theology with a diminished view of God nor one that will lead people not to worship God. I have not sidestepped the centrality of God's work in Christ, so the cross and resurrection remain at the heart of the gospel. I have not reduced the importance of faith in Christ nor the mission-ary calling of the church. I have not undermined the authority of the Bible. I have not "gone soft" on God's wrath nor got rid of hell. I have not tinkered with any of the key doctrines of orthodox Christianity. If I am wrong, then anyone who mistakenly comes to think that I am right will love and wor-ship the triune God, study and follow the Scriptures, proclaim Christ to the lost, and seek to walk in holiness, just like any non-universalist evangelical. Hopefully, neither they nor those around them will be adversely harmed by their mistaken universalist beliefs. I have made a provisional case for accept-ing universalism, but in the end one must make a wager and take a position. Here I stand, and I can do no other. I realize that most of my Christian family do not stand with me in the extent of my hope for the future, and I certainly do not think that true Christian faith requires agreement with my views! Belief in universalism is most certainly *not* a requirement for Christian ortho-doxy, but neither does it amount to an exclusion from orthodoxy *even if it is wrong*. I hope that this book may persuade some at least to tolerate evangeli-cal universalism as a legitimate Christian position—a view that is true to the message of the gospel—even if they themselves feel unable to accept it.

In conclusion, let me ask you to hold in your mind traditional Christian visions of the future, in which many, perhaps the majority of humanity, are excluded from salvation forever. Alongside that hold the universalist vision, in which God achieves his loving purpose of redeeming the whole creation. Which vision has the strongest view of divine love? Which story has the most powerful narrative of God's victory over evil? Which picture lifts the atoning efficacy of the cross of Christ to the greatest heights? Which perspective best emphasizes the triumph of grace over sin? Which view most inspires worship and love of God bringing him honor and glory? Which has the most satisfac-tory understanding of divine wrath? Which narrative inspires hope in the human spirit? To my mind the answer to all these questions is clear, and that is why I am a Christian universalist.

A Reply to William Lane Craig's Argument that Molinism is Compatible with Non-Universalism

I T WILL be recalled that in chapter 1 I argued:

> 1. God, being omniscient, knows, via his middle knowledge, how to bring all people freely to accept salvation in Christ.

> 2. God, being omnipotent, is able to actualize a possible world in which all persons freely accept salvation in Christ.

> 3. God, being omnibenevolent, wants to bring all people to salvation through Christ.

1–3 entail that if God creates creatures with free will, then all people will be brought to salvation through Christ. Thus, 1–3 are inconsistent with:

> 4. Some persons do not receive Christ and are eternally damned.

If, however, one were to reject proposition 2 because one thought that God could not actualize a possible world in which all persons freely choose to accept salvation in Christ, then we could add proposition 5:

> 5. God prefers a world in which there are no persons at all to a world in which there are persons some of whom fail to receive Christ (and are damned).

Proposition 5 is also inconsistent with proposition 4. And if 5 does not seem compelling, we could substitute 6.

> 6. God prefers a world, W, in which any people who do not accept salvation in Christ freely (in a libertarian sense) will nevertheless accept it freely (in a compatibilist sense) to a world, W*, in which those who do not accept salvation in Christ freely (in a libertarian sense) are condemned to hell for eternity.

Proposition 6 is also incompatible with proposition 4, and proposition 6 seems, to me at least, to be true.

William Lane Craig seeks to show that the God of traditional theism (omnipotent, omniscient, omnibenevolent, etc.) is not, in fact, incompatible with proposition 4. To do this, he denies that propositions 2 and 5 are necessarily true (he does not consider 6).

Craig claims that the Christian who accepts middle knowledge is free to reject 2; because, although it is *logically* possible that God could actualize any possible world, it may not be *"feasible"* for him to do so. It may be that an omnipotent God could not actualize the possible world in which all people *freely* accept Christ if the counterfactuals of creaturely freedom are such that when God tries to create such a world its inhabitants, as a matter of contingent fact, choose to reject Christ. God could compel them; but if he did so, he has not actualized a world in which all people *freely* choose to accept Christ.

To show that the propositions[1]

7. God is omniscient, omnipotent, and omnibenevolent

and

8. Some persons do not receive Christ and are damned

are compatible, Craig must be able to produce a proposition that is consistent with 7, and that, together with 7, entails 8. Craig's proposal is:

9. God has actualized a world containing an optimal balance between the saved and the unsaved, and those who are unsaved suffer from transworld damnation.

It is important to understand 9 clearly. It may be that God is unable to create a world in which all people *freely* accept Christ (i.e., such a world is logically possible but not feasible). It may be that our world is the world that has the optimal balance of saved and lost. There could be possible worlds in which fewer people are damned, but they may be worlds in which very few are saved. God seeks the optimum balance, and this world may be it. It could be objected that God knows, for any individual, in what circumstances they would freely accept Christ. It does seem unfair that God knew how to bring about this person's free acceptance of the gospel but did not do so. The problem here is that of those who have either never heard the gospel or who have been presented with a distorted version of it. Why would God refuse to put such people in circumstances in which he knows, via his middle knowledge, that they *would* freely choose salvation? However, Craig maintains that some people may suffer from what he refers to as "transworld damnation." Such people would not freely choose to be saved *in any world that God could create.* Perhaps *all* the people who reject Christ in this world suffer from transworld damnation. Thus, there is no situation in which they would freely accept Christ. In this case *every* person who does not freely accept

---

[1] The numbering of the premises here differs from Craig's numbering.

Christ is a person God knows would never accept Christ *in any circumstances.* Thus, he does them no injustice by damning them.[2]

Proposition 9 does not seem to contradict anything in 7; and, when combined with 7, it entails 8. Thus 8 *seems* logically compatible with 7.

In contrast to 5, Craig maintains that a theist *could* hold:

> 10. God prefers certain worlds in which some persons fail to receive
> Christ and are damned to certain worlds in which all receive Christ
> and are saved.

This is because the price to be paid for *a multitude* in heaven may be that *some* are eternally damned, and God is faced with the tragic choice of saving only a small number or of saving a large number at the expense of some people being lost.

> Now we have seen that it is possible that God wants to maximize the number
> of the saved: He wants heaven to be as full as possible. Moreover, as a loving
> God, He wants to minimize the number of the lost: He wants hell to be as
> empty as possible. His goal, then, is to achieve an optimal balance between
> these, to create no more lost than is necessary to achieve a certain number of
> saved.[3]

It is important to realize that all Craig claims to offer is a defense and not a theodicy.[4] Thus, all that his argument needs to show is that the God of theism is logi-

---

[2] There is a plausibility problem with the notion of transworld damnation. The claim that all people who reject, or never hear, the gospel suffer from a condition according to which there is no feasible world in which they would freely accept it seems to be massively implausible. To seriously believe, or even think plausible, the suggestion that someone who never heard the gospel before they died would never have freely responded to it in any circumstances God could have actualized is beyond my ability. However, this objection does not decimate Craig's argument because, as Craig says in a later article, he sees the doctrine of transworld damnation as an auxiliary doctrine proposed in response to an objection based on what I regard as the very dubious assumption that necessarily, an omnibenevolent God would not create persons who actually reject His grace and are lost, but who would have been saved under other circumstances (Craig, "Middle Knowledge and Christian Exclusivism," *Sophia* 34 [1995] 120–39).

So Craig thinks his argument can survive the loss of transworld damnation for, it may still be the case that every feasible world in which John Smith chooses to be saved is a world in which Julie Smith chooses to reject salvation. This is possibly the case *even if Julie Smith does not suffer from transworld damnation* and there are some John-Smith-free worlds in which she does freely accept salvation. Hence, the argument goes that perhaps God could not create a world in which John *and* Julie Smith freely choose salvation. In a similar way, perhaps there is no feasible world in which some people freely choose salvation without others freely rejecting it.

[3] Craig, "'No Other Name': A Middle Knowledge Perspective on the Exclusivity of Salvation Through Christ," *F&Ph* 6 (1989) 172–88.

[4] Following Plantinga we can say that a theodicy is an attempt to answer the question, "Why does God allow evil?" while a defense is the more modest task of attempting to show that God and evil are not logically contradictory.

cally consistent with the eternal damnation of some. For the purposes of a defense he does not have to show that his propositions 9 and 10 are plausible or probable.

This leads us to the first weakness with Craig's strategy: Let us suppose, for the sake of argument, that we cannot demonstrate that Craig's defense fails. The position we find ourselves in is that we cannot *prove* that God and traditional views of hell are logically contradictory. But this would be a limited victory for Craig. It does not follow that God and hell are *not* logically contradictory—that would only follow if we *knew* that Craig's propositions 9 and 10 were possible, and we do not know this.[5] So even if we could not *show* that Craig is wrong, he may still *be* wrong.

My second problem is that Craig says, in response to proposition 5 and in defense of 10, that the only feasible worlds in which all people freely choose salvation may be worlds with few inhabitants. "Is it not at least possible," he asks, "that such a world is less preferable to God than a world in which great multitudes come to experience His salvation and a few are damned because they freely reject Christ?"[6] I'm not sure that it is, but even if it were, he still has a problem; for Craig says earlier in his article, "if we take Scripture seriously, we must admit that the vast majority of persons in the world are condemned and will be lost forever."[7] So the question Craig *really* needs to ask is, "Is it not at least possible that such a world is less preferable to God than a world in which great multitudes come to experience His salvation and *massively* greater multitudes are damned because they freely reject Christ?" A negative answer to *this* question seems very reasonable. Craig suggests that this grisly lack of balance may in fact be the best that God can achieve—the optimum balance between saved and unsaved. There are several problems lurking in this neighborhood. First is that, as with transworld damnation (see p. 180, fn. 2), it seems very hard to believe that the suggestion is plausibly, let alone probably, true. That, of the infinity of feasible worlds God could have actualized, there is none with a better balance of saved and lost than one in which, to quote Craig, "the *vast majority* of persons in the world are condemned and will be forever lost,"[8] I find this staggering. Craig, however, says he finds it plausible; so I'll leave this concern alone and move on.

A third problem: How does God calculate this optimal balance? It seems to me that what Craig has in mind is that (a) God aims to achieve the best balance of the misery of the lost (which God wishes to minimize) and the ecstasy of the saved (which God wants to maximize) with one caveat—(b) that God wants to save a multitude. Now God may be able to achieve (a) without (b) and save everyone, but this is worse than to achieve (a) and (b). Now the joy of the saved must be *very* intense to

---

[5] To Craig it is obvious that they are possible but this point is moot (on this see Talbott, "Craig on the Possibility of Eternal Damnation," *RelSt* 26 [1992] esp. 496–99). It may actually be impossible that a free agent would reject God forever (in which case proposition 9 is not possible). In fact, that is exactly what I *do* think (see later). It may also, for all I know, be impossible for God, given his perfect nature, to prefer a world in which some are damned to a world in which all are saved (in which case proposition 10 is not possible).

[6] Craig, "No Other Name," The Virtual Office of Dr. William Lane Craig, http://www.leaderu.com/offices/billcraig/docs/middle2.html.

[7] Ibid.

[8] Ibid.

balance out the misery of the vast majority. This is a utilitarian calculation aimed at bringing about the greatest balance of bliss over misery in the universe but without bringing about the greatest bliss *for the greatest number*! Such a calculation may well be just (given that hell is deserved), but is it loving? Suppose that you could create either:

(i) 10 really happy children, or

(ii) 100 really happy children and 1,000 really miserable children.

Is it obvious that (ii) is the better choice? Is it right or loving to make the few extremely happy at the expense of the many? And what of God's sorrow at the loss of the 1,000? He will bear the pain for eternity, never to be healed. Marilyn Adams maintains that our feelings are a valuable (though not an infallible) source of information on value questions. She says that she is "appalled at Craig's . . . valuations, at levels too deep for words."[9] For those who share her gut instincts, Craig's cold calculations will cut little ice.

However, the fourth problem, and the real Achilles heel in Craig's argument, lies in his claim that perhaps God could not create a world in which all people freely choose to accept salvation. Both Craig's proposition 9 and his proposition 10 are parasitic on the plausibility of the notion that a free agent could choose forever to reject God. If it could be demonstrated that the notion of a rational agent freely rejecting God *forever* is incoherent, then it follows that we have demonstrated that God could indeed create a world in which all people freely accept salvation. From this it would follow that propositions 9 and 10 were *necessarily* false. Proposition 9 (combined with 8) would be *necessarily* false; because if God could create a world in which all freely embrace salvation, then the world with the optimal balance between lost and saved would be one in which *all* were saved and *none* lost. A world in which some are damned *could not* be the world in which the optimal balance of lost and saved is achieved.

Similarly, proposition 10 would also be *necessarily* false; because if God is able to save all and wants to save all, it follows that he would *not* prefer a world in which some persons are not saved.

So everything hinges on this question: "Is there a possible world in which some people freely choose to reject God forever?" Following Thomas Talbott, I argued in Chapter 1 that if we grant that free will requires (a) a certain amount of rationality and (b) an adequate appreciation of the facts relevant to the choice in question, then a *fully informed*, free decision to reject God is an incoherent notion. This means that so long as God brings people to a point where they appreciate the consequences of their decision to accept or reject salvation, there is no possible world in which any people choose to reject God *forever*; and Craig's argument collapses.[10] Following Eric

---

[9] Marilyn Adams, "The Problem of Hell: A Problem of Evil for Christians," in *A Reasoned Faith*, ed. E. Stumpt (New York: Cornell University Press, 1993) 326.

[10] Of course, one could still argue that God may have good reasons not to put any/all agents in the situation in which they were fully informed about the consequences of this decision

Reitan, I further maintained that even if, along with Craig, we mistakenly wished to retain an unpredictable, random element in human free choices, God could *still* guarantee that in the long run all people would freely choose to accept salvation; and Craig's argument still collapses.

(Craig argues precisely this). On this objection see the discussion in Chapter 1 but especially in the articles by Talbott and Reitan cited there.

Christ, Cosmos, and Church:
The Theology of Ephesians

I WISH TO argue that a very similar theology as that described in Chapter 2 can be found in Ephesians. Ephesians has been written by someone familiar with the content of Colossians—Paul or perhaps one of his disciples. Like Colossians, it has a Jewish doctrine of creation modified by its Christology. It also has a strong focus on the "new creation" work of God available "in Christ." It, too, has a doctrine of the final "summing up" of the whole cosmos in Christ, which, I shall argue, ought probably to be understood salvifically. Finally, like Colossians, it conceives of the church as the "firstfruits" of this eschatological "summing up." However, in Ephesians we will find a stronger statement of the conflict between God and the powers and a stronger statement of the condition of those outside of Christ than we find in Colossians. I will try to show that this is consistent with the apparent universalism of 1:10.

Ephesians 2 draws a strong contrast between the previous condition of the readers in their non-believing way of life and their new condition "in Christ." The description of the unbelieving state in 2:1-3 is very strong indeed:

> As for you [probably the readers in general but especially Gentile readers], you were dead in your transgressions and sins, in which you used to live when you followed the ways of this world and of the ruler of the kingdom of the air, the spirit who is now at work in those who are disobedient. All of us also lived among them at one time, gratifying the cravings of our sinful nature and following its desires and thoughts. Like the rest, we were by nature objects of wrath.

The unbeliever is "dead" in sin (cf. Col 2:13; Rom 6:16, 21, 23). The wages of sin is "death" (Rom 6:23), by which is meant eschatological death at the day of judgment—separation from the life of God. Just as those who are in Christ can share in the life of the age to come in the present, so those who are outside of Christ share in the death of the age to come in the present. A very similar theme is found in John's Gospel. John says:

> Whoever believes in him is not condemned, but whoever does not believe *stands condemned already* because he has not believed in the name of God's one and only Son. (John 3:18)

> Whoever believes in the Son has eternal life, but whoever rejects the Son will not see life, for God's wrath *remains* on him. (John 3:36)

> I tell you the truth, whoever hears my word and believes him who sent me has eternal life and will not be condemned; he has crossed over *from death* to life. (John 5:24)

It is clear that, in John's Gospel, the end-time verdict of condemnation and the consequent death sentence in which God's wrath is expressed are present realities for non-Christians (though, of course, *they* will not conceptualize their condition this way). This seems to be so in Ephesians also. The world stands outside of the eternal life God offers. Unbelievers are also under the control of spiritual forces—the "ruler of the kingdom of the air" (cf. Gal 4:3, 8)[1] and are dominated by "the flesh" (cf. Rom 7:5): slaves to their own sinful cravings. By nature such people are "children of wrath." This expression is a Hebraism meaning that the believers in their previous lives were deserving of God's wrath (Eph 5:6; Col 3:5-6). "The children of wrath, then, are those who, through their condition of sinful rebellion, deserve his righteous judgment."[2] And this is a condition people are born into—they are children of wrath "by nature."

There can be no doubt that Ephesians has a strong doctrine of human sinfulness and of the desperate plight of humanity. The situation is very dark indeed, but many have been too quick to conclude from this that Ephesians is incompatible with universalism. 2:1-10 does paint a bleak picture of life outside of Christ, but it does so in order to contrast it with the amazing grace that the readers now experience. Like the rest of humanity, they too shared in the death, the wrath, and the slavery to sinful desires and spiritual forces; *but no longer!* They were dead, *but now* they are alive! They were children of wrath, *but now* they are children of mercy. Obviously, this teaching in no way implies universalism, but neither does it rule it out. Nothing here states that God will make *all* people alive with Christ, but nothing excludes that possibility either. The writer is not, in this context, interested in the question of how many will experience God's grace, but focuses instead on the fact that the readers of the letter have done so. What I would like to draw attention to is the undeniable fact that the writer can say that his descriptions were once apt descriptions of people who went on to become Christians. The obvious implication is that being dead in sin as a child of wrath does *not* mean that one must remain that way forever. What it does mean is that any change can only come through the grace of God available in Christ.

---

[1] Scholars debate the exact meaning of the expression in v. 2. We need not concern ourselves with that debate.

[2] Andrew Lincoln, *Ephesians*, WBC 42 (Dallas: Word, 1990) 99.

To the writer of Ephesians the present time can be described as "this present evil age." For now, evil has its way, but not forever. The great future vision of the chapter is found in 1:10.

> And he made known to us the mystery of his will according to his good pleasure, which he purposed in Christ, to be put into effect when the times will have reached their fulfillment—*to bring all things in heaven and on earth together under one head, even Christ.* In him we were also chosen, having been predestined according to the plan of him who works out everything in conformity with the purpose of his will, in order that we, who were the first to hope in Christ, might be for the praise of his glory. (1:9-12 NIV)

The crucial Greek verb used in 1:10 translated as "to bring together," "unite," or "sum up" in the translations is *anakephalaiōsasthai.* It is composed of an adjective, *kephalaion,* meaning "the main point," "the summary" (Heb 8:1; Acts 22:28), or "completion," plus a prefix, *ana.*[3]

The verbal noun *anakephalaiōsis* is found in secular rhetorical texts books such as those of Aristotle (*Fragments* 123), Quintilian (6:1), and Dionysius of Halicarnassus (*De Lysia* 9). They use it in the sense of "repetition" and "drawing together" in the context of "summing up" an argument. Paul uses it in a similar way in Romans 13:9 when he writes that all of the commandments of the law are "summed up" in the command to love. The love command draws together and unifies all the other commands.

Thus, Ephesians 1:10 teaches that God's purpose is the "bringing together," "the uniting," or "the summing up" of all creation in Christ. In some sense, all things

---

[3] The prefix *ana* could be understood indifferent ways. Kitchen suggests the following four possibilities (M. Kitchen, *Ephesians*, London: Routledge, 1994):
- directional—"up"—summing up (only metaphorically "up")
- repetitive—to return to a previous state—thus to "recapitulate,"
- intensive—to intensify the verb
- stylistic—little or no denotative significance

It has been suggested that *Kephalaion* as a noun has been derived from *kephalē* meaning "head." *Kephalē* can be used of a literal head (Callias, *Cycl.*5.1), metaphorically in the sense of "chief" (Plutarch, *Life of Pericles* 3). In light of the emphasis in Ephesians on Christ as "head" of the cosmos (1:22) and of the church (4:15; 5:23) some have suggested a translation that brings out the "headship" dimension of Ephesians 1:10. For instance, Markus Barth translates the verb as "to comprehend under one head" (Markus Barth, *Ephesians*, AB 34 [Garden City, N.Y.: Doubleday, 1974] 89–92). The idea here is that God's central purpose for creation is to bring it all under subjection to Christ. The problem with this approach is that it is a linguistically dubious procedure to determine the meaning of the word on the basis of the etymology of one of its component parts. In this particular case it is possible that *kephalaion* is derived from *kephalē* (head) but this is no sure guide to the meaning of *anakephalaiōsasthai.* Better to examine other contemporary uses of *anakephalaiōsis* before resorting to such procedures.

are "brought to their conclusion" in him.[4] Schnackenburg thus speaks of Christ as "the unifying power of the universe."[5] Andrew Lincoln concludes that

> The summing up of all things in Christ means the unifying of the cosmos or its direction towards a common goal. In line with the letter's close links with Colossians, a similar thought about Christ and the cosmos had been expressed in the Colossian hymn in terms of reconciliation and with explicit soteriological connotations (Col. 1:20). Both passages appear to presuppose that the cosmos has been plunged into disintegration on account of sin and that it is God's purpose to restore the original harmony in Christ.[6]

The parallel with Colossians 1:20 has been observed by many scholars and makes a salvific interpretation likely.

God's purposes in redemptive history are to restore "all things" to their proper purpose. That "all things" is to be taken in its strongest sense is indicated by the following clause, which expands the phrase as follows: "things in heaven and things on earth in him" (see also the use in 1:22; 4:10; Rom 11:36; 1 Cor 8:6; 15:27; Phil 3:21; Heb 1:3; 2:10; Rev 4:11). This restoration is achieved "in Christ." Christ represents all creation, and in the Christ-event all creation is already restored. It is, to our author, a present reality that creation has been redeemed in Christ.[7] Christ has been exalted to heaven, all things have already been placed beneath his feet, and he has been made head of all things (1:22). He fills all things (1:23; 4:10). This is the emphasis on realized eschatology in Ephesians as in Colossians. However, Ephesians is also aware that at present we do not *see* all things subject to Christ. There is a tension between the "now" and the "not yet" of God's achievements in Christ. Thus, although the powers are placed under Christ's rule (1:22), they are still in rebellion (1:21; 2:2; 6:12). In just the same way, although all things are summed up in Christ already, at the present time we certainly do not see all the effects of this victory.

Returning to the interpretation of 1:10, although I have argued that *anakephalaiôsis* ought to be translated as "summed up" or some equivalent and not as "headed up" (p. 186, fn. 3), I do think that the eschatological goal envisaged by Ephesians in 1:10 can be filled out by examination of other key texts such as 1:22. Kitchen sets 1:10 in the context of the argument of chapters 1–2. He argues that chapters 1 and 2 are really expanding on the theme of God's summing up all things in Christ. Ephesians 1:3-10 concern God's purposes of election and redemption worked out in Christ, with v. 10 as the climax[8] in which the ultimate goal of God's grand purposes is made clear. "The *anakephalaiôsis* thus comes as the climax of the divine plan, and

---

[4] The LXX uses it once in Ps 71:20 (MT Psalm 72) in the version of Theodotion and the Quinta in the sense of "to come to an end." The *Epistle of Barnabas* 5:11 uses the verb in the sense of "to bring to completion" or "to bring to an end."

[5] Rudolf Schnackenburg, *The Epistle to the Ephesians: A Commentary*, trans. Helen Heron (Edinburgh: T. & T. Clark, 1991) 60.

[6] Lincoln, *Ephesians*, 33.

[7] Schnackenburg, *Ephesians*, 61; Lincoln, *Ephesians*, 34–35; and Ernest Best, *Ephesians*, ICC (Edinburgh: T. & T. Clark, 1998) 142

[8] So too Best, *Ephesians*, 139.

involves redemption, forgiveness of sins and enlightenment."[9] Part of the Christian experience of redemption is the blessing of understanding God's redemptive plan (vv. 9-12) and v. 10 is the revelation of that plan to the church.

The grand purpose of God involves the bringing together of things in heaven and earth. Kitchen proposes that chapter 2 expands on both themes with an eye to the place of the church. In 2:1-10 we see some of the implications of unification in the heavens. Believers are reunited with God and empowered for good works as a renewed humanity. Ephesians 2:11ff. work out some of the implications of unification on the earth. Jew and Gentile are made one new man in Christ, and the wall of hostility is broken down. There is an ecclesiological focus as the implications of 1:10 are explored, but it is clear that the rupture between humans and God and within humanity are healed in Christ. This is, at present, only the experience of a limited number within humanity, but 1:10 looks forward to a broader goal embracing the whole of creation.

The subjection of creation to Christ as the reigning head of the cosmos (1:22 ff.) is also part of this eschatological vision. As Schnackenburg notes, "The unification of the universe takes place in its subordination to the Head."[10] The divine rule is restored in Christ, and this is an essential element of the reunification that is achieved.

It is often argued that this subjection of creation indicates God's condemnation and destruction of the hostile powers rather than their reconciliation. For instance, Moritz argues that *anakephalaiôsis* means "subjection under Christ" for sinners and hostile powers and "incorporation into the body of Christ" for believers.[11] It is true that the theme of the restoration of the powers is not as clear in Ephesians as it is in Colossians; but, that said, there are reasons to think that the redemption of the powers achieved through their subjection to Christ is in view. First of all, we note the fact that 1:10 is most naturally understood redemptively. The terminology used certainly seems salvific (see above), and the parallel with Colossians 1:20 supports that thesis. We may also draw attention to 3:10-11, which explains that

> through the Church the manifold wisdom of God should now be made known to the principalities and authorities in the heavenly realms, according to the eternal purpose which he accomplished in Christ Jesus our Lord. . . .

This text is not totally perspicuous. Dahl argues that it concerns the making known of God's purposes to the angelic powers present when the Church meets in worship, although such angels do not seem to be the hostile powers referred to here. More plausibly, Walter Wink argues that as the gospel is preached to the Gentiles it

---

[9] Martin Kitchen, *Ephesians*, NTR (London: Routledge, 1994) 48.

[10] Schnackenberg, *Ephesians*, 60.

[11] Thorsten Moritz, "'Summing Up All Things': Religious Pluralism and Universalism in *Ephesians*," in *One God, One Lord: Christianity in a World of Religious Pluralism*, ed. Andrew D. Clark and Bruce W. Winter, 2d ed., THS (Carlisle: Paternoster Press; Grand Rapids: Baker, 1992) 101–24.

is simultaneously being preached to the angelic guardians of the Gentile nations.[12] Perhaps more likely still, Andrew Lincoln maintains that

> the writer's thought is . . . best understood as being that by her very existence as a new humanity, in which the major division of the first-century world has been overcome, the church reveals God's secret in action and heralds to the hostile heavenly powers the overcoming of cosmic divisions with their defeat . . . the Church provides hostile cosmic powers with a tangible reminder that their authority has been decisively broken and that all things are subject to Christ. The overcoming of the barriers between Jews and Gentiles, as they are united through Christ in the Church, is the pledge of the overcoming of all divisions when the universe will be restored to harmony in Christ (cf. 1:10). In this way the Church as the focus of God's wise plan could give the readers an essential clue to the meaning of this world's history.[13]

So, following either Wink or Lincoln, one can see that the proclamation through the Church to the hostile heavenly powers is one that declares the future reunification of all creation (including the powers). This is not something the Powers desire at present, but it is already achieved in Christ and is being made manifest in the Church community. There is nothing they can do about it.

The key text behind Moritz's claim that being "summed up in Christ" could work itself out for salvation *or subjection* is Ephesians 1:20-23. The text speaks of the mighty power of God available to believer:

> 20 . . . which He brought about in Christ, when He raised Him from the dead and seated Him at His right hand in the heavenly places, 21 far above all rule and authority and power and dominion, and every name that is named, not only in this age but also in the one to come. 22 And He put all things in subjection under His feet, and gave Him as head over all things to the church, 23 which is His body, the fullness of Him who fills all in all.

These verses have proven very difficult for scholars to interpret. Clearly Moritz understands the subjection spoken of to be non-salvific, but I shall question this and suggest a different way of understanding Paul's thought.

The background to the head-body metaphor is probably best sought, as already mentioned in our discussion of Colossians, in the Hellenistic views about the cosmos as God's body (Orphic Fragment 168; Philo, *Quaest. In Exod.* 2.117). From the Old Testament the term "head" also inherits associations with authority and rule. In 1:22 Christ is spoken of as "head of all things" that is to say, "ruler of the whole cosmos." This point is driven home in the exaltation of Christ to God's right hand "far above all rule and authority and power and dominion, and every name that is named, not only in this age but also in the one to come." 1:23 speaks of how Christ fills "all in all" or "everything in every way." Christ is the one who fills the whole of created reality in every way. This is indeed the same "summing up of all things" found in 1:10, even though the conceptualization is slightly different. So far so good.

---

[12] Walter Wink, *Naming the Powers: The Language of Power in the New Testament* (Philadelphia: Fortress, 1984) 89–96.

[13] Lincoln, *Ephesians*, 187, 194.

The next step is to note an interesting parallel that appears in Ephesians, just as we found it did in Colossians, between Christ as head of the cosmos and Christ as head of the Church. In 1:23 we read that the Church is Christ's body (cf. 2:16; 3:6; 4:4, 12, 16; 5:23, 29). It is not said there that he is head of the Church, but Ephesians makes this very clear elsewhere (4:15; 5:23). As Christ is head of his cosmic body (all creation) so he is head of his body the Church (cf. Col. 1:18; 2:19). The Church is Christ's body and also his fullness (1:23). That is to say, the Church is full of Christ, and in this too there is a parallel with all creation. Just as Philo saw God as permeating the whole universe with his power (*Leg. Alleg.* 3.4; *De Vit. Mos.* 2.238) and the Stoics conceived of a unified cosmos saturated with the divine Spirit (Seneca, *De Benefac.* 4.8.2; Aristides, *Or.* 45.21, 24), so Paul thinks of the Church as a unified body (notice his emphasis on unity in the body references above) filled with Christ (cf., Col. 2:10; Eph. 4:13; 3:19). And as Christ has filled his Church, so also he is in the process of filling all things in every way (1:23).

So what exactly is the relationship between Christ, Church, and cosmos in Ephesians? Andrew Lincoln says,

> ecclesiological and cosmic perspectives are juxtaposed in a way that under-lines the Church's special status, for although Christ is in the process of filling the cosmos, at present it is only the Church which can actually be called his fullness. The Church appears, then, to be the focus for and medium of Christ's presence and rule in the cosmos . . . The writer does not make clear exactly how the Church participates in the process of Christ's cosmic rule, but he does see it as the community which manifests Christ's presence and as the community in which the consummation of Christ's rule is anticipated.[14]

So the train of thought seems to be that God's ultimate purpose is to fill all things with Christ and to bring all things together in Christ. This will involve the re-establishment of the fractured harmony of creation. Christ will be acknowledged as ruler of all things. In the emphasis on realized eschatology the writer speaks of how this has already been accomplished in Christ, for he has *already* been exalted by God and *already* rules. However, this rule is presently only manifested in the Church. The Church is a scale model anticipating the grander re-unification of creation. This explains the parallels between Church and creation noted above. It also may explain why Paul speaks of how God, "gave [Christ] as head over all things to the church" (1:22). This is a most perplexing claim, but we need to recall that the focus of 1:20-23 is the Church. Paul is praying that the Ephesians may know God's power available to them. 1:20-23 expound on the nature of the divine power available to the Church. In that context he says that God has given all rule and authority to Christ and then has given this Christ to the Church, making all that power and authority available to them. What hostile powers and authorities can resist a Church to whom God has given Christ as head of all things? None, of course.

---

[14] Lincoln, *Ephesians*, 77–78.

So what are we to make of the language of all things being subjected to Christ? The language is drawn from a combination of Ps 8:4-7[15] and Ps 110:1.[16] Through the allusion to Psalm 8 Christ is presented as the last Adam in whom God's rule over the cosmos is restored. From the Psalm 110 allusion we see that this restoration comes through the defeat of the hostile powers. This theme of the defeat of the powers followed by their subjection is clearer in 1 Corinthians 15 (See Chapter Four for a discussion). Both that text and Ephesians 1 are open to being read in one of two ways. Either the hostile authorities are defeated and subjected by being annihilated or they are defeated, subjected, and, in this way, are restored. It is not at all obvious that the subjection language is non-salvific. For a start, Paul says that Christ is head of both all things *and the Church*. The nature of the rule implied by such headship is spoken of as being "far above all rule and authority and power and dominion, and every name that is named, not only in this age but also in the one to come. And He put all things in subjection under His feet" (1:21-22). The exaltation over and subjection of all things here must not be thought to exclude the Church. As a microcosm of the cosmos the Church is presumably also subjected to him, and yet this subjection is compatible with salvation. That the subjection simply indicates a restoration of divine order in the cosmos is indicated by 1 Corinthians 15:20-28, to which this text is indebted.[17] In 1 Corinthians the hostile cosmos is subjected to Christ, and then "the Son himself will be made subject to him who put everything under him, so that God may fill all things in every way" (15:28). Just as the cosmos is subjected to Christ, so Christ is made subject to the Father. The focus is on the re-establishment of divine rule and harmony. If it implies the annihilation of the hostile powers, that is certainly not made clear. I suggest that the language about God's purpose to sum up all things under Christ as head and to fill all things with the presence of Christ implies restoration and salvation for the cosmos just as it does for the church and inclines us to seeing the defeat and subjection of the powers as a means to that end.[18]

The high view of the Church in both Colossians and Ephesians should be clear by now. The Christian community is to make manifest in its life and worship the reunification of creation with God and with itself. The Church is called to be a taste of things to come. An ecclesiology like that is truly inspirational for Christian communal aspirations.

---

[15] "What is man that you are mindful of him, the son of man that you care for him? You made him a little lower than the heavenly beings and crowned him with glory and honor. You made him ruler over the works of your hands; you put everything under his feet: all flocks and herds, and the beasts of the field, the birds of the air, and the fish of the sea, all that swim the paths of the seas"

[16] "The LORD says to my Lord: 'Sit at my right hand until I make your enemies a footstool for your feet.'"

[17] Ephesians 1:20-23 combines Psalms 8 and 110 in just the way 1 Corinthians 15 does. Also the language of filling all things in every way is picked up by Ephesians.

[18] That Paul speaks of Christ exaulted over the powers in this age and the age to come suggests that they are not annihilated. The annihilation of the powers would suggest that there are dimensions of creation which God does not seek to redeem.

The Lamb's Book of Life

GIVEN REVELATION 21:27, it is clear that a universalist interpretation of Revelation will only work if a non-Calvinist interpretation can be given to the Book of Life (BOL). The BOL is mentioned in 3:5; 13:8; 17:8; 20:12,15; 21:27. The following points are clear and agreed by all:

> a) Some people have their names written in the BOL and some people do not.
>
> b) Those whose names are written in the BOL enter the new Jerusalem.
>
> c) Those whose names are not written in the BOL will not enter the new Jerusalem.

One could interpret the BOL in a predestinarian sense: God, before the foundation of the world, chooses whom he will save and records their names. This could be supported by 17:8 and perhaps 13:8.[1] If that is correct, then, as Beale notes, universalism will have a problem in Revelation; for the universalist needs a BOL with flexible contents—one in which names can be deleted and, more importantly, added. The universalists want to say that the kings of the earth are first thrown into the lake of fire because their names are not recorded in the BOL (20:15). They then want to say that the same kings of the earth are allowed to enter because their names have now been added to the BOL (21:27). If the content of the book is fixed before creation, then this is impossible. So is the content fixed?

> a) The first indication that it is not fixed is the plausibility of the universalist interpretation of 21:24-27 (defended above). That would clearly indicate the possibility of being added into the

---

[1] Revelation 13:8 is possibly translated as, "those whose names were not written in the book of life of the Lamb who was *slain from the foundation of the world*" though it is more likely to mean, "those whose names were not *written from the foundation of the world* in the book of life of the Lamb who was slain."

BOL. For those who see the reading of 21:14-17 offered above as plausible then it will lend weight to a flexible BOL view.

b) A more important observation is that 3:5 strongly suggests that one could have one's name removed from the BOL. This interpretation is strengthened by the following observations:

(i) The Old Testament background to the notion of the BOL clearly envisages the real possibility of being "blotted out" from it (Ps 69:28; Exod 32:32-33; Dan 12:1-2).

(ii) The book of Revelation is clear in its warnings that Christian apostates will be thrown into the lake of fire.[2] To suggest that such apostates were not real Christians does not, in my view, do justice to the way in which they are described[3] and the severity of the warnings to the churches not to apostatize.

All this strongly suggests a non-fixed content for the BOL. However, 17:8 speaks of those "whose names have not been written in the book of life from the creation of the world" (cf. 13:8), and this seems to suggest that one's presence or absence from the BOL is determined before creation. What is the universalist to make of this? I am unsure. Let me suggest two possibilities that are compatible with universalism. though they owe more to a theological interpretation than straightforward exegesis.

1. Perhaps the BOL is a record of those who will receive eternal life, and within it we see the following, and only, entry—"Christ." Before creation, God ordains that those "in Christ" (to resort to Pauline terminology) would receive eternal life—share in the resurrection life of Christ. When a person believes the gospel they are in Christ and share in that promise of his life. *In Christ* they are in the book from before creation. If they apostasize, they are out of Christ and are thus

---

[2] In the letters to the churches it is only the overcomers (i.e., those who do not give in to compromise with the "world") who inherit the blessings of the new creation. Notice how the lists of sins in 21:8 and 22:15 closely mirrors the sins found in the churches in Revelation 2–3. This indicates that John's primary focus is warning the churches against apostasy so that they do not end up in the lake of fire. This is confirmed by warnings found throughout the book such as that in 18:4-5. One could also think of other texts found within this particular Christian community which clearly envisage Christian apostasy resulting in purging in the fire (John 15:1-8). It is interesting that universalism provides a fruitful way of resolving a blatant tension between NT texts that claim God will bring the Christian to ultimate salvation and that nothing can thwart this (Phil 1:6 etc.) and texts that claim Christians can end up in hell (Heb 6:1-8 etc.). This tension has given rise to the debate about whether Christians can lose their salvation. To the universalist genuine Christians could fall away and end up in hell and yet still be ultimately saved.

[3] For instance, the compromising church members in 2:20 are described by Christ as *his servants*.

no longer in the book from creation. The moment a person believes he
or she moves from the state of "not being (in Christ) recorded in the
BOL from before the creation of the world" to the state of "being (in
Christ) recorded in the BOL from before the creation of the world." I
put this forward as a tentative proposal that could possibly make sense
of the problematic data. Although the theology of indwelling Christ
and sharing in his life is not prominent in the Apocalypse, it is a major
theme in John's Gospel, which probably arose in the same Christian
circle; and that could lend weight to this proposal.[4]

Thomas Talbott has suggested that:

> Perhaps all the descendents of Adam, all who come into the world as "chil-
> dren of wrath," also go by a name that is not written in the BOL. Yes some
> names are written there from the foundation of the world and some are not.
> But is "Abram" written there? Or is it "Abraham"? In Revelation 2:17 we
> read: "To him who conquers I will give some of the hidden manna, and I will
> give him a white stone, with a new name written on the stone, which no one
> knows except him who receives it." Evidently then, people can receive a new
> name, and this is certainly consistent with the idea of a new birth or a new
> creation in Christ. So is not the following consistent with the teaching about
> the Lamb's BOL? Even though no new names are ever added, people can (as
> all Christians do) receive a new name, one that has always been written in the
> Book of Life from the foundation of the world.[5]

---

[4] The proposal is based upon Roger Forster and Paul Marston's interpretation of being "chosen
in Christ before the foundation of the world" (Eph 1:4) in *God's Strategy in Human History*
(Minneapolis: Bethany, 1973) chap. 15.

[5] An email to me dated 23 / 7 / 01.

Bibliography

Adams, M. M. "Hell and the Justice of God." *Religious Studies* 11 (1975) 433–47.
———. "The Problem of Hell: A Problem of Evil for Christians." In *A Reasoned Faith*, edited by E. Stump. Ithaca, N.Y.: Cornell University Press, 1993.
———. *Horrendous Evils and the Goodness of God*. Ithaca, N.Y.: Cornell University Press, 1999.
Allison, D. C. "The Problem of Gehenna." In D. C. Allison, *Resurrecting Jesus*, 56–110. London: T. & T. Clark, 2005.
Atkinson, B. F. C. *Life and Immortality*. Taunton: Phoenix/Goodman, n.d.
Barth, Karl. *Church Dogmatics*. Vol. 3. Translated by G. W. Bromley and T. F. Torrance. Edinburgh: T. & T. Clark, 1956–76.
Barth, M. *Ephesians*. Vol. 1. Anchor Bible 34. Garden City, N.Y.: Doubleday, 1974.
Bauckham, R. J. "Early Jewish Visions of Hell." *Journal of Theological Studies* 41 (1990) 357–85.
———. "The Rich Man and Lazarus: The Parable and the Parallels." *New Testament Studies* 37 (1991) 225–46.
———. *The Theology of the Book of Revelation*. New Testament Theology. Cambridge: Cambridge University Press, 1993.
———. "Life, Death and the Afterlife in Second Temple Judaism." In *Life in the Face of Death: The Resurrection Message of the New Testament*, edited by R. N. Longenecker. Grand Rapids: Eerdmans, 1998.
Beale, G. K. *The Book of Revelation: A Commentary on the Greek Text*. New International Greek Testament Commentary. Grand Rapids: Eerdmans; Carlisle: Paternoster, 1999.
———. *The Temple and the Church's Mission: A Biblical Theology of the Dwelling Place of God*. Leicester: Apollos; Downers Grove, Ill.: InterVarsity, 2004.
Bell, R. "Rom 5.18-19 and Universal Salvation." *New Testament Studies* 48 (2002) 417–32.
———. *The Irrevocable Call of God: An Inquiry into Paul's Theology of Israel*. Wissenschaftliche Untersuchungen zum Neuen Testament 184. Tübingen: Mohr/Siebeck, 2005.
Berkhof, H. *Christ and the Powers*. Scottdale: Herald, 1962.
Best, E. *Ephesians*. International Critical Commentary. Edinburgh: T. & T. Clark, 1998.
Beuken, W. A. M. van. "The First Servant Song and Its Context." *Vetus Testamentum* 22 (1972) 1–30.

————. "The Confession of God's Exclusivity by All Mankind: A Reappraisal of Is. 45:18-25." *Bijdragen* 35 (1974) 335–56.

————. "The Main Theme of Trito-Isaiah: The Servants of Yahweh." *Journal for the Study of the Old Testament* 47 (1990) 67–87.

Bonda, J. *The One Purpose of God.* Grand Rapids: Eerdmans, 1998.

Boring, M. E. "The Language of Universal Salvation in Paul." *Journal of Biblical Literature* 105 (1986) 269–92.

Brueggemann, W. *Reverberations of Faith: A Theological Handbook of Old Testament Themes.* Louisville: Westminster John Knox, 2002.

Buckareff, A., and A. Plugg. "Escaping Hell: Divine Motivation and the Problem of Hell." *Religious Studies* 41 (2005) 39–54.

Carson, D. A. *Divine Sovereignty and Human Responsibility: Biblical Perspectives in Tension.* Grand Rapids: Baker; London: Marshall Pickering, 1994.

————. *The Gagging of God: Christianity Confronts Pluralism.* Grand Rapids: Zondervan; Leicester: Apollos, 1996.

Chae, D. J.-S. *Paul as Apostle to the Gentiles.* Carlisle: Paternoster, 1997.

Clines, D. J. A. *The Theme of the Pentateuch.* 2d ed. JSOT Supplements 10. Sheffield: Sheffield Academic, 1997.

Collins, A. Y. *The Combat Myth in the Book of Revelation.* Harvard Dissertations in Religion 9. Missoula, Mont.: Scholars, 1976.

Cook, R. "Devils and Manticores: Plundering Jüng for a Plausible Demonology." In *The Unseen World: Christian Reflections on Angels, Demons and the Heavenly Realm*, edited by A. N. S. Lane. Carlisle: Paternoster.

Craig, W. L. *The Only Wise God: The Compatibility of Divine Foreknowledge and Human Freedom.* Grand Rapids: Baker, 1987.

————. "'No Other Name': A Middle Knowledge Perspective on the Exclusivity of Salvation Through Christ." *Faith and Philosophy* 6 (1989) 172–88.

————. "Talbott's Universalism." *Religious Studies* 27 (1991) 297–308.

————. "Talbott's Universalism Once More." *Religious Studies* 29 (1993) 497–518.

————. "Middle Knowledge and Christian Exclusivism." *Sophia* 34 (1995) 120–39.

————. *The Problem of Divine Foreknowledge and Future Contingents From Aristotle to Suarez.* Brill's Studies in Intellectual History 7. Leiden: Brill, 1997.

Crisp, O. "Divine Retribution: A Defense." *Sophia* 42 (2003) 36–53.

————. "Augustinian Universalism." *International Journal for Philosophy of Religion* 53 (2003) 127–45.

————. "On Barth's Denial of Universalism." *Themelios* 29 (2003) 18–29.

Cross, F. M. *Canaanite Myth and Hebrew Epic: Essays in the History of the Religion of Israel.* Cambridge: Harvard University Press, 1973.

Daley, B. E. *The Hope of the Early Church: A Handbook of Patristic Eschatology.* Cambridge: Cambridge University Press, 1991. Reprinted, Peabody, Mass.: Hendrickson, 2003).

Das, A. A. *Paul and the Jews.* Library of Pauline Studies. Peabody: Hendrickson, 2003.

de Boer, M. C. *The Defeat of Death: Apocalyptic Eschatology in 1 Corinthians 15 and Romans 5.* JSNT Supplement Series 22. Sheffield: Sheffield Academic, 1988.

DeRose, K. "Universalism and the Bible." <http://pantheon.yale.edu/%7Ekd47/univ.htm>.

Dumbrell, W. *Covenant and Creation.* Exeter: Paternoster, 1984.

Dunn, J. D. G. *Romans 1–8*. Word Biblical Commentary 38A. Waco, Tex.: Word, 1988.

———. *Romans 9–16*. Word Biblical Commentary 38B. Waco, Tex.:Word, 1988.

———. "The 'Body' in Colossians." In *To Tell the Mystery: Essays on New Testament Eschatology in Honor of Robert H. Gundry*, edited by T. E. Schmidt and M. Silva. JSNT Supplement Series 100. Sheffield: Sheffield Academic, 1994.

———. *The Epistle to the Colossians and to Philemon*. New International Greek Testament Commentary. Carlisle: Paternoster; Grand Rapids: Eerdmans, 1996.

Eaton, J. H. *Festal Drama in Deutero-Isaiah*. London: SPCK, 1979.

Eller, V. *The Most Revealing Book in the Bible*. Grand Rapids: Eerdmans, 1974.

———. "How the Kings of the Earth Land in the New Jerusalem: The World in the Book of Revelation." *Katallagete / Be Reconciled* 5 (1975) 21–27.

Ellul, J. *Perspectives on Our Age: Jacques Ellul Speaks on His Life and Work*. Toronto: Canadian Broadcasting Corporation, 1981.

Evans, C. A. "Jesus and the Continuing Exile of Israel." In *Jesus and the Restoration of Israel: A Critical Assessment of N. T. Wright's Jesus and the Victory of God*, edited by C. C. Newman. Downers Grove, Ill.: InterVarsity, 1999.

———. *Mark 8:27-16:20*. Word Biblical Commentary. Nashville: Thomas Nelson, 2001.

Evans, C. F. *Saint Luke*. London: SCM; Philadelphia: Trinity, 1990.

Fekkes, J. *Isaiah and Prophetic Traditions in the Book of Revelation: Visionary Antecedents and their Development*. Sheffield: JSOT Press, 1994.

Findlay, G. G. *The Epistles to the Thessalonians*. Cambridge: Cambridge University Press, 1891.

Fletcher-Louis, C. "The High Priest as Divine Mediator in the Hebrew Bible: Dan 7:13 as a Test Case." *Society of Biblical Literature Seminar Papers* (1997) 161–93, 190–91.

Forster, R. T., and V. P. Marston. *God's Strategy in Human History*. Minneapolis: Bethany, 1973.

Fudge, E. W. *The Fire that Consumes: The Biblical Case for Conditional Immortality*. Rev. ed. Carlisle: Paternoster, 1994.

Gelston, A. "Universalism in Second Isaiah." *Journal of Theological Studies* 43 (1992) 377–98.

Gleason, R. "The Eschatology of the Warning in Hebrews 10:26-31." *Tyndale Bulletin* 53 (2002) 97–120.

Gorman, M. *Cruciformity: Paul's Narrative Spirituality of the Cross*. Grand Rapids: Eerdmans, 2001.

Gray, T. "The Nature of Hell: Reflections on the Debate Between Conditionalism and the Traditional View of Hell." In *Eschatology in Bible and Theology: Evangelical Essays at the Dawn of a New Millennium*, edited by K. E. Brower and M. W. Elliot. Downers Grove, Ill.: InterVarsity, 1997.

Green, G. L. *The Letter to the Thessalonians*. Pillar New Testament Commentary. Leicester: Apollos; Grand Rapids: Eerdmans, 2002.

Green, J., and M. Baker. *Recovering the Scandal of the Cross: Atonement in New Testament and Contemporary Contexts*. Downers Grove, Ill.: InterVarsity, 2000.

Hall, L. *Swinburne's Hell and Hick's Universalism: Are We Free to Reject God?* London: Ashgate, 2003.

Harmon, S. *Every Knee Should Bow: Biblical Rationales for Universal Salvation in Early Christian Thought.* Lanham, Md.: University Press of America, 2003.

Helm, P. "The Logic of Limited Atonement." *Scottish Bulletin of Evangelical Theology* 3 (1985).

Hick, J. *Evil and the God of Love.* London: Macmillan; New York: Harper and Row, 1966.

Hilborn, D., editor. *The Nature of Hell.* Carlisle: Paternoster, 2000.

Hill, C. E. "Paul's Understanding of Christ's Kingdom in 1 Corinthians 15:20-28." *Novum Testamentum* 30 (1988) 297–320.

Hillert, S. *Limited and Universal Salvation: A Text Oriented and Hermeneutical Study of Two Perspectives in Paul.* Coniectanea biblica: New Testament Series 31. Stockholm: Almqvist & Wiksell, 1999.

Hugenberger, G. P. "The Servant of the LORD in the Servant Songs of Isaiah." In *The Lord's Anointed: Interpretation of Old Testament Messianic Texts*, edited by P. E. Satterthwaite, R. S. Hess, and G. J. Wenham. Grand Rapids: Baker; Carlisle: Paternoster, 1995.

Johnson, T. "A Wideness in God's Mercy: Universalism in the Bible." In *Universal Salvation? The Current Debate*, edited by R. A. Parry and C. H. Partridge. Carlisle: Paternoster; Grand Rapids: Eerdmans, 2003.

Kierkegaard, Søren. *Christian Discourses: The Crisis and A Crisis in the Life of an Actress.* Translated and edited by H. V. Hong and E. H. Hong. Princeton: Princeton University Press, 1997.

Kitchen, M. *Ephesians.* New Testament Readings. London: Routledge, 1994.

Kvanig, J. "Heaven and Hell." In *Companion to the Philosophy of Religion*, edited by P. Quinn and C. Taliaferro. Oxford: Blackwell, 1999.

Levine, M. "Swinburne's Heaven: One Hell of a Place." *Religious Studies* 29 (1993) 519–31.

Lewis, C. S. *The Problem of Pain.* New York: Macmillan, 1944.

Lincoln, A. T. *Ephesians.* Word Biblical Commentary 42. Waco, Tex.:Word, 1990.

———. *Colossians.* New Interpreter's Bible 11. Nashville: Abingdon, 1998.

Ludlow, M. *Universal Salvation: Eschatology in the Thought of Gregory of Nyssa and Karl Rahner.* Oxford: Oxford University Press, 2000.

———. "Universalism in the History of Christianity." In *Universal Salvation? The Current Debate*, edited by R. A. Parry and C. H. Partridge. Carlisle: Paternoster; Grand Rapids: Eerdmans, 2003.

Malherbe, A. J. *The Letters to the Thessalonians.* Anchor Bible 32B. New York: Doubleday, 2000.

Marshall, C. *Beyond Retribution: A New Testament View of Justice, Crime and Punishment.* Grand Rapids: Eerdmans, 2001.

Marshall, I. H. "Does the New Testament Teach Universal Salvation?" In *Called to One Hope: Perspectives on the Life to Come*, edited by J. Colwell. Carlisle: Paternoster, 2000.

———. "The New Testament Does not Teach Universal Salvation." In *Universal Salvation? The Current Debate*, edited by R. A. Parry and C. H. Partridge. Carlisle: Paternoster; Grand Rapids: Eerdmans, 2003.

———. "For All, For All My Saviour Died." In *Semper Reformandum: Studies in Honor of Clark H. Pinnock*, edited by S. E. Porter and A. R. Cross. Carlisle: Paternoster, 2003.

Moltmann, J. *The Way of Jesus Christ: Christology in Messianic Dimensions*. Translated by M. Kohl. London: SCM; Minneapolis: Fortress, 1993.

———. *The Coming of God: Christian Eschatology*. Translated by M. Kohl. London: SCM; Minneapolis: Fortress, 1996.

Moritz, T. "'Summing Up All Things': Religious Pluralism and Universalism in Ephesians." In *One God, One Lord: Christianity in a World of Religious Pluralism*, edited by A. D. Clark and B. W. Winter. Carlisle: Paternoster; Grand Rapids: Baker, 1992.

Motyer, A. *The Prophesy of Isaiah*. Leicester: InterVarsity, 1993.

Murray, J. *The Epistle of St Paul to the Romans*. Vol. 1. Grand Rapids: Eerdmans, 1960.

Murray, M. "Three Versions of Universalism." *Faith and Philosophy* 16 (1999) 55–68.

Niehaus, J. J. *God at Sinai: Covenant and Theophany in the Bible and the Ancient Near East*. Grand Rapids: Zondervan, 1995.

Nolland, J. *Luke 9:21—18:34*. Word Biblical Commentary 35B. Dallas: Word, 1993.

Norris, F. "Universal Salvation in Origen and Maximus." In *Universalism and the Doctrine of Hell*, edited by N. M. de S. Cameron. Grand Rapids: Baker; Carlisle: Paternoster, 1992.

Oaklander, N., and Q. Smith. *Time, Change, and Freedom*. London: Routledge, 1995.

Oswalt, J. N. *The Book of Isaiah Chapters 40–66*. Grand Rapids: Eerdmans, 1998.

Packer, J. I. "Good Pagans and God's Kingdom." In *Celebrating the Saving Work of God*, J. I. Packer. Carlisle: Paternoster, 1998.

———. "The Love of God: Universal and Particular." In *Celebrating the Saving Work of God*, J. I. Packer. Carlisle: Paternoster, 1998.

———. "The Problem of Universalism Today." In *Celebrating the Saving Work of God*, J. I. Packer. Carlisle: Paternoster, 1998.

Pao, D. *Acts and the Isaianic New Exodus*. Grand Rapids: Baker, 2002.

Parry, R. A., and C. H. Partridge, editors. *Universal Salvation? The Current Debate*. Carlisle: Paternoster; Grand Rapids: Eerdmans, 2003.

Perriman, A. *The Coming of the Son of Man: New Testament Eschatology for an Emerging Church*. Milton Keynes: Paternoster, 2005.

Powys, D. *Hell: A Hard Look at a Hard Question*. Carlisle: Paternoster, 1997.

Reisner, M. *Jesus and Judgment: The Eschatological Proclamation in Jewish Context*. Minneapolis: Fortress, 1997.

Reitan, E. "Universalism and Autonomy: Towards a Comparative Defense of Universalism." *Faith and Philosophy* 18 (2001) 222–40.

———. "Human Freedom and the Impossibility of Eternal Damnation." In *Universal Salvation? The Current Debate*, edited by R. A. Parry and C. H. Partridge. Carlisle: Paternoster; Grand Rapids: Eerdmans, 2003.

———. "A Guarantee of Universal Salvation?" Unpublished, 2005.

Richards, J. W. "A Pascalian Argument Against Universalism." In *Unapologetic Apologetics*, edited by W. A. Dembski and J. W. Richards. Downers Grove, Ill.: InterVarsity, 2001.

Rissi, M. *The Future of the World: An Exegetical Study of Revelation 19.11—22.15*. Studies in Biblical Theology 2/23. London: SCM, 1972.

Robinson, J. A. T. *In the End God: A Study of the Christian Doctrine of the Last Things.* Theology for Modern Men 4. London: James Clarke, 1950.

Roloff, J. *Revelation of John.* Translated by John E. Alsup. Continental Commentaries. Minneapolis: Fortress, 1993.

Russell, C. A. *Cross Currents: Interactions Between Science and Faith.* Leicester: InterVarsity, 1985.

Schnackenburg, R. *Ephesians: A Commentary.* Translated by H. Heron. Edinburgh: T. & T. Clark, 1991.

Schweizer, E. *The Letter to the Colossians.* Translated by A. Chester. Minneapolis: Augsburg, 1982.

Seymour, C. *A Theodicy of Hell.* Boston: Kluwer Academic, 2000.

Smith, Hannah Whitall. *The Unselfishness of God: My Spiritual Autobiography,* chapter 22 (London: Nishet, 1903; first edition only). <http://www.godstruthfortoday.org/Library/smith/hwsmith9.html>.

Snaith, N. H. "The Servant of the Lord in Deutero-Isaiah." In *Studies in Old Testament Prophecy Presented to Professor Theodore H. Robinson,* edited by H. H. Rowley. Edinburgh: T. & T. Clark, 1950.

Stott, J., and D. L. Edwards. *Essentials: A Liberal-Evangelical Dialogue.* London: Hodder & Stoughton, 1988.

Strange, D. "A Calvinist Response to Talbott"s Universalism." In *Universal Salvation? The Current Debate,* edited by R. A. Parry and C. H. Partridge. Carlisle: Paternoster; Grand Rapids: Eerdmans, 2003.

Stump, E. "Dante's Hell, Aquinas' Moral Theory and the Love of God." *Canadian Journal of Philosophy* 16 (1986) 181–96.

Sweet, J. P. M. *Revelation.* London: SCM; Philadelphia: Westminster, 1979.

Swinburne, R. "A Theodicy of Heaven and Hell." In *The Existence and Nature of God,* edited by A. J. Fredosso. Notre Dame: Notre Dame University Press, 1983.

———. *Providence and the Problem of Evil.* Oxford: Oxford University Press, 1998.

Talbott, T. "Providence, Freedom and Human Destiny." *Religious Studies* 26 (1990) 227–45.

———. "The Doctrine of Everlasting Punishment." *Faith and Philosophy* 7 (1990) 19–42.

———. "Craig on the Possibility of Eternal Damnation." *Religious Studies* 28 (1992) 459–510.

———. *The Inescapable Love of God.* Universal Publishers, 1999.

———. "Freedom, Damnation and the Power to Sin With Impunity." *Religious Studies* 37 (2001) 417–34.

———. "Universalism and the Supposed Oddity of our Earthly Life: A Reply to Michael Murray." *Faith and Philosophy* 18 (2001) 102–9.

———. "Towards a Better Understanding of Universalism," "Christ Victorious," "A Pauline Interpretation of Divine Judgment," and "Reply to my Critics." In *Universal Salvation? The Current Debate,* edited by R. A. Parry and C. H. Partridge. Carlisle: Paternoster; Grand Rapids: Eerdmans, 2003.

———. "Misery and Freedom: Reply to Walls." *Religious Studies* 40 (2004) 217–24.

———. "Libertarian Freedom and the Problem of Hell." A paper delivered at the 52nd Annual Wheaton College Philosophy Conference, 21 October 2005.

Thiselton, A. C. *First Epistle to the Corinthians*. New International Greek Testament Commentary. Grand Rapids: Eerdmans; Carlisle: Paternoster, 2000.

Travis, S. *Christ and the Judgment of God*. Basingstoke: Marshall, Morgan & Scott, 1986.

———. "Wrath of God (NT)." In *Anchor Bible Dictionary* 6:996–98. New York: Doubleday, 1992.

Vogelgesang, J. M. "The Interpretation of Ezekiel in the Book of Revelation." Ph.D. diss., Harvard University, 1985.

Walls, J. *The Logic of Damnation*. Notre Dame: Notre Dame University Press, 1992.

———. *Heaven: The Logic of Eternal Joy*. New York: Oxford University Press, 2002.

———. "A Philosophical Critique of Talbott's Universalism." In *Universal Salvation? The Current Debate*, edited by R. A. Parry and C. H. Partridge. Carlisle: Paternoster; Grand Rapids: Eerdmans, 2003.

———. "A Hell of a Choice: Reply to Talbott." *Religious Studies* 40 (2004) 203–16.

Ware, K. *The Inner Kingdom*, 193–215. Collected Works 1. New York: St. Vladymir's Seminary Press, 2000.

Watts, J. D. W. *Isaiah 34–66*. Word Biblical Commentary 25. Waco, Tex.:Word, 1987.

Wenham, G. J. *Genesis 1–15*. Word Biblical Commentary 1. Waco, Tex.:Word, 1987.

———. "Sanctuary Symbolism in the Garden of Eden Story." In *"I Studied Inscriptions From Before the Flood: Ancient Near Eastern Literary and Linguistic Approaches to Genesis 1–11,"* edited by R. J. Hess and D. T. Tsumara. Sources for Biblical and Theological Study 4. Winona Lake, Ind.: Eisenbrauns, 1994.

Wenham, J. W. *The Goodness of God*. London: InterVarsity, 1974.

Whybray, R. N. *Isaiah 40–66*. New Century Bible. Grand Rapids: Eerdmans, 1975.

Williamson, H. G. M. *Variations on a Theme: King, Messiah and Servant in the Book of Isaiah*. Carlisle: Paternoster, 1998.

Wink, W. *Naming the Powers: The Language of Power in the New Testament*. Philadelphia: Fortress, 1984.

Winkle, D. W. van. "The Relationship of the Nations to Yahweh and to Israel in Isaiah XL–LV." *Vetus Testamentum* 35 (1985) 446–58.

Wolterstorff, N. *Divine Discourse: Philosophical Reflections on the Claim That God Speaks*. Cambridge: Cambridge University Press, 1995.

Wright, N. G. "Charismatic Interpretation of the Demonic." In *The Unseen World: Christian Reflections on Angels, Demons and the Heavenly Realm*, edited by A. N. S. Lane. Carlisle: Paternoster, 1996.

Wright, N. T. "Towards a Biblical View of Universalism." *Themelios* 4 (1979) 54–61.

———. *Colossians*. Leicester: InterVarsity, 1987.

———. *The Climax of the Covenant: Christ and the Law in Pauline Theology*. Edinburgh: T. & T. Clark; Minneapolis: Fortress, 1991.

———. *The New Testament and the People of God*. London: SPCK; Minneapolis: Fortress, 1992.

———. *Jesus and the Victory of God*. London: SPCK; Minneapolis: Fortress, 1996.

———. *New Heavens, New Earth: The Biblical Picture of Christian Hope*. Grove Biblical Series 11. Cambridge: Grove, 1999.

Also available from SPCK

JESUS THROUGH MIDDLE EASTERN EYES
Cultural Studies in the Gospels

Kenneth Bailey

Beginning with Jesus' birth, Ken Bailey leads us on a kaleidoscopic study of Jesus in the four Gospels. Bailey examines the life and ministry of Jesus with attention to the Lord's Prayer, the Beatitudes, Jesus' relationship to women and especially Jesus' parables.

Throughout the author employs his trademark expertise as a master of Middle Eastern culture to lead us into a deeper understanding of the person and significance of Jesus, lifting away the obscuring layers of modern Western interpretation to reveal Jesus in the light of his actual historical and cultural setting.

KENNETH E. BAILEY is an author and lecturer in Middle Eastern New Testament studies. An ordained Presbyterian minister, he also serves as Canon Theologian of the Diocese of Pittsburgh of the Episcopal Church, USA. He has written many books in English and in Arabic, including *The Cross and the Prodigal, Poet and Peasant, Through Peasant Eyes, Jacob and the Prodigal* and *Finding the Lost: Cultural Keys to Luke 15*.

ISBN: 978–0–281–05975–1

Also available from SPCK

THE LAST WEEK
What the Gospels Really Teach About Jesus's Final Days in Jerusalem

Marcus J. Borg and John Dominic Crossan

What was the last week of Jesus's life about? And what does it mean for us now?

Two of today's leading experts on Jesus, Marcus J. Borg and John Dominic Crossan, offer what they believe is the real story of Jesus's final week in Jerusalem. Using the Gospel of Mark as their guide, they present a day-by-day account of Holy Week—the most sacred time of the Christian year.

The Last Week reveals a radical and little-known Jesus who gave up his life to protest against power without justice and to condemn the oppression of the poor by the rich. Indeed, the Jesus uncovered here is far more dangerous than the one enshrined in the Church's traditional teachings. In *The Last Week* we do not simply meet the Jesus of history but a passionate and engaging Jesus who invites us to follow him today.

"*The Last Week* shows one of the most careful and insightful readings of the Bible I've ever come across . . . Readers across the spectrum will be challenged, educated, stretched, and perhaps disturbed (in a constructive way) by this important, fascinating and well-written book."

Brian McLaren, author of *A New Kind of Christian*

"If there is to be one book for the redemption of Holy Week, this is it. This is a 'must-read' for clergy and laity."

Peter J. Gomes, Harvard University

MARCUS J. BORG is Hundere Distinguished Professor of Religion and Culture at Oregon State University and the author of many books, including *Meeting Jesus Again for the First Time* and *The Heart of Christianity*. JOHN DOMINIC CROSSAN is the author of several bestselling books including *God and Empire* and *The Historical Jesus*. He lives in Minneola, Florida.

ISBN: 978-0-281-05983-6

Also available from SPCK

THE FIRST CHRISTMAS
What the Gospels Really Teach About Jesus's Birth

Marcus J. Borg and John Dominic Crossan

In *The First Christmas*, two of today's top Jesus scholars, Marcus J. Borg and John Dominic Crossan, show how history has biased our reading of the nativity story as it appears in the Gospels of Matthew and Luke. *The First Christmas* explores the beginning of the life of Christ, peeling away the sentimentalism that has built up over two thousand years around this most well known of all stories to reveal the truth of what the Gospels actually say.

Borg and Crossan help us to see this familiar narrative afresh by answering the question "What do these stories mean?" from the perspective of both the first and the twenty-first centuries. They successfully show that the Christmas story, read in its original context, is far richer and more challenging than people imagine.

ISBN: 978–0–281–06004–7

Also available from SPCK

PASSIONATE CHRISTIANITY
A Journey to the Cross

Cally Hammond

Fear, resentment, humiliation, cruelty, love and compassion: these are some of the raw emotions exposed in the Gospel stories of Christ's Passion.

Passionate Christianity explores key moments in the Passion as experienced by those caught up in the world-changing events of the last hours of Jesus' life, and relates them to life and faith today.

Cally Hammond invites you to experience afresh the events of the Passion—the agony in the garden of Gethsemane, the scourging of Jesus, the crowning with thorns, the carrying of the cross and the crucifixion. In doing this, she leads you to discover new depths of meaning in these events, to develop a deeper commitment to your faith, and to meet the challenges of life with passionate Christianity.

ISBN: 978–0–281–05882–2

Also available from SPCK

THE EASTER STORIES

Trevor Dennis

The resurrection accounts are not only about God's triumph over evil and death. They are also stories of encounter with God—the recovery of that ancient intimacy briefly enjoyed in the Garden of Eden.

This absorbing volume, which includes some of the author's own poetry and reflective pieces, suggests that in entering into the resurrection stories from the Gospels, we step outside time and place into a strange and wonderful world where death no longer holds sway. Here we meet a wounded God, scarred with the marks of crucifixion—a risen Christ, in whom God once more becomes familiar. And through the wonderful intimacy we are able to enjoy with this truly close yet ever mysterious God, we gain the energy and courage to strive to establish his topsy-turvy kingdom on this, his own dear earth.

The Easter Stories is a companion volume to *The Christmas Stories*, also published by SPCK.

Praise for the author's previous book, *The Book of Books*:

"Trevor Dennis's retelling of the Bible is exceptional in its range, from the mysterious and poetic to the down-to-earth and funny . . . [his skill] as a storyteller . . . is undeniable."
Church Times

TREVOR DENNIS is Vice Dean of Chester Cathedral.

ISBN: 978–0–281–05849–5

Also available from SPCK

SURPRISED BY HOPE

Tom Wright

What do Christians hope for? To leave this wicked world and go to "heaven"? For the "kingdom of God" to grow gradually on earth? What do we mean by the "resurrection of the body", and how does that fit with the popular image of sitting on clouds playing harps? And how does all this affect the way we live in the here and now?

Tom Wright, one of our leading theologians, addresses these questions in this provocative and wide-ranging new book. He outlines the present confusion about future hope in both church and world. Then, having explained why Christians believe in the bodily resurrection of Jesus himself, he explores the biblical hope for "new heavens and new earth", and shows how the "second coming" of Jesus, and the eventual resurrection, belong within that larger picture, together with the intermediate hope for "heaven". For many, including many Christians, all this will come as a great surprise.

Wright convincingly argues that what we believe about life after death directly affects what we believe about life *before* death. For if God intends to renew the whole creation— and if this has already begun in Jesus' resurrection—the church cannot stop at "saving souls", but must anticipate the eventual renewal by working for God's kingdom in the wider world, bringing healing and hope in the present life.

Lively and accessible, this book will surprise and excite all who are interested in the meaning of life—not only after death but before it.

TOM WRIGHT is Bishop of Durham and is a regular broadcaster on radio and television. He is the author of over forty books, including the popular FOR EVERYONE guides to the New Testament and the magisterial series CHRISTIAN ORIGINS AND THE QUESTION OF GOD.

ISBN: 978–0–281–05617–0

Also available from SPCK

RADICAL ORTHODOXY
A Critical Introduction

Steven Shakespeare

Radical Orthodoxy is a new, exciting, sometimes baffling and always controversial trend in theology. It also has a fearsome and off-putting reputation for complexity. Its books are full of detailed arguments and are crammed with philosophical terms in a range of languages.

Here, Steven Shakespeare makes accessible Radical Orthodoxy's key arguments and offers an explanation and critique of its theology. This jargon-free introduction will help students, clergy and those with an interest in theology to engage with both the movement and with the wider debate about the place of the Church in the world.

"This is an excellent one-stop reference book to an important contemporary theological movement. Shakespeare's clear analysis and summaries are matched by his fair and incisive critical questions."
Kevin J. Vanhoozer, Research Professor of Systematic Theology
Trinity Evangelical Divinity School, Illinois

"Steven Shakespeare presents in delightfully lucid prose the complex and sometimes opaque theology of Radical Orthodoxy. In an engaging and creative manner he probes its significant problems and ends by presenting an alternative approach. Shakespeare's work will serve the initiated and uninitiated alike."
Gavin D'Costa, Professor of Christian Theology
University of Bristol

THE REVD DR STEVEN SHAKESPEARE is the Anglican Chaplain at Liverpool Hope University, UK. He is the author of *Kierkegaard, Language and the Reality of God* and co-author (with Hugh Rayment-Pickard) of *The Inclusive God: Reclaiming theology for an inclusive Church*.

ISBN: 978–0–281–05837–2

Also available from SPCK

THE SPCK INTRODUCTION TO KARL RAHNER

Karen Kilby

"Karen Kilby's book will be invaluable to teachers and students because of its lucid, learned, and penetrating understanding of one of the most important theologians of the twentieth century. It is the best single slim volume on Rahner that I know."

Gavin D'Costa, University of Bristol

"Karen Kilby's book is an imaginative, clear and succinct work. It offers many illustrative and accessible analogies which I have found invaluable in communicating important aspects of Rahner's thought to students."

Philip Caldwell, Ushaw College, Durham

"I have never come across a more useful tool in presenting Rahner to undergraduates than Kilby's book. It is a model of succinctness and precision, but far more importantly, it succeeds in accurately identifying and unpacking the key to Rahner's thought in a very reader-friendly way."

Eamonn Mulcahy, Missionary Institute, London

"Lucid, perceptive, thickly textured, theologically rich, and refreshingly concise—Kilby's presentation of Rahner's theology is a must for students of Rahner, be they first year seminarians or senior theologians. I have taught her book for years and I still learn something new from it every time I return—it's brilliant reading."

Serene Jones, Yale Divinity School

"This is an excellent book, very useful for students and one of the clearest introductions to Rahner."

John McDade, Principal of Heythrop College, London

KAREN KILBY is an Associate Professor in the Department of Theology and Religious Studies at the University of Nottingham. She is the author of *Karl Rahner: Theology and practice.*

ISBN: 978–0–281–05842–6

Also available from SPCK

CHRISTIANITY'S DANGEROUS IDEA
The Protestant Revolution: A History from the Sixteenth Century to the Twenty-First

Alister McGrath

Protestantism is one of the world's largest and most dynamic religious movements, currently experiencing major growth and expansion in many parts of the world. This book sets out to explore the inner identity of this movement, and its implications for the religious future of humanity. The "dangerous idea" lying at the heart of Protestantism is that every individual has the right and responsibility to interpret the Bible. With no overarching authority to rein in "wayward" thought, opposing sides on controversial issues appeal to the same text, yet interpret it in very different ways. The spread of this principle has led to five hundred years of remarkable innovation and adaptability—but also to cultural incoherence and instability.

Christianity's Dangerous Idea is the first book that attempts to define this core element of Protestantism, and the religious and cultural dynamic that this "dangerous idea" has unleashed. Its three major sections explore the history of the movement, engage with the distinctive features of Protestant belief and practice, and offer a provocative assessment of Protestantism's global future.

"An original and important book . . . the most readable introduction to the history, theology and present-day practices of Protestantism."
Publishers Weekly

"Alister McGrath invariably combines enormous scholarship with an accessible and engaging style."
Rowan Williams, Archbishop of Canterbury

"It is great, good news that I, without human intermediaries of any kind, can enter into full fellowship with God. And, it is great, good news that I, with full soul competency, can come to the Bible and understand its spiritual treasures, apply its life-giving message to my heart, and live in joy-filled obedience to its wonderful words of life. This is the powerful reality Alister McGrath explores so well and so helpfully in *Christianity's Dangerous Idea*."
Richard Foster, author of *Celebration of Discipline*

"Alister McGrath presents a daringly ambitious idea, nothing less than a systematic history of Protestantism and its variant forms—evangelicalism, Pentecostalism—from the Reformation through the modern-day rise of world Christianities. This highly readable survey is at once wonderfully wide-ranging, and impressively fair-minded."
Philip Jenkins, author of
The Next Christendom: The Coming of Global Christianity

ALISTER McGRATH is Professor of Historical Theology at Oxford University and Senior Research Fellow of Harris Manchester College, Oxford. A prolific author, his recent book (with Joanna Collicutt McGrath), *The Dawkins Delusion? Atheist fundamentalism and the denial of the divine* (SPCK), has become an international bestseller.

ISBN: 978-0-281-05968-3

John Stott vs evil things.